RECLAIMING
HIGHER
GROUND

Other Works by Lance Secretan

The Masterclass: Modern Fables for Working and Living

The Way of the Tiger: Gentle Wisdom for Turbulent Times

Managerial Moxie: The 8 Proven Steps to Empowering Employees and Supercharging Your Company

Living the Moment: A Sacred Journey

If you would like to contact the author, or if you wish to order videos, audio-cassettes, seminars, consulting, retreats, or any of his other books, please do so at the following address:

Dr. Lance H. K. Secretan
The Secretan Center Inc.
R.R. #2
Alton, Ontario, L0N 1A0
CANADA

E-mail: 73002,3575@compuserve.com
World Wide Web: http://www.secretan.com

For Public Speaking engagements, please contact:

Leigh Bureau
50 Division Street, Suite 200
Sommerville, New Jersey, 08876-2955
USA

Telephone: (908) 253-8601

RECLAIMING HIGHER GROUND

Creating Organizations that Inspire the Soul

LANCE H. K. SECRETAN

McGraw-Hill

New York   San Francisco   Washington, D.C.   Auckland   Bogotá
Caracas   Lisbon   London   Madrid   Mexico City   Milan
Montreal   New Delhi   San Juan   Singapore
Sydney   Tokyo   Toronto

McGraw-Hill

A Division of The **McGraw·Hill** Companies

1 2 3 4 5 6 8 9 0 DOC/DOC 9 0 2 1 0 9 8 7

ISBN 0-07-057919-9

The sponsoring editor for the book was Susan Barry, the production supervisor was Claire Stanley. It was set in Sabon by North Market Street Graphics.

Printed and bound by Donnelley/Crawfordsville.

McGraw-Hill books are available at special quantity discounts to use as premiums and sales promotions, or for use in corporate training programs. For more information, please write to the Director of Special Sales, McGraw-Hill, 11 West 19th Street, New York, NY 10011. Or contact your local bookstore.

Contents

Our deepest fear is not that
we are inadequate.
Our deepest fear is that we are powerful
beyond measure.
It is our light, not our darkness that frightens us.
We ask ourselves, who am I to be brilliant,
gorgeous, talented and fabulous?
Actually, who are we not to be?
You are a child of God. Your playing small
doesn't serve the world.
There's nothing enlightened about
shrinking so that other people
won't feel insecure around you.
We were born to make manifest the glory
of God that is within us.
It's not just in some of us, it's in everyone.
And as we let our own light shine,
we unconsciously give other people
permission to do the same.
As we are liberated from our own fears,
our presence automatically
liberates others.

Marianne Williamson, *A Return to Love*

Acknowledgments

Reclaiming Higher Ground has been an extraordinary project. I'm not sure if it was born during a walk along a beach in paradise with Trish, or during my richly rewarding work with marvelous clients around the world. Or it may simply be a message from the soul. But as soon as it started, it took me for the ride of my life. It seemed as if a hidden hand reached into my quiver and dispatched a single arrow to the bull's-eye. The reaction of my friends and business associates astonished me. Each in their own way described the great yearning they saw in our society, for hope, healing, and balance. I have been influenced and educated by many great thinkers, some of whom have been cited in this book. I am grateful to many who reviewed early manuscripts, gave me valuable insights, and sharpened my focus including Dave Blair, Dan Bollom, Dale Brewster, Clare Cremer, Vern Dale-Johnson, Simon Dean, Bob Dryburgh, Cameron Fellman, Margot Franssen, David Fugate, Anky Graydon, Lynne Hallinan, Ed Hardison, Alan Harman, Steve Heise, Roberta Kent, Rocky Kimball, Rob Kozinets, Scott Ladd, Janet Laughton MacKay, Carole and Malcolm MacLeod, Patrick McCabe, Ross Morton, Christine Moss, Karen Neal, Brenda Nylund, Ray Patrick, Ray Pedersen, Kathy Schultz, David Sersta, Denis Shackel, Sue Sheldon, Peter Somers, Hugo Sorensen, Ralph Stayer, Bill Sutton, Frank Syer, Michael Trueman, Donn Winn, Warner Woodley, and Mark Yeatman. Many thanks to the team at Macmillan Canada, especially Denise Schon, Karen O'Reilly, Liza Algar, and Anne Nelles and to the McGraw-Hill team: Susan Barry, Claudia Rainer Butote, Lynda Luppino, Claire Stanley and to my colleague, Zorina Swallow, all of whom steered me with great Mastery through the production of this book and to Ron Szymanski of the Leigh Bureau. Special thanks to my wonder dog Spirit, who supervised most of my writing. Of course nothing I do on this planet would make any sense or have real meaning without Trish, my greatest critic, editor, supporter, friend, and lover. I am her Skin Horse (see page 41).

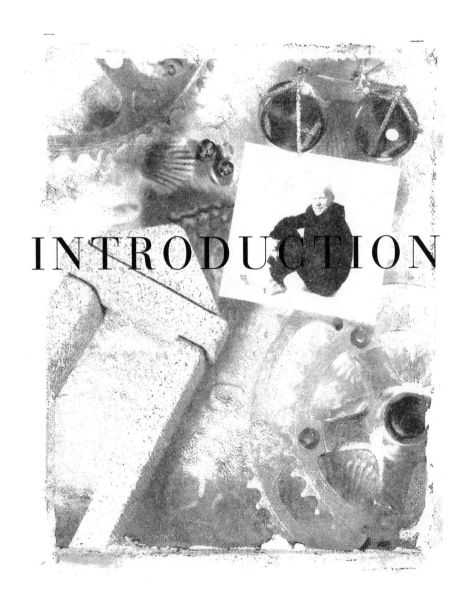

INTRODUCTION

What's Wrong with This Picture?

Four-fifths of the world's population are suffering from a hunger of the body and one-fifth is suffering from a hunger of the soul. Something strange is going on: our personalities are becoming richer and richer, while our souls become poorer and poorer. Our personalities are being whipped into a frenzied spiral of acquiring more, doing more, and being faster, while our souls feel empty and yearn for renewal. Voices within us warn of the growing conflict between our personality and our soul. We are precariously poised at a moment of great danger and great hope. *Reclaiming Higher Ground* is a book about hope.

Somewhere along our journey of human experience, we abandoned our souls in favor of our personalities. Nowhere has this been more true than in our work, resulting in a great emptiness within the human spirit. Yet our sense of loss and lack of fulfilment is temporary. By honoring our souls once again, we will restore joy and grace throughout our work and the rest of our lives.

Loneliness and the feeling of being unwanted are the most terrible poverty.

MOTHER TERESA

In modern times, this will be a challenge for many of us, because our experience has been forged through polishing our skills of manipulation and exploitation to unparalleled brilliance. Even though the cult of personality has ruled our lives for two hundred years, we can reclaim higher ground by revering our souls once again. This will be a new experience in our time and therefore a difficult change, but making our work a spiritual practice will yield a quantum leap in human fulfilment, producing a change so profound that it will seem like a revolution.

I think that maybe in every company today there is always at least one person who is going crazy slowly.

JOSEPH HELLER

Questions and Answers

For most of my professional career, I have been a corporate soothsayer, and I like to believe that my prescriptions have usually contributed to the good fortunes of my clients. During the last few years, however, I have come to question the value of the ready answer. We are well experienced

3

in providing answers but it is likely that we have enough of them. It seems to me that our greater challenge is to ask the right questions. This is not easy, because although an expert maintains an inventory of answers, there is no inventory of questions. Knowing and remembering to ask the right questions requires wisdom and judgment. *Reclaiming Higher Ground* suggests some of the questions and the source of many answers.

In the Arthurian legends, young Perceval's mother teaches him the importance of asking questions. The lesson was affirmed during his younger years, when he escaped from a group of knights by asking questions rather than giving answers. By the time Perceval had become a brave knight of King Arthur's Round Table, however, his teachers had convinced him to curb his questioning. This seemingly reasonable instruction led to many trials for Perceval because, in following this advice and living by the rules of others, he began to lead a life that lacked authenticity. One evening, while at the Grail Castle, invisible to all but those who are worthy, he dined with the impotent Fisher King who suffered from wounds that never healed. As the king and the knight conversed, a procession passed before them in which he saw the fabulous Holy Grail. Perceval was being tested, for if he asked the most important question, "Whom does it serve?" the Fisher King would be healed and the surrounding wasteland restored to a paradise on Earth. But he failed to do so. As a punishment for adhering to someone else's rules and not being true to his inner promptings, he was cast under a five-year spell, during which he was required to deal with a succession of strange and terrible events. Eventually, tired, exhausted, and dispirited, not being aware even of the day, time, or season—though it was Good Friday—Perceval stopped to ask a stranger, "What day is today?" At that moment, the act of asking a question broke the spell and shortly after, Perceval rejoined King Arthur to continue a long life of adventure and romance.

Today, we are under a similar spell. Every year, consultants, authors, and business academics offer us answers suggesting that by doing "more-of-the-same" (MOTS), only faster and with less resources, we will cure the current ailments of modern organizations and heal the pain of the souls within them. They offer a plethora of ready answers and quick-fix solutions: excellence, Total Quality Management (TQM), teams, downsizing, restructuring, customer service, empowerment, re-engineering and more.

If re-engineering was the answer, what was the question? The definition of re-engineering is, "the fundamental rethinking and radical redesign of business processes to achieve dramatic improvements in critical, contemporary measures of performance, such as cost, quality, service and speed,"[1] all classic issues driven by the personality. Re-engineering is the quintessential prototype of the "answer" that does not deal with the question of the soul. At our current levels of angst, it is not another answer we need, but the right questions. The incessant stream of "answers" we have been producing has not been able to heal what ails us because they are the very reason for our current condition.

You can't dig a hole in a new place by digging the same hole deeper.

EDWARD DE BONO

They are answers that do not fit the questions; they propose specific answers for broad issues. They are used by those who "manage by fad-flitting" and those who are possessed by the need to "fix things." But fad-flitting fixes few failings. What we need is not re-engineering but *regenerating*. The dictionary defines regeneration as, "*spiritual rebirth; to give new life or energy; renewing or restoring, especially after a decline to a low or abject condition.*" We no longer need answers for the personality. Instead, we need to sit with the soul and ask the right questions.

We don't need to look far for confirmation that the old answers no longer work. The American Quality Foundation has been disbanded. Applications for the Baldrige award, America's prize for quality, have slumped — down a third in three years. More than three million Americans have been fired over five years. IBM alone, vowing for most of its corporate existence never to lay off an employee, fired 200,000 employees at a balance sheet cost (not to mention the human cost) of nearly $20 billion.[2]

The truth is that the spell we are under cannot be broken until we begin to ask the right questions and to follow our inner voices. The right questions reveal much more than the right answers. Socrates taught geometry to his slave by asking questions. He would feign ignorance, encourage others to talk, and then, by cross-examination, expose their inconsistencies — the so-called Socratic method. The Greeks were so intimidated by Socrates' questioning approach that in 399 B.C., having become the greatest philosopher of his time, he was accused of impiety and corrupting the young and sentenced to die by drinking hemlock. It is not the answers that we fear. We are afraid of asking questions. We are in awe of those with the courage to ask them. As a result, we have relied for too long on answers alone to guide us. We will be informed more deeply, learn and grow and break the spell we are under, when we learn to ask questions as skilfully as we offer answers.

Reclaiming Higher Ground is a book that raises questions appropriate to the fundamental shift that is occurring in the attitudes of people who know that most of the old answers no longer work. A new path is needed for the future, in which we are guided more by the right questions than by ready answers.

Hitting the Wall — The Decline of Personality

Most management-by-cliché approaches merely provide answers that fiddle with the cosmetics of what we have already been doing, achieving gains by adding an ever-increasing component of speed. The employees who have survived and remain after the downsizing and restructuring of the last fifteen years simply cannot dance any faster. Today the real breakthroughs are being made by those who realize that people everywhere are seeking much more from their working lives — something that inspires the soul more than the personality. Inspired leaders are not force-fitting old answers onto new problems; they are asking timeless, yet contemporary questions for a new era. They are determined to break the spell.

We have succeeded beyond our wildest dreams in meeting the needs of the personality, but in the process, we have abandoned the soul. Percy Barnevik, former CEO and president of Asea Brown Boveri says, "Our organizations are constructed so that most of our employees are asked to use 5 percent to 10 percent of their capacity at work. It is only when those same individuals go home that they can engage the other 90 percent to 95 percent — to run their households, lead a boy scout troop, or build a summer home. We have to be able to recognize and employ that untapped ability that each individual brings to work every day."[3]

> **The brain is a wonderful organ; it starts working the moment you get up in the morning, and does not stop until you get into the office.**
>
> ROBERT FROST

People are tired of bringing their exhausted minds to work but leaving their hearts at home. They are also tired of being told what to do by managers who have attended empowerment seminars but who still don't understand what the word means. For years, employees have been doing more with less, increasing their productivity, quality, and customer service, even while feeling used and abused. Now we have hit the wall and employees are saying, "It's my turn, I want some." *We have reached the end of man-*

agement theory. In short, it's time for a quality program for people. There has never been a more urgent need for change and MOTS is not an option.

The sad truth is that work has been degenerating for thirty years. For most people, work has ceased to become a source of inspiration, joy, leadership, integrity, and authenticity. For many people, organizations have adopted an anti-people approach, with their leaders viewing customers as nothing more than opportunities for manipulation and exploitation. A major consumer products company wiretaps a Cincinnati newspaper reporter because he writes unflattering articles about them. Even as world oil prices decline, oil companies coincidentally raise gasoline prices, by the same amount, on the same day. The tobacco industry contributes to pollution and the death of millions. Banks charge their credit-card customers an interest rate that is 300 percent of prime. A multinational food company battles the Food and Drug Administration in court for the right to label as "fresh" a processed product with a two-year shelf-life.

> **As a splendid palace deserted by its inmates looks like a ruin, so does a man without character, all his material belongings notwithstanding.**
>
> MOHANDAS K. GANDHI

How Did We Lose Our Souls?

How has this condition arisen and what are the solutions? We will explore many parts to this puzzle in this book, all of which are the result of focusing on the personality at the expense of the soul and failing to ask the right questions. One example is the way we have compressed time in our lives. Time frames have been shrinking consistently over the last twenty-five years so that today, especially in organizations, two main time frames rule our lives. The first is the organization's quarter: financial institutions expect organizations to account for their performance every ninety days. Once this task is accomplished, less than ninety days will pass before we are required to do it all over again. All decisions are therefore geared to a ninety-day ritual and every fourth quarter we are summoned to an annual rite called the fiscal year-end, which is celebrated or rationalized in the annual report.

Life revolves around the quarters. We get the behavior we reward and since we reward time-based behavior so well, we should not be surprised by the behavior it generates. What happens when we are driven by short-term criteria? In 1994, Orange County, California, became the largest municipal bankruptcy filing in U.S. history. Former Treasurer Robert L. Citron had built a $7.5-billion portfolio based largely on the advice of Wall Street brokerage, Merrill Lynch, which, in some cases, even underwrote the securities that it sold. Some of the investments were an exotic species known as "inverse floating derivatives." According to one report in 1992, Merrill Lynch "warned Citron that his investment tactics were risky and twice offered to buy back some of the diciest investments." Of course, while they proffered this advice, they continued to sell the same high-risk investments while collecting millions in annual fees and commissions. The fall-out from this short-term strategy was a $1.7-billion loss, a pack of lawsuits, the termination of 400 employees, and the elimination of 300 other positions. "I had no responsibility in these financial decisions, so it does not seem fair that I am now being punished," said Manucheh Yazdi, a sixty-two-year-old research analyst in the County Administrative Office who was fired after fourteen years of employment.

Sheriff Brad Gates cut 129 jobs from his department as well as ninety-eight phones, six fax machines, ten cellular phones, and bottled-water deliveries, and limited jail inmates to coffee with breakfast only. He observed, "There has been a death in the family called Orange County." What we learn from this kind of thing, as if we didn't know already, is that people get hurt when there is extreme pressure to perform in the short term at the expense of the long term.

The other time cycle to which we gear our lives is the eighth-minute time frame. We have all been raised, to a greater or lesser degree, on a diet of television. Although formats vary, especially on cable channels, the interval between commercial breaks (called programming content) is usually around eight minutes. This means that television viewers do not usually watch television for more than eight minutes before their concentration is distracted. As a result, our attention span has been programmed to eight minutes and few of us can concentrate on one thing for much longer. Our work lives pulse to the rhythm of the quarter and the eighth minute, resulting in a generation of short-term thinkers, many of whom now occupy executive positions in modern organizations.

There's three moments in a man's life: when he buys a house, a car, and a new color TV. That's what America is all about.

ARCHIE BUNKER

Environmental issues are not measured in ninety-day increments — they are eternal. The lives of human beings are not enriched by re-engineering, delayering, restructuring or downsizing — all of which serve near-term, not long-term, goals. Bilking little old ladies by siphoning their pension funds into fraudulent savings and loan companies may have served the short-term greed of these institutions but it didn't build the long-term viability of the financial services industry, nor did it create sustained wealth for the elderly. To add insult to industry, it has cost U.S. taxpayers $150 billion. To put this into perspective, the U.S. government spends about $17 billion on family support, $10 billion on farm price supports, and $7 billion for child nutrition annually. Most importantly, these short-term perspectives are driven by the need to nourish the personality and the ego — greed and power — and this is often expressed as a tendency to exploit society rather than serve it. In our workplaces today, there is too little awareness of the need to meet the requirements of the soul, which has anything but a short-term interest.

The Fallacy of Geometric Progression

Growth has been an assumed cornerstone of management theory for the last two hundred years. Try suggesting to leaders, bankers, or politicians that growth will no longer be one of their perennial touchstones and watch the look of bewilderment and disbelief on their faces. It is a message we do not want to hear because we simply have no idea how to run organizations, or our lives for that matter, if they are not continuously growing. All modern management and leadership theories, indeed the very workings of our financial system and our society, depend on it.

The truth that makes men free is for the most part the truth which men prefer not to hear.
HERBERT AGAR

But the theory of endless growth is illogical. The screws of corporate psychosis, dysfunctionality, stress, and exhaustion can only be tightened so far. Eventually, human and corporate implosion occurs. It is simply not possible to keep growing at geometric rates forever. To illustrate this point, I have selected some data at random, and converted them into the charts below. Any other data would have served as well, but these demonstrate the foolishness of our illusion.

Figure 1 shows that the average per-capita consumption of resources in the Western world is 100 times greater than it was at the beginning of the Industrial Revolution two hundred years ago. If we continue at current rates of growth, our consumption will be 200 times greater by the year 2110.

Figure 1
300 Years of
Growing Resource
Utilization

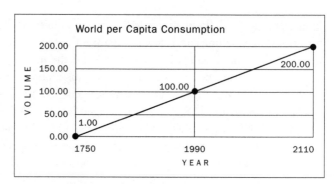

Figure 2
300 Years of
Population Growth

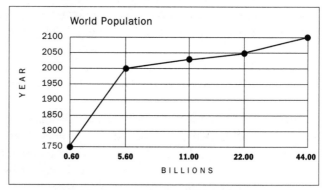

During the same time, as shown in Figure 2, the population has grown ten times. Factor these two expansion curves together and the result is a 1,000-fold increase in growth, pollution, waste, bio-deterioration, stress, and so on.[4] Extrapolate these numbers into the future, with a forecast world population of eleven billion, and even after allowing for significant improvements in waste and pollution controls, it is evident that humans are in danger of overwhelming themselves and the planet.

Figure 3
30 Years
of Rising Crime...

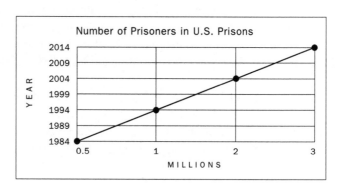

Figure 4
... has led to
ballooning litigious
expansion

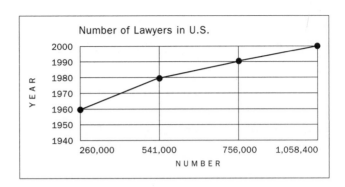

Number of Lawyers in U.S.

Dostoevsky said that prisons are the barometer of society, and Lord Brougham described a lawyer as someone who rescues your money from your enemies and keeps it himself. Figures 3 and 4 show how the growth of both is set to tilt our society. In 1960,

There is hardly a shortage of lawyers. In Washington, where I live, there may actually be more lawyers than people.

JUSTICE SANDRA DAY O'CONNOR

there were 260,000 lawyers in the United States. By 1980, the number had grown to 541,000 and by 1990, there were 756,000. The number of lawyers per 100,000 population in 1970 was 120. It now stands at over 300 and the number of federal lawsuits has tripled. In 1950, the District of Columbia Bar Association had 1,000 lawyers, today there are 61,000. California's 116,000 lawyers each use an average of one ton of paper every year—a total of two million trees.

There is wide dissatisfaction today with the *work more, spend more, enjoy it less,* syndrome. At current rates of increase, the average length of the workweek has the potential to pose a greater health risk than drugs, traffic, or war. At the same time, it is unrealistic to assume that 40 million North Americans will sit idle as the rest of us enjoy the material fruits of overwork.

Figures 5 and 6 simply illustrate what happens if we are naive enough to expect an extrapolation of current growth rates: we cannot simply keep growing at these geometric rates—it is completely illogical.

The chart in Figure 7 shows the rate of new product introduction over eighteen years. In 1980 3,000 new products were introduced; by 1988 the number had grown to 10,000 and by 1993 it stood at 17,000.[5] Maintaining this rate of progression will lead to 29,000 new products being introduced each year to U.S. grocery stores by 1998. The number of items (called stock keeping units or SKUs) in the average grocery store has risen from 15,000 in 1980 to 30,000 in 1994. There are 57 different kinds of

Figure 5
Some of us will
kill ourselves from
overwork . . .

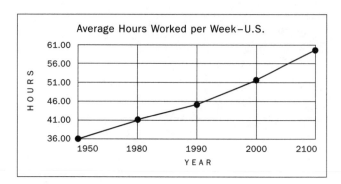

Figure 6
. . . while others kill
for lack of it

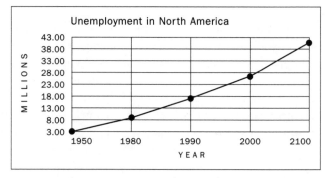

Figure 7
The Proliferation of
New Products

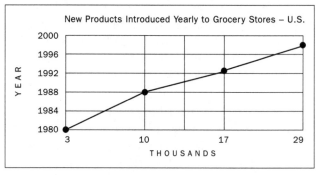

Crest toothpaste alone. We will drown in the confusion of choice if this momentum is maintained.

If we think about it rationally, the mathematics of continued growth, forever and ever, simply do not compute, which is why the figures I have extrapolated previously will not be achieved. Unchecked growth, as in the case of the cancer cell, which is another example of the triumph of a greedy individual at the expense of the rest, leads to collapse of the system and death. We are not the cancer of the planet. We are the hope of the planet.

Figure 8
The Growth of Chip
Memory

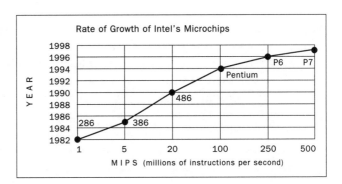

A 5 percent annual growth rate in production or profits, considered modest by many organizations, when compounded for twenty years, results in 165 percent growth and in one hundred years, this growth reaches 13,000 percent. This amounts to silly math when viewed over the long term.

Intel's history of new product innovation and introduction (Figure 8) demonstrates the growth dilemma at the corporate level. Even if continued geometric growth were sustainable for one organization, it cannot be sustainable for all, or even the majority, of organizations. Growth cannot keep climbing onto the shoulders of previous growth forever. If we continue under our spell, these extrapolations chart a frightening picture of the future. But we are awakening from our spell. This is why there is more cause for hope today than at any time during the last 100 years.

We want something that we cannot have: continuous growth. Yet we have become chronic co-dependents of growth. This co-dependency is corrosive to our souls because we know in our hearts that it is a terminal condition for any form of life. We are temporary travelers, on what Buckminster Fuller called "a little automated Spaceship Earth," designed not to be burned out, but to be balanced, in equilibrium with our hearts, our minds, and the bottom line. It is time for regeneration and for us to redesign work so that we can balance our material and spiritual aspirations and integrate them into the larger, and longer-term picture — our lives and souls depend on it. It is time to choose between standards of living and quality of life. On Spaceship Earth, we are not the passengers — we are the crew.

The Dangers of Corporate Anorexia

The waves of downsizing and re-engineering that have hit North America and most of the industrialized world have taken their toll on the soul. We have created the anorexic organization, which, like the anorexic person, is firm and solid on the outside but lacks balance and control on the inside. Medical research now suggests that body fat serves to support our immune system, helps to sustain us when our reserves are low, keeps us warm, and contributes to longer life. Organizations are the same. The "fat," which we might more properly call regeneration, is the unscheduled time we need for reflection and play; our freedom to experiment, take risks, and make mistakes without penalty; our capacity for being creative, dreaming, and playing, and our organizational culture. "Lean-and-mean" organizations have lost this elbow room along with their spirit and are therefore less able to inspire the remaining souls within.

Some traditional managers claim that re-engineering and downsizing can be done humanely, but "humane downsizing" is still an oxymoron. The very term "being downsized" is the ugly euphemism that hides a lie — it cannot disguise the act of firing, terminating or laying off a colleague. Much effort is often expended in attempting to alleviate the personal trauma of loss through outplacement (another euphemism), psychological counseling, and numerous other palliative techniques, just as victims of war or terrorism receive post-trauma care. But the cause of the trauma still remains an act of violence. We need to heal, not amputate; to regenerate, not re-engineer.

This terrorism against the soul can be avoided. New Jersey Governor Christine Todd Whitman's ambitious efforts to reduce the costs of government are a case in point. When a home for veterans was scheduled for privatization, the unionized employees developed a plan for keeping the facility in-house by reducing operating costs by more than $600,000 a year. This facility continues to be run and owned by the state and no-one has lost their job. We all have the imagination to regenerate instead of re-engineer — our souls depend on it.

Perhaps the greatest damage caused by years of downsizing and re-engineering has been the tragic loss of wisdom from within organizations. In restructuring we have fired our elders and they were the keepers of our organizational wisdom. Over the next few years, we will honor our elders once again, rehiring those still willing to return, because, after we have restructured our organizations so that they are as efficient as possible, and they all look the same, spirituality and wisdom will be the only distinguishing features between them.

The pressure to strive for ever-higher performance each quarter is aggravated by the rising competition for jobs. In downsizing, we fire our own customers, many of whom will not find the same level of income again, and in doing this, we reduce the opportunities to create jobs and markets. Each time we raise the stakes for staying in the game of business, the desperation of managers increases, forcing them to cut more corners and settle for lower moral and ethical standards. From this flows the alienation of business by society and their very own employees upon whom they depend for success. Many organizations have abandoned their ascent to higher ground, settling for the lower ground of mediocrity. *The mediocre person is one who has stopped climbing.*

The Evolved Individual

Evolution: An unfolding, opening out, or working out;
process of development, as from a simple to a complex form, or of
gradual, progressive change, as in a social or economic structure

Traditionally, we have attempted to change our personal circumstances by changing our environment — changing what is on the outside instead of what is within. We attempt to reinforce our self-esteem, which is an inner dimension, by spoiling ourselves with a new suit or hair style, which are external dimensions. In the same way, we hope that a change in our organization, which is an external dimension, will enhance our self-esteem. This is a backwards approach — personal evolution must precede corporate evolution.

> **By a willingness to learn and not by dogmatism the love of the spirit is increased. The roads are many but the goal is one, and that is realized by every soul that really seeks for the Divine.**
>
> ANNIE BESANT

To reclaim the higher ground where we can renew our souls, we must first complete our inner work. Once we open ourselves to self-renewal and regeneration, personal evolution can commence, enabling us to ask the important questions of contemporary life: Why is this happening to me? What is going on? Why is everything so chaotic? How can I protect myself? How can I thrive? What is my purpose? What will my legacy be? How do I contribute? How can I be of service?

Personal evolution is the path of personal transformation. In my work I notice that many people are what I call perennial seekers. These are

> **It is an error to imagine that evolution signifies a constant tendency to increased perfection. That process undoubtedly involves a constant remodeling of the organism in adaptation to new conditions; but it depends on the nature of those conditions whether the direction of the modifications effected shall be upward or downward.**
>
> THOMAS HENRY HUXLEY

people who, although they attend seminars, read many books, and study with great masters, fail to *integrate their learning* into their lives. *They know all the answers but none of the questions.* They seem to be stuck and, regardless of their experiences, fail to evolve. The key to personal development and evolution lies not outside ourselves but within. I have found that others are born, live, and die, without ever pausing along the way to meet their soul.

Personal evolution is the result of emotional and spiritual reinvention. It is self-generated. By giving ourselves permission to change our attitudes and our skills, and making it safe for each other to do so, we can begin the inner work that leads to spiritual renewal. We all evolve whether we like it or not. Some of us evolve more and sooner than others, but the choice for each of us is whether we evolve positively or negatively and whether we direct our evolution or not. We cannot expect the teams we lead in organizations to become anything we are not becoming first. Personal evolution precedes corporate evolution.

The path of personal evolution moves through three stages.

Immature: In The Immature Phase, we do not explore consciousness, but simply defer to power and penalty.

Traditional: In The Traditional Phase, our self-doubt and insecurity drive us to behave in ways that are shaped by personality and ego that enable us "to fit in," so that we are accepted by others. Many of us do not progress beyond this phase during our lives. We remain addicted to compensating for our insecurities rather than having the courage to experiment and discover. Many executives become stuck in this mode and I call them Traditional Managers.

Evolving: The Evolving Phase is the most advanced human condition, in which we gain a measure of consciousness by challenging traditional logic, aligning our beliefs, searching for the connection between soulfulness and work, and seeking deeper meaning in our lives. When we think of "an evolved person," we are thinking of a pioneer — a seeker — who is more interested in asking the right questions than offering answers. The evolved individual has left behind mediocrity to follow a path to higher ground—the path of regeneration. These are the new missionaries of corporate life; they ask the challenging questions that cause us all to examine the existing paradigms that have led to spiritual poverty. The questions of the missionary lead to regeneration.

In the Legend of the Holy Grail, Perceval travels the same heroic journey, from the youthful absence of consciousness (Immature), to the doubt caused by the absence of questioning and learning (Traditional), and finally to personal transformation and illumination (Evolving).

The Evolved Organization

There are no evolved organizations—or moral or successful ones for that matter—only evolved, moral, or successful individuals who create them. In my work, nine times out of ten, our research shows that individuals believe that they are more truthful, honest, hardworking, clever, and loyal than the rest of their organization. In survey after survey, the sum of the scores of individuals is greater than the sum of the scores they give for the organization. We live under the illusion that organizations are "them" when, in reality, they are "us." If we wish to work in evolved organizations, we must each be the first to start the journey.

Most traditional managers approach personal as well as organizational leadership as an intellectual process—a subject best handled by the mind. We think that if we can articulate a rational theory of leadership, it will be embraced because of its unassailable logic and elegance. The Quality Movement is a good example of this. Total Quality Management is often treated as a process, complete with mathematical formulae, measurement tools, process controls, statistical analysis, data collection tools, cybernetic systems, and feedback loops. TQM becomes a "program" that is "good for the organization," frequently championed by a senior executive such as the CEO, who, out of the blue one Monday morning, announces the "Corporate Quality Program" to a group of wide-eyed, uninvolved skeptical employees.

Over a number of years, I worked very closely with the leaders of a large agricultural cooperative, guiding them through a journey of strategic renewal. The vice president of human resources was asked to create a proposal for changing the corporate culture into one that would inspire and motivate all employees. The resulting proposals presented to the executive team some weeks later described an elaborate plan to hire consultants to redesign the merit increase compensation systems and the pension plan! It will take more than technical adjustments to the pension plan to change corporate culture, let alone inspire the soul!

Many processes, such as re-engineering, customer service, downsizing, and just-in-time inventory, are viewed the same way—as issues of the mind that treat organizations as an intellectual game. *But the mind will only do what the heart tells it to.* We have lost sight of the fact that work is a game of the heart as well as the mind. Playing the game well has a beneficial effect on the bottom line—but it is not the only, or even the primary, goal. It is a union between what I call "The Heart, Mind, and Bottom Line" and the purpose of the evolved organization is to inspire the soul—hence the organization of this book into three similar and symbiotic parts. We cannot continue to separate the three components of Heart, Mind, and Bottom Line if we wish to develop high-performance individuals and organizations and make work fun again. Only by integrating all three can we help people to evolve at the personal level, thus empowering them to create enlightened teams and therefore transform their organizations. Through this integration, we can create organizations that inspire the soul and therefore the planet.

Whom Does It Serve?

For leaders of western organizations, the thought of reconnecting business with the soul requires an enormous leap of faith and courage. *Reclaiming Higher Ground* suggests that the era of personality is over and a new era is about to commence, in which we will need to completely redesign work and organizations, as well as our leadership style, so that they speak to the needs of the soul. For many, this will be a big dose to swallow. For them, it will be frightening to walk away from the comfortable, if outdated, beliefs in the valley, to grope along an unfamiliar path leading to the higher ground where there are radical ideas, contrary thinking, and new ways of being. Many will counter these ideas with cynicism, the definition of which is *creativity that is repressed.* Cynics cannot imagine an alternative possibility that contradicts their current beliefs. They will be afraid of change, but we need to be sensitive to their fears, because, to them, they are real. As organizational

Courage is grace under pressure.
ERNEST HEMINGWAY

missionaries, it is our responsibility to hold their hands and guide them safely to higher ground. This is the responsibility of all of us, since we are all missionaries.

Our souls are crying for less restraint, fewer strictures, and more capacity. We are yearning for regeneration, which is achieved through truthfulness, courage, grace, joy, rewards, beauty, collaboration, knowledge, freedom, creativity, community, and honor — the subjects of this book. The soul does not like to run a marathon in a hair shirt. For many people today, the awesome gifts bestowed on them by business, not the least of these being derived from the wonders of modern technology, have come with too many strings attached. Today's employees, customers, and suppliers (whom I prefer to describe as *partners* since they are members of our team) view organizations with a curious combination of hope and distrust. On the one hand, no other sector of our society holds as much potential to ravage the soul and our planet. In its current form, dedicated as it is to the cult of personality, the modern organization is heading for an evolutionary dead-end. On the other hand, no other sector of our society could do as much to bring about the positive changes that would uplift the human spirit. The reinvented modern organization has the global reach, influence, talent, knowledge, assets, and the technology to make the world a better place through service to humanity. More than any other group in society, it has the potential to reclaim higher ground and inspire the soul.

> **My great religion is a belief in the blood, the flesh, as being wiser than the intellect. We can go wrong in our minds. But what our blood feels and believes and says is always true.**
>
> D. H. LAWRENCE

No one is comfortable when they begin the journey from the known to the unknown, but we can be comforted by the knowledge that the summit is not really new. We are not leaving home; we are coming home. We used to live on this higher ground long ago — we are simply reclaiming it. It beckons us to return. First though, we must learn to ask the right questions, beginning with, "Whom does it serve?"

PART ONE

THE HEART

The world is too much with us; late and soon,
Getting and spending, we lay waste our powers:
Little we see in nature that is ours;
We have given our hearts away, a sordid boon.
WILLIAM WORDSWORTH

1

Body and Soul

Moving from Personality to Soul

Our personality is our exterior. For many people, it is all that we see in each other. It is shaped by our environment, our genes, our parents, and our life experiences. We express our personalities through our lifestyle, (occupation, status, material assets, car, home, and other toys), the way we interact with each other, our physical presence (health, fashion, and style), and our values and beliefs. Our personality reacts to need fulfilment and we meet our needs by using our personality to manipulate and control our environment, as well as each other, through the use of five senses: taste, hearing, smell, touch, and sight.

Since the seventeenth century, and especially during the last 100 years, which gave birth to modern psychology and behavioral studies, organizational theory has been centered on improving our effectiveness in manipulating, controlling, and fulfilling the needs of employees, customers, and partners. Consumer marketing is based on appeals to the personality and we manage organizations in much the same way — for and by the personality. We try to make people run faster (you will earn a prize if you meet your sales quota), be more efficient (you will get a bonus if you bring this project in on time), meet the needs of the customer (you will get the order if you throw in the warranty), and so on. We are appealing to the status, ego, survival, and recognition needs of the personality.

Our history of leadership theory is firmly rooted in the psychology of personality — to the exclusion of the soul. In a recent newsletter, one of the world's largest firms of industrial psychologists wrote, "Some executives allow emotion to override reason. Their conclusions are based more on their feelings at the time the conclusion was drawn than on the relevant facts. Conversely, more effective executives are better able to contain their emotions and base their conclusions on facts rather than feelings."[1] The implication is that "good" decisions should not be compromised by emotions or feelings. Yet people in organizations everywhere are crying out for *more,* not less, emotion — for *greater* consideration of feelings, not less. They want their souls to be *included,* not excluded. More than anything else, what people detest about their work is that it is driven too much by the mind and not enough by the heart. We are delivering answers from the mind, and forgetting to ask questions that come from the heart. We have yet to learn the advantages of giving control to others over "having it all" ourselves.

Generally speaking, we live in an age in which the personality has eclipsed the soul. We have come to believe that people's self-worth is no more than their net worth. Although the fields of psychology and psychoanalysis have amassed an immense body of knowledge, much of this work has been limited to crude concepts of motivation, performance, and leadership based on personality. All our techniques are dedicated to refining these appeals.

But what if we replaced this tired paradigm with a new understanding of individuals, not as personalities or egos alone, but as souls as well? Suppose we adapted organizations so that they met the needs of the soul of the customer, as well as the personality? Suppose we learned to relate with each other through a sixth sense: soul-to-soul communication? Suppose we became skilled at integrating soul with personality in our work and throughout our lives? Since there has been no precedent in corporate history for such a breakthrough, it is hard to comprehend the implications for personal and therefore organizational transformation — the new vistas open to us from the vantage point of this higher ground would steal our breath away.

Asking the Right Questions

The path of the soulful missionary is strewn with hazards. But who puts them there — others or ourselves? This question can be illuminated by further questions. Let's see if we can ask some appropriate questions together.

Relax for a few moments. Take a few deep breaths and dissolve your tensions. Feel the positive energy flowing into your body. Reflect on your organization and your role within it. Run your eyes over the questions below. Dig deep into your heart and resonate with your answers. Stretch — be as ambitious as possible for your soul. When you are ready, write down each answer using no more than one or two words.

Now probe deeper by asking yourself some additional questions. What would it take to achieve the changes you yearn for? What is really stopping them from happening? Apart from the excuses of traditional thinkers where we work and our entrenched ways of doing things, what

1. Do I stand up for what I believe in?	
2. Do I honor equally my female and male energies?	
3. Do I regard people inside and outside our organization as sacred?	
4. Is my organization an expression of love?	
5. How does my work help to heal the planet?	
6. What would make my work more soulful?	
7. What could I do to become a more soulful person?	
8. Who is the most soulful person where I work? How can I help everyone's souls to grow as much?	
9. What would really inspire my soul?	
10. What else?	
11. ... and what else – something that I have never told anyone before?	
12. What could my company do differently that would reach my soul?	
13. What could my employees do to inspire my soul?	
14. How could my colleagues create magic for my soul?	
15. How could I make our workplace more soulful for our employees?	

prevents you from making a breakthrough for the soul? Who is preventing change — you or your organization? Your personality or your soul? What are you prepared to risk to make your life more soulful? Would it be worth it? Or is it more comfortable to protect the material gains achieved in life so far? As you answer each question, ask *why*? Keep asking why until it comes from your soul.

The decisions we make in our lives tend to reflect both our material and spiritual values. The instructions and advice we receive from the personality tend to be driven by the need to gratify our egos: material comforts, personal worth, career progress, approval, status, power, control, and reputation — the things that preoccupy us when we have lost sight of the essential. Our soul gives instructions that are derived from sacredness, reverence, integrity, love, meaning, compassion, and values. We make these decisions based on these different choices every day and our emphasis varies depending on how far we have each traveled on our journeys of personal learning, discovery, and evolvement. A useful means for choosing is to consider these three questions:

1. "What are the instructions from my personality? If I were to follow the instructions from my personality, how would I make this decision?"
2. "What are the instructions from my soul? If I were to follow the instructions from my soul, how would I make this decision?"
3. "Which of these instructions shall I follow?"

An adaptation of Perceval's question can be a useful guide. "Whom does it serve — the personality or the soul?" We have unlimited power to make choices and we exercise these choices every day by following the instructions of the personality or the soul. The outcomes can redirect and change our lives, as well as those of others — forever. We *can* break the spell we are under.

Why the Soul Is Shut Out

Traditional managers dismiss the notion of a workplace with soul, which I prefer to call a Sanctuary, believing that this is a role more appropriate to organized religion. (For more on the Sanctuary, please see page 37.) This attitude is based on the misconception that spirituality and other "soft stuff" have no place in organizations. *Reclaiming Higher Ground* will show that an awesome opportunity awaits those who are tired of the MOTS approach to leadership and who have the courage to blaze a promising new trail.

We have traditionally believed that "business is business" and that spirituality should not be a part of work. This belief, of course, does not square with the experience of millions of uninspired souls who yearn for a new generation of evolving leaders, who will assume their true roles as custodians of the human spirit. We long for leaders who will regenerate our organizations and create the appropriate environment in which our souls can flourish. The evolved individuals who offer a soaring vision of their organization's purpose on this planet will create soulful workplaces — Sanctuaries — that invite employees to bring their souls to work as well as their minds. The ambition driving this approach is the need to reward people both in the pocketbook *and* in the soul. Until now, we have tended to focus mainly on the former.

> **Spiritual ignorance is often so complete that people do not realize they are ignorant.**
>
> T. D. MUNDA

What Exactly Is the Soul?

Psychotherapist Thomas Moore has written, "It is impossible to define what the soul is. Definition is an intellectual enterprise anyway; the soul prefers to imagine. We know intuitively that soul has to do with genuineness and depth, as when we say certain music has soul or a remarkable person is soulful. When you look closely at the image of soulfulness, you see that it is tied to life in all its particulars — good food, satisfying conversation, genuine friends and experiences that stay in the memory and touch the heart. Soul is revealed in attachment, love, and community, as well as in retreat on behalf of inner communing and intimacy."[2]

> **Four thousand volumes of metaphysics will not teach us what the soul is.**
>
> VOLTAIRE

With something as resistant to definition as soul, how can we prescribe a path that leads to greater soulfulness? Most of us have an innate understanding of soul, even though each of us might define it in a very different and personal way. We intuitively understand that we have a body and a soul and that each needs nourishing. Taking care of the body alone leaves us feeling empty and unfulfilled. It is a feeling that is hard to describe, but one that is frequently experienced.

For me, the soul is the immortal or spiritual part of us. It is our essence — our moral and emotional fiber, our warmth, and our force. It is the vital part of us that transcends our temporary existence; it is our nobleness within. We are souls with bodies, not bodies with souls, or as Pierre Teilhard de Chardin put it, souls seeking a human experience not humans seeking a spiritual experience. The soul pursues values that respect the sacredness in everything, including humans. The soul reveres the truth and honors promises. The soul embodies a continuous state of grace, rejecting violence and competition and celebrating harmony, cooperation, sharing, and reverence for life, because it sees the sacredness of things. It seeks balance and freedom and yearns to be whole with the universe.

Our minds are limited to dealing in possibilities, but our souls are capable of reaching beyond the traditional, to the magical and the richly elaborated dream. What the limited mind considers a miracle, the soul considers routine. The soul flourishes in beauty. The soul thrives on information, learning, and growth as well as the opportunity to share its essence with others. The soul is the essential "more" that exists in our work, our play, our friends, our families, our environment, material objects, and all of life's activities. It is this "more," this magic that inspires the soul, that is missing from our work and therefore our lives. We must all seek to reclaim it.

> This country will not be a good place for any of us to live in unless we make it a good place for all of us to live in.
>
> THEODORE ROOSEVELT

The word "spirit," which the dictionary defines as having the same meaning as soul, derives from the Latin *spiritus* or *spirare*, meaning "to breathe, to give life." "Inspire" is a closely related word that means "to breathe in." Unless we breathe in, there is no life, just as without spirit or soul, there is no life. Hence the subtitle of this book, *Creating Organizations That Inspire the Soul.*

Balance: Restoring Our Female Energy

The Chinese believe that there are two forces in the universe: yin, the feminine, passive, negative force; and yang, the masculine, active, positive force. Yin and yang are based on the principles of balance and interdependence, and a perfect system is evenly represented by both. They are a unified system, with all things having aspects of yin as well as yang, and their energy rules everything in the natural world. In the Arthurian legends, the chalice represents male energy (yang) and the blade represents female energy (yin). Just as time is composed of day (yang) and night (yin), so too are humans composed of the soul (yin) and the personality (yang).

Though linked, and ideally aligned, with the personality, the soul is different from it. Where the soul has a life that transcends the body, preceding and surviving it, the personality is temporary, expiring when the body does. The personality is an accumulation of external, social conditioning and the values of our time blended with the drives and aspirations of the ego. The personality enables us to manage the basic tasks of life and is susceptible to the influences of others. *A personality that is successful by all exterior measures may not indicate a fulfilled soul.* And a personality, radiating the confidence of male energy, may hide the soul's truth—that it yearns for the balance that includes the female energy.

In the Arthurian legend of the Holy Grail, young Perceval learns the knightly code of religion, ethics, chivalry, and the art of arms from the

Figure 9: Yin and Yang

vavasor Gurnemant of Gohort, who teaches him that he must be merciful to any knights he may vanquish, observe his faith, avoid being too talkative, and aid anyone in distress. Perceval tells Gurnemant that his mother gave him the same advice. Gurnemant advises Perceval that in order to realize his full potential of becoming one of the greatest knights in the land, he must not say that he learned the code of chivalry from his mother because people will think him foolish. Instead, he should say that he was taught by Gurnemant. In following this advice, Perceval, like many of us, became inauthentic. He denied his female energy and became a partial person.

We still follow this advice today—no less among women than men. Our society judges the asking of questions (yin) to be a sign of weakness, and the offering of answers as a sign of strength. This partly explains why many men refuse to take women seriously as competent senior executives. Ironically, as many women ascend the corporate ladder and assume positions of executive responsibility and leadership, they often distance themselves from the female energy of their souls. Male and female energy is not deter-

Perhaps everything that frightens us is, in its deepest essence, something helpless that wants our love.
RAINER MARIA RILKE

mined by gender, but by the balance between yin and yang in each of us. The yang is evident in characteristics such as ambition, drive, competition, and power; the yin manifests itself in compassion, love, relationships, and nature. We attain balance in our lives through the equilibrium between yin and yang, but traditionally, the personality drives our female energy away from our soul, causing yin to give way to yang.

We tend to be afraid of the energy that is complementary to our gender. The personalities of traditional men guard against appearing to be wishy-washy to others. The personalities of traditional women fear the rejection that results from macho behavior. Yet we can only achieve personal balance when yin and yang are in harmony — we are not whole until this balance is reached. So the question for men is, How can I honor my female energy? And the question for women is, How can I honor my male energy? These questions, when answered by each of us in our own ways, lead to personal evolution and growth, providing the inner peace and balance that is essential for our time.

So Rich, Yet So Poor

Our society is experiencing a paradox of wealth: we have never been so rich, yet we have never been so poor. We are experiencing both the greatest period of material prosperity and scientific achievement as well as the greatest period of social breakdown. In January 1995, a Time/CNN poll reported that 53 percent of Americans agreed that the country is in "deep and serious trouble," compared to 40 percent a decade ago.[3]

On the one hand, we are rich with the material assets that smooth our physical existence: money, time, holidays, technology, and science. On the other hand, we suffer the extreme poverties of the soul: stress, burnout, isolation, substance abuse, prejudice, crime, and lack of balance and meaning.

> **It was the best of times, it was the worst of times, it was the age of wisdom, it was the age of foolishness, it was the epoch of belief, it was the epoch of incredulity, it was the season of Light, it was the season of Darkness, it was the spring of hope, it was the winter of despair, we had everything before us, we had nothing before us...**
>
> CHARLES DICKENS, *A TALE OF TWO CITIES*

As change accelerates, we feel more alienated and confused. There is emptiness in our lives — in our souls in fact — and we hunger for meaning. At work, we yearn for more but we are reaping less. In our search for personal meaning, we do not identify with the essence of our work, but with the trappings that appeal to the personality: the status of the company, our proximity to the corner office, our title, our income — all used to measure our acceptance, achievement, and personal worth. We even gain identity from merely surviving in the dangerous world of downsizing and restructuring. There is scant meaning in the intrinsic value of our work and its beneficial effect on humans and the planet.

This paradox contains another dilemma: we continue to rely on material rewards as our principal means of appealing to and motivating the personalities of others, despite the clear and growing evidence that our souls crave regeneration: spiritual, not material, rewards. This is true throughout our lives, but especially at work. This subject will be addressed more fully in Chapter 7, Soul Provider.

We are getting richer and richer . . .	
Success	Power
Wealth	Consumer choice
Ambition	Technology
Pride	Entertainment
Prestige	Science
Speed	Lower costs
Information	Freedom
Vacations	

. . . as we get poorer and poorer	
Burnout	Loss of spirit
Stress	Less wonder
Lack of balance	Crime
Loneliness	Prejudice
Fear	Lack of meaning
Less time	Ecological
Absence of wisdom	Degradation
Unhappiness	Selfishness
Lack of renewal	Less fun

Figure 10 So poor and yet so rich

The Mechanical Organization

Organizations today may be broadly categorized into three types:

- the mechanical organization
- the chaotic organization
- the Sanctuary

We owe much of our life-view to Sir Isaac Newton. During the seventeenth century, he gave us the laws of gravity and motion, the binomial theorem, differential and integral calculus, and a new spin on the humble apple. He also created the scientific revolution. Before Newton, the mysteries of life were largely explained by the wisdom within each of us. Mystics, healers, spiritual teachers, theologians, priests, magicians, and storytellers—the keepers of female energy—were our guides, and our decisions were based on inner knowing, intuition, meditation, prayer, and service. We relied more on folklore, wisdom, and myth.

Since Newton, the scientific model, based on the yang characteristics of controlled observation, experimentation, and mechanics, has ruled our lives. We ask for proof before accepting an explanation, requiring scientific evidence for our decisions, saying, "I'll believe it when I see it." This causal, logical approach to science, and therefore life, introduced by Newton, taught us to look outside ourselves for meaning and perception instead of within. In time we replaced instinct, metaphysics, and self-awareness with scientific evidence: "If you prove it to me, I'll believe it."

The Newtonian worldview is based more on mechanics than metaphysics. We respect and understand the universe by thinking of it as a machine made from separate parts and we have come to dismiss other methods of learning and knowing. Consequently, we tend to view everything as a giant clockwork or engine, whether it is nature, religion, government, wellness, supply and demand in the marketplace—even raising children or training a puppy.

Change your thoughts and you change your world.

NORMAN VINCENT PEALE

The Newtonian worldview is based on the male energy of scientific, mechanical cause and effect: if you do this, then this will happen—if you are good, you will go to heaven; if we pay you a commission, you will sell more; if you like my advertisement, you will buy my product. Because this causal approach leads us to translate our experiences into mechanical cause-and-effect models, our capacity to explain is very limited. We only see "parts," never seeing the yin and the yang of the whole or accepting what we cannot explain with our mechanical reasoning.

Guided by Newtonian logic, mechanical organizations are built on the same kind of command and control structures originated by the Roman army and perfected by the Roman Catholic Church. These machinelike cultures provide policy manuals, hierarchies, job descriptions, titles, and goals. Typically, mechanical organizations develop financial yardsticks and performance measures, strategic planning models, organization charts, PERT diagrams, and elaborate systems — all means of gathering information in order to control. Charismatic leaders do the thinking and everyone else follows the policies and procedures manual. The "corporation-as-machine" metaphor has become the basis of our modern models of the organization, the subject of most management research, the archetype for MBA programs, and the media stereotype of the modern corporate leader.

Organizations viewed as machines are the perfect venue for, largely male, engineers and financial specialists to apply Newton's theories of motion to management. Planning, organizing, implementing, and controlling became the curricula of every course and the theses of every text. There is little room for activities that promote the soul in mechanical organizations, where innovation, creativity, fun or adventure are sometimes admired but seldom fostered. These tend to be denigrated as "warm fuzzies" or "touchy-feely thinking." We ridicule our essential female energies and therefore suppress them. Consequently, the soul is not generally inspired at work in mechanical organizations, only regaining its inspiration and coming alive again as soon as it finds a Sanctuary.

Among shareholders and traditional managers, there has been little buy-in to the notion that a change of approach is necessary. By most traditional measures, mechanical organizations have been an outstanding success. By controlling the inputs, processes, and outputs, just like a machine, certain predictable results can often be forecast, including the financial returns for shareholders and the productivity ratios for employees. John Bryan, CEO of Sara Lee for over twenty years, believes that, "There's a problem in big and successful companies. The people in them want to take charge. You have to fight that all the time."[5] Bryan has built his frozen foods and famous brands like Playtex, Hanes, and Coach leatherware, into a $16-billion powerhouse. Empowering, inspiring, and lifting the spirits of Sara Lee's 138,000 employees will probably be a hard-sell to the company's shareholders, who have been receiving annual returns of over 20 percent. *The music is irrelevant if the audience is deaf.*

Change will not gather pace until we honor the female energy within ourselves and our organizations. As we reflect on the changes we need to make, employees have already hit the wall and are demanding a new quality program — this time for people. So we do not have long. A revolutionary movement dedicated to restoring our rights to honor our souls has already begun. The evolved leader will adapt, release the long-imprisoned female energy and help others to do the same, while the traditional managers will be passed by.

The Chaotic Organization

In the early 1970s, a new scientific kid on the block arrived to challenge Newton's Laws. It was called Chaos Theory. The Newtonian idea that nature operates in a cause-and-effect manner assumed that if scientists could identify all the major components of an event, they could forecast all the potential outcomes. Edward Lorenz, a meteorologist from the Massachusetts Institute of Technology, discovered that minute variations in data could produce massive variations in weather systems, not just small ones, as had been previously believed. Lorenz called this the butterfly effect, because, through the use of computer simulations, he postulated, a butterfly flapping its wings in China could materially affect the weather across North America. He proved that there is a kind of order in disorder.[6]

Chaos Theory suggests that the apparent randomness of simple things is not as random as it seems. A plume of smoke rising from a chimney appears to swirl and drift in a chaotic manner but the underlying equations, if their complexity can be understood, can explain each seemingly chaotic eddy. As children, when we built a cone-shaped sandpile and added more handfuls of sand, little sand-slides would cascade downwards. The same mathematical formula that explains the activity of the swirling smoke from the chimney can describe activity anywhere: the sand grains; the collision of electrons with atoms in an electrical resistor; the flaring of spots on the sun; the movement of share prices or currency exchange rates; or the way people behave in organizations. According to Dr. Per Bak of the Brookhaven National Laboratory in New York, the sandpile is constantly trying to organize itself, hence the term, "self-organized criticality." In this example, the grains of sand have what physicists define as "a large number of degrees of freedom."[7] Yet only a few forces seem to be at work: handfuls of sand are being scooped up and dropped on approximately the same place at varying intervals.

Start-up and entrepreneurial organizations are hybrids, sharing many of the characteristics of Newtonian, machinelike models and Chaos Theory. A few key factors are at work: high energy, enthusiasm, innovation, risk-taking, survival, growth, focused strategy, commitment to the customer, hands-on practices, lack of complexity. At first blush, only these and a few other seemingly simple and very measurable things are happening, but in reality, the complexity and therefore the chaos beneath the surface is almost infinite. The organization does not have the capacity or the experience to implement a command and control, "know-all-the-facts-and-predict-the-future" model — the mechanical organization. I call this type of organization, the chaotic organization.

Despite these limitations, chaotic organizations, in their dash for growth and survival, unconsciously blend the features of mechanical (autocratic, goal-dominant, purposeful, linear behavior) and soulful practice (having fun, achieving rewards, being in flow, learning and growing, operating with integrity, developing friendships and camaraderie, celebrating mastery, and making a difference while making money). The energy and fun generated while parlaying minimal resources into customer satisfaction and profitability translates into mechanical, yet soulful, and therefore, chaotic work. If control and power are the defining characteristics of mechanical organizations, fun and spontaneity are the characteristics of chaotic organizations. Different personality types are drawn to and thrive in these entirely different environments.

> **You will derive your supreme satisfaction not from your ability to amass things or to achieve superficial power but from your ability to identify yourselves with others and to share fully in their needs and hopes. In short, for fulfillment, we look to identification rather than acquisition.**
>
> NORMAN COUSINS

The chaotic organization, during the early years at least, can inspire the soul like few others. Microsoft is a chaotic organization. Of Microsoft's nearly 20,000 employees, most staff members with over six years' seniority are independently wealthy, and more than 2,000 are millionaires — having exercised 50 million stock options worth over $3 billion. Yet most are not inspired by the money. Senior executive Mike Maples says, "We are able to keep [these employees] because their jobs are meaningful, not because they need more money." Says Stewart Konzen, a

Microsoft veteran, "Who wants to retire? What is the point of that? I do cool stuff already." Software legend Charles Simonyi, the designer of Multiplan, which was the predecessor of Excel, adds, "The possibilities to change the world are even greater now than in the 1980s."[8] A sense of meaning is one of the most powerful human motivators and a common characteristic of chaotic organizations.

Possibilities and Voids

While the scientific community is replacing the Newtonian model with the new laws of quantum physics, the business community clings to the old, machine-based paradigm. The Newtonian model has long ceased to be at the cutting edge of science; it is not even taught anymore in the science courses of leading universities because it is considered to be more appropriate to elementary history than science classes.

Yet leadership theory has yet to catch up. Let me illustrate with the following example. Newton believed that the world was made up of matter consisting of discrete particles — atoms — that attract, repel, or resist each other like billiard balls. In quantum physics, however, matter is either a wave (when it is in motion, such as light or sound) or a particle (when it is stationary), and one of the strange concepts of quantum physics is that atoms are both, all the time. The Uncertainty Principle of quantum physics, articulated by Werner K. Heisenberg, suggests that one can measure the exact position of something or its speed, but not both. Electrons and other subatomic entities are neither particles nor waves but a combination of both called a "wave packet." Heisenberg and others, such as Niels Bohr, suggested that there is therefore no reality, only possibility. This concept replaces Newtonian determinism.

> An important scientific innovation rarely makes its way gradually winning over and converting its opponents: it rarely happens that Saul becomes Paul. What does happen is that its opponents gradually die out and that the growing generation is familiarized with the idea from the beginning.
>
> MAX PLANCK

Since all matter consists of waves and particles, including people, markets, customers, unions, governments, interest rates, and so forth, how can we measure them like billiard balls? How can we have faith in research or strategic plans? All we can be sure of is that there are possibilities, not realities. Nothing is certain, only possible. The entire universe, of which modern organizations are a small part, works in this way. As we begin to grasp this unfamiliar notion, we will start to rethink our entire approach to people and work — and therefore the soul.

In quantum field theory, the basic, underlying reality of everything is called a quantum vacuum. One might think of it as a sea of possibilities waiting to happen, which, when they do, become particles, then atoms, and eventually, the reality of everything in the universe. Before something can exist, it remains a possibility, waiting to happen. The quantum vacuum is the container for all of these possibilities. Therefore, one can speculate that consciousness is born within the quantum vacuum, and therefore that the soul emanates from the same place — deep within all of us at the subatomic level of quantum physics. This concept is not dissimilar to the philosophy of the Buddhist void. In fact, since the quantum void consists only of possibilities, there is ample room within it to accommodate all of the religious, mystical, and scientific theories that purport to explain the origin of the soul.

Carl Jung introduced the concept of synchronicity as an appropriate explanation of certain life events. Synchronicity, he argued, is a relationship between events or possibilities, based not on mechanics, but on their participation in a pattern of events — it is the pattern that relates them. It is the same with our souls. The internet is a striking contemporary example.

When a number of possibilities come together, they start to take form. From here, ideas, actions, space, and time result. These are awkward concepts for most of us to grasp because we have been reared on Cartesian reductionism — the practice of attempting to understand things by breaking them down into their smallest component parts — and our heads are not used to contemplating a world without labels, let alone one in which there is no reality, space, or time, only possibilities. Yet when we do think this way, we are presented with a world in which nothing is a given and everything is a possibility. This permits us to make choices.

The Sanctuary: A Community of Souls

One of those choices is to replace our old human configurations with Sanctuaries. A Sanctuary is a special place that is different from the rest of our environments. A Sanctuary is not a collection of parts but an integrated system of souls — not so much a place but a state of mind in which they may flourish. A Sanctuary is a state of consciousness, embracing the concepts described in *Reclaiming Higher Ground*, shared by a community of souls. It is a place that beckons, and even the thought of a visit there is eagerly anticipated. The Sanctuary renews our soul and refreshes us because it is even more than a physical location — it is an attitude. Sanctuaries are often formed by groups of like-minded individuals who seldom meet, but who share values; people who love, trust, and respect each other and enjoy a common code — like clubs, tribes, or communities. Synchronicity draws them to a Sanctuary. Sanctuaries are led and populated by people who have made personal breakthroughs and are liberating and being liberated by their souls.

In organizations, these enlightened Sanctuary dwellers realize that loss of morale, market share, obsolescence, declining profits, employee resignations, and corporate neuroses cannot be resolved by focusing on controls and cost-cutting alone. They create Sanctuaries because they know that the questions they wish to raise about the issues troubling people and organizations today are just as likely be found in the heart as they are in the mind, or in the soul as much as in the personality. Members of a Sanctuary are not afraid to let go — to surrender control and to be honest about their vulnerabilities as well as their strengths. A Sanctuary embraces human solutions just as much as technological solutions. The members of a Sanctuary don't re-engineer and put people last, they re-conceptualize, regenerate, and put people first. In a Sanctuary, celebrating and respecting the diversity of individual color, race, religion, social style, belief, and so on, is not as important as understanding the value of unity. We are all part of the universe; we are part of one, interdependent, universal, and eternal soul.

In many entrepreneurial organizations functioning in survival mode, the idea of helping each other to thrive may be considered valid only in California, but this is the very hallmark of a Sanctuary. In a Sanctuary, the old-fashioned myth of rugged individualism and heroic leadership has been replaced by a more inclusive set of values, emphasizing what is good for you as well as what is good for me. (This Values Shift *from me to you* is described more fully in the following chapter.)

The Role of Corporate Democracy in Freeing the Soul

With the fall of the Berlin Wall and the democratization of the Eastern Bloc, some believe that the Western corporate oligarchy is the last remaining nondemocratic institution. For many, democracy is not a word associated with organizational hierarchy. Yet there is an emerging awareness that there is more to life than working for a machine that makes you feel like one. The clockwork, mechanical view of people and work is alienating and obsolete, and alienation is one of the most grievous diseases of the soul. It is time to listen to our hearts as attentively as we have been listening to our minds.

The modern commercial organization — our most powerful and influential institution — almost certainly faces extinction unless we consciously gather our spiritual resources. As Ben Cohen, co-founder of Ben and Jerry's Homemade Ice Cream, has pointed out, "Business is the only institution that is capable of solving social and environmental problems. Business is the most powerful force in the country; business controls the country. It's business and business [people's] money that funds political campaigns and pays for most of the lobbyists in Congress. It's businesses that do most of what goes on in the country. Most of our daily interactions involve business. Businesses have created most of our social and environmental problems. If business were instead trying to solve these problems, they would be solved in short order."[9]

Rome fell because of a leaching away of meaning and a loss of faith.
LEWIS MUMFORD

A Public Agenda Forum study found that four out of five people agree with the statement, "I have an inner need to do the very best job I can regardless of pay." However, the same study revealed that although people believe they have some discretion and control over the effort they give to their jobs, fewer than one in five use this freedom of choice to fulfil their inner need to do the very best job. Forty-eight percent of respondents surveyed by Gallup said they would work harder and do a better job if they were more involved in decisions relating to their work. When asked why they didn't do so, they said that any increase in output would only benefit someone else — management, customers, or shareholders. As pollster Daniel Yanklevich states, "The leaders who run our institutions do not really understand today's workforce: tens of millions of well-educated Americans, proud of their achievements, zealous of their freedoms, motivated by new values, with substantial control over their own production, and ready to raise their level of effort if given the proper encouragement."[10]

Business has done more to integrate culture and values on our planet than organized religion or government. With values that are directed from the soul, the modern organization is our primary, and best-adapted, agent of world change. Business States may conceivably replace Nation States someday — if they can evolve successfully into soulful Nation States.

Creating a Sanctuary

Today, people are afraid in the workplace and there is a profound yearning to feel secure again. We are all looking for a Sanctuary — a haven from which fear has been banished. Enlightened leaders who want to create a Sanctuary begin by removing fear from the workplace. A fearful organization that is under siege from downsizing, competition, loss of market share, low morale, and intimidation cannot lift its collective soul.

The process of creating a safe Sanctuary is arduous and long, and it is started by enlightened leaders systematically introducing the changes in culture described in the following chapters. Other organizations simply blink at these notions, dismissing them as "new age" fluff. Clinging to their old mechanical beliefs, these dinosaur organizations hunker down one last time in a futile attempt to survive.

Personality is a great servant but a lousy master. The personality-driven organization, relying only on its five senses and the Newtonian model, is merely waiting to die, or evolve into the new conceptual framework in which organizations are run for and from the soul. Evolved organizations gather their courage and walk boldly and bravely into the future by creating a Sanctuary for employees, customers, and suppliers. In creating these safe spaces, we are not naively intending to change the entire world, just our day-to-day part of it. We can get to the larger task later. For now, the best place to start is with ourselves, and then, when we are ready, we can add one other person. Together, we can then make a pact committing us to living by an agreed code, a set of values, on which we build a sacred relationship. Over time, we are able to add another soulmate, and then another, until we finally create a team that is a Sanctuary. Others do the same, and we help them, and as time passes, our organizations include many Sanctuaries. Eventually, the entire organization is transformed into a natural and sacred place — a Sanctuary.

By these acts we are creating a safe space in an otherwise unsafe world — a place so unique that it commands us to spring from our beds in the morning and be a part of its comforting embrace. A Sanctuary is a condition of serenity, inspiration, love, and personal development. It is a place that beckons us because it speaks directly to the needs of the soul. In a personality-driven, mechanical organization, 80 percent of the employees hate their work and distrust their leaders because the organization has lost its soul. In a Sanctuary, work and life are sacred. This is the environment in which the soul is able to exercise its one essential birthright, which is to express itself — to be real.

The Skin Horse had lived longer in the nursery than any of the others...He was wise, for he had seen a long succession of mechanical toys arrive to boast and swagger, and by and by break their mainsprings and pass away, and he knew that they were only toys, and would never turn into anything else. For nursery magic is very strange and wonderful, and only those play-things that are old and wise and experienced like the Skin Horse understand all about it.

"What is REAL?" asked the Rabbit one day... "Does it mean having things that buzz inside you and a stick-out handle?"

"Real isn't how you are made," said Skin Horse, "It is a thing that happens to you. When a child loves you for a long, long time, not just to play with, but REALLY loves you, then you become Real."

"Does it hurt?" asked the Rabbit.

"Sometimes," said the Skin Horse, for he was always truthful. "When you are Real, you don't mind being hurt."

"Does it happen all at once, like being wound up," he asked, "or bit by bit?"

"It doesn't happen all at once," said the Skin Horse. "You become. It takes a long time. That's why it doesn't often happen to people who break easily, or have sharp edges, or who have to be carefully kept. Generally, by the time you are real, most of your hair has been loved off, your eyes drop out, you get loose in the joints and very shabby, But these things don't matter at all, because once you are Real, you can't be ugly, except to people who don't understand."

"I suppose *you* are Real?" said the rabbit. And then he wished he had not said it, for he thought the Skin Horse might be sensitive. But the Skin Horse only smiled.

FROM *THE VELVETEEN RABBIT* BY MARGERY WILLIAMS
SIMON & SCHUSTER

2

Values-Centered Leadership

The walls of my library are lined with hundreds of books written by the world's great management theorists. Many are from one of my former lives as a business school professor. I no longer read most of them because they are virtually irrelevant to the burning issues of working life. Since I love books so much, however, I cannot bear to toss them out, even though they are the intellectual debris from an earlier era and a metaphor for the confusion that currently immobilizes modern leaders of organizations.

As we pass from the old era of morally deficient and redundant management philosophies, we are faced with the need for a new paradigm. Rampant materialism, consumption, and rationalism is giving way to a new, humanistic approach rooted in values. As we observe the weaknesses of our political, religious, or business leaders with increasing horror, we might be tempted to conclude that none of them is capable of leading the moral renaissance for which we all yearn. Yet corporate leaders, more than any other group, have the potential to heal the wounds that ail us. And there are growing signs that a new breed of corporate leader is ready to renounce the old ways and rise to this formidable challenge.

The personality-driven philosophy, based on ego and greed, views customers as opportunities for exploitation. In the Sanctuary, customers, partners, and employees are viewed as people. These people come to work each day for more than just money. They come to be inspired, to create friendships, to learn, to have fun — in short, they yearn for an uplifting experience. Corporate leaders today, therefore, are being called upon to be the new custodians of the human spirit. And all of us are the missionaries of regeneration.

How do customers and partners feel about the personality-driven mechanical organization? Do they respect and trust the traditional managers within them? Or do they grit their teeth, hold their noses, and count their change carefully when doing business with them? As the unwilling collaborators of these contemporary buccaneers, how does it feel to be an employee these days? Do employees secretly fear that their managers will treat them the same way — that they will be the victims of similar cynicism? The answer may be revealed in Gallup's annual poll, which points out that 80 percent of employees dread returning to work on Monday mornings. In some European countries, the figures cluster around 90 percent. A recent study of 30,000 workers by Opinion Research of Princeton, New Jersey, revealed that 47 percent of respondents either disliked or were ambivalent about the company they worked for and extensive research has concluded that the largest incidence of heart attacks and strokes occur at nine o'clock on Monday mornings. Some people hate their work so much that they wait until Monday morning to die! The statistics are not merely coincidental. The number-one predictor of heart attacks is the level of a person's happiness at work — his or her job satisfaction.

Our current managerial bankruptcy is the result of our infatuation with quick-fix solutions. We are convinced by charismatic seminar leaders, who shed more heat than light, that there are quick-and-ready cures in the modern mantras of downsizing, reorganizing, re-engineering, empowerment, TQM, corporate slogans, frequent-user points, merging, and refinancing. The fad-flitter's list is never-ending. The reality is different. We will get ourselves out of managerial hock only when we embrace values that are good for people and our planet.

> **Give me chastity and continence, but not just now.**
>
> SAINT AUGUSTINE,
> *CONFESSIONS, VIII, 7*

We are also managerially bankrupt because many traditional managers and the theories they espouse are morally bankrupt. Traditional managers destroy their credibility when they ask employees to salute the latest corporate code of ethics while deceiving their customers at the same time. We cannot embrace the new religion of service and quality while failing to respect, trust, and love our employees, customers, partners and our fragile ecosystem. We cannot receive the outer rewards without first doing the inner work.

What has gone wrong? Clearly, we need to make changes; MOTS won't change much. The "microwave approach" to management, in which one plugs in quality, customer service, or leadership and presses "start," will not cure what ails us. Nor can we continue to indulge our moral deafness. The quality and direction of an organization is almost exclusively determined by the values of its leaders. Over the years, I have developed a model called the Values Cycle, which realigns the qualitative thrust of individuals and their organizations, permitting them to concentrate on the most important things we must each do in our work and personal lives every day. It looks simple and it is — but *it isn't easy!*

The Values Cycle — A Model for Work and Life

The Primary Values

The metaphor for my model is the bicycle. If your team* were a bicycle, it would derive its power from the back wheel and its direction from the front wheel. From the back wheel we derive the values that are the life skills that energize individuals, teams, and organizations. They are called *Primary Values* and they help us to kick-start personal development and change attitudes. Most of us know and use these Primary Values every day, but we need to increase our practice of them. They are:

Mastery: **Undertaking whatever you do to the highest standards of which you are capable.** *Mastery* is possessing a commitment to do what it takes to be the best in whatever we do, being devoted to continuous personal and professional improvement, to setting standards for personal development, polishing one's skills, competencies, and practices, being an expert and respecting knowledge, wisdom, and learning. *Mastery* embodies a commitment to excellence in everything one does. Walt Disney used to tell his employees, "Do what you do so well, that others will come to see you do it again." Isn't that what we all need to do in every corner of our lives? Can you imagine people at Disney getting up in the morning, recalling Walt Disney's dictum, and then doing shoddy work? The mission of all of us is the same: to do what we do so well that others will come to see us do it again — no matter what we do in our personal and working lives.

Chemistry: **Relating so well with others that they actively seek to associate themselves with you.** People with *Chemistry* possess characteristics and attitudes which favor building strong relationships. They place a high value on harmonious interaction with others, taking the initiative to repair, maintain, and build friendships, and they seek to fathom the depths of their relationships, going beyond the usual superficialities. They know that interest is the most sincere form of respect. Truth-telling and promise-keeping are keystones of *Chemistry* and result in the establishment of emotional bonds with others built on trust. Those with *Chemistry* enjoy the company of others as much as their own solitude, being a team player as much as a soloist.

---

* In using the term *team*, I am referring to any team — a business, government, department, church, school, family, or spousal couple.

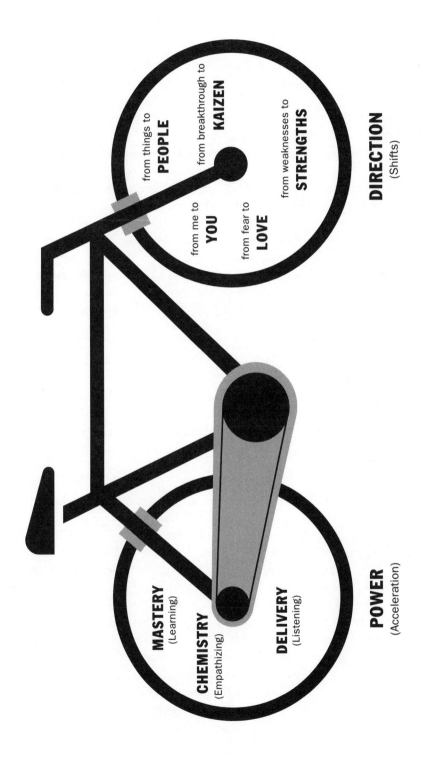

Figure 11: The Values Cycle – A Model for Work and Life

DIRECTION (Shifts)

from things to **PEOPLE**

from breakthrough to **KAIZEN**

from weaknesses to **STRENGTHS**

from me to **YOU**

from fear to **LOVE**

MASTERY (Learning)

CHEMISTRY (Empathizing)

DELIVERY (Listening)

POWER (Acceleration)

45

Delivery: **Identifying the needs of others and meeting them.** *Delivery* is being respectful of the needs of others and having a passion for meeting them. This focus on the needs of others is motivated by enlightened self-interest and altruism. *Delivery* honors meeting the needs of customers over mere profit-making. *Delivery* is founded on "win/win" deals and relationships that treat customers, employees, and suppliers as partners rather than adversaries. *Delivery* is being concerned with doing the right thing more than doing things right.

> **We don't care. We don't have to. We're the phone company.**
>
> LILY TOMLIN

To summarize the three *Primary Values*, *Mastery* is the act of doing everything we do as well as we can, in every corner of our lives; *Chemistry* is the practice of relating well with others, always behaving like their friend; and *Delivery* is the assiduous application of unfiltered listening to, and meeting, the needs of others. If we do these three things with gusto, personal and organizational excellence and leadership will result — and the soul will rejoice.

The Accelerators

Becoming proficient in *Mastery*, *Chemistry*, and *Delivery* requires that we first adopt three other behaviors and habits, called the *Accelerators* (because they accelerate the Primary Values). *Mastery*, *Chemistry*, and *Delivery* are driven by these three Accelerators and gain their momentum from them. They are:

1. Mastery is driven by **Learning**: Seeking and practicing knowledge and wisdom. If mastery is chopping wood, then learning is sharpening the ax. The dictionary defines leading as "showing the way to" and teaching as "showing how to." Therefore, leading *is* teaching and teachers show learners how to learn. To acquire greater *Mastery*, this learning must come from masters — in person and through their teachings. *Mastery* is never perfect, just as there is no perfect knowledge or wisdom. Knowledge and wisdom are always incomplete and so continuous learning — that is, life-long learning — is essential if continuous *Mastery* is to flourish in all areas of our work and personal lives. Notice that the value is learning not training: training is for dogs — learning is an attitude.

2. Chemistry is dependent on **Empathizing**: Considering the thoughts, feelings, and perspectives of others. To be a friend (*Chemistry*), we must

walk in the moccasins of others, because to relate well with them, we must first understand them. This is often best achieved by imagining their feelings, emotions, and sensitivities, thinking how we would feel if we were in their situation, and then trying to behave as we would want them to. So our goal is to be in a continuous state of empathy, behaving in a way that would make each of us the kind of person with whom we would want to be friends if our roles were reversed. This leads to great *Chemistry.*

3. Delivery is supported by **Listening**: Hearing and understanding the communications of others. We cannot meet the needs of others (*Delivery*) if we do not pause to hear what those needs are. Listening is not simply "not talking." To truly listen, we must

The first duty of love is to listen.

PAUL TILLICH

shut down our "mental chatter" and genuinely, and non-judgmentally, listen to each other. Then, and only then, can we hear the speaker's needs, and only then will we be in a position to take the appropriate actions to meet these needs. Of all human skills, listening is perhaps the most difficult.

In one exercise in my seminars, participants are required not to talk, but only to listen to each other. They always tell me how exhausting they find a full day of enforced silence. This is because it is an unfamiliar activity for them. The fact that it is such hard work probably explains why we do so little of it — there is a reason why we have only one mouth but two ears!

We are experiencing a growing social ailment — a sense that we are not being heard. It starts in our youth, with our parents and friends, and continues throughout our lives. Unconditional and totally attentive listening is a beautiful gift to the soul of another. Arguments and conflicts are caused when people stop listening to each other and focus instead on convincing others of their points of view, explaining them to each other in as many different ways as possible until they "win." Conversely, conflicts are always resolved as soon as both parties agree only to ask questions, cease making assertions, and listen.

The Values Shifts

The values on the back wheel provide power and acceleration to our lives and our organizations. But our motives can be flawed unless they are tempered by the values on the front wheel, which provide our direction. Most of us are familiar with the back-wheel values, to a greater or lesser degree; we simply need to increase our practice of them. This cannot be said of the front-wheel values; they are qualitatively different. Most of us are not committed practitioners of the values on the front wheel — in fact, we need to shift from "old" values to these "new" ones. This is why we call them "Values Shifts." They represent a shift from personality to soul:

1. *You Before Me*. We are emerging from one of the most self-absorbed eras in human history. The personality-driven way is dangerously egocentric. The Values Cycle is other-centered and seeks win/win combinations. It assumes that when we help others to win, we all win. It recognizes that a proposition that is good for me but bad for you is ultimately bad for both of us. It eschews egocentric forms of structure such as "self-directed teams," favoring instead a holistic systems approach in which the members of any team are sensitive to their impact on all other parts of the system. The shift from me to you assumes that a customer is more than a walking credit card.

For each of us, our mission is to meet the needs of employees, customers, and partners, and if we do so brilliantly, all the time, we will be rewarded with a team of dedicated and loyal employees who no longer dread work but celebrate its rewards and have fun — a growing legion of customers who become our fans and a support team of partners who love doing business with us. More importantly, a shift from me to you offers a much needed balance to the preoccupations flowing from our personalities, by shifting our focus from increasing market share, sales, cash flow, or power to being of service to others and our planet.

2. *People Before Things*. Helmsley, Milken, and Trump perfected the science of questing for things. The genius of Western management has been our unsurpassed ability to acquire, measure, analyze, and count things. But in revering analysis and acquisition, we have forgotten that organizations are the sum of people, not of things.

Now we must catch up by developing the soft technologies of the Values Cycle. The things approach obeys politics, procedures, policies, manuals, formal systems, and salary levels. The things approach prompts retailers to forbid customers from taking more than three garments into a change room. The people approach, as practised by Don Cooper, a Toronto fashion retailer, is a sign proclaiming, "Please — take as many items into the change room as you wish." The things approach assumes that you can't trust people and that systems must be established to protect retailers from the dishonesty of customers. The people approach recognizes the universal desire of people to be trusted, respected, and loved. In the Sanctuary, "people are our most important asset" is a genuine concept. Traditional managers in mechanical organizations have not yet made this discovery. If they really believed this much in the value of people they would be included in the balance sheet. The financial concept of goodwill is the personality's definition of people in the balance sheet, and a clumsy and inadequate measurement of the most precious asset in any organization. Until we consider people to be a superior asset to things, we cannot be taken seriously when we proclaim that "people are our most important asset."

3. *Kaizen* and **Breakthrough**. Creativity nourishes the soul and there are two ways to be creative: by innovating (finding a *different* way) and by *kaizen* (finding a *better* way). The favorite heroes of management gurus are breakthrough specialists: great inventors, entrepreneurs, promoters, and marketers. They are the hares who turn their innovative breakthroughs into personal fortunes. But we also need to celebrate tortoises — and just as passionately. As Aesop said, "Slow and steady wins the race."

The capacity to do the same thing a little bit better every day, may not look like a spectacular achievement in the short run, but it is in the long run. The Japanese call this *kaizen* — continuous improvement in personal life, home life, social life, and work life, involving everyone. *Kaizen* is a Japanese word that literally translates as "better way." But it is not simply a Japanese idea; it is an *intelligent* idea.

A *kaizen* team at a ball-bearing manufacturer detected a minor problem on the assembly line. Bearings of different sizes were dropped from a hopper on the assembly line, and then into the boxes that were eventually sold in stores. The entire process of production and packaging was automated. But customers were complaining that they sometimes got a box containing no ball bearings. This would occur once in every 100,000 to 200,000 boxes (a quality ratio that most Western executives can only dream about). Although the cost of replacing empty boxes after delivery was minimal, the *kaizen* team convinced the company that an empty box could seriously damage the company's reputation.

The *kaizen* team originally suggested installing an X-ray system to detect the empty boxes, but they abandoned this idea because of its high cost. They tried many other ideas but these failed to meet cost/benefit criteria. After discussing it further, they came up with the solution: a small, inexpensive fan. They installed it at the side of the assembly line so that it blew the empty (and therefore lighter) boxes right off the line. Later they upgraded the process by using pressurized air, which was readily available in the factory. Now, with minimal expense, the company was error-free — 100 percent of the time — as a result of maximum heart- and mind-power from the *kaizen* team.

Such dedication to continuous improvement builds the self-esteem of individuals and teams and propels organizations to excellence. While acknowledging the importance of being a world-class innovator (by finding a **different way**), the Values Cycle recognizes that it is just as important to practise *kaizen* (by finding a **better way**). This subtle difference nourishes the souls of individuals and therefore propels them and their organizations into a unique spiritual plane.

4. *Strengths Before Weaknesses*. Researchers claim that during an average business meeting each new idea is met with nine criticisms. According to Dr. Marylin L. Kourilsky, former dean for teacher education at UCLA's Graduate School of Education, 97 percent of U.S. kindergarten children think creatively, while only 3 percent form their thoughts in a conforming, structured manner. By the time students complete high school, the balance has begun to shift — 46 percent think creatively while a more rigid, structured style is preferred by 54 percent. The process of losing our individuality, passion, and creativity is completed in the workplace: by the time we are age 30, a mere 3 percent enjoy the freedom of practising holistic, original thought processes, while 97 percent subject our thinking to a structure that screens for orthodoxy and social correctness — "group-think."

In other words, we are like Perceval — we begin our lives honoring the magic of questions but eventually, by overlooking questions and only being open to answers, we fall under a spell of spiritual impotence. We do not start out thinking like traditional managers — it is something we acquire. By criticizing, judging, and jeering, we suck the self-esteem from the souls of individuals and, therefore, organizations. When we get the financial statements, we immediately hunt for the red ink, the brackets, the negative performance data. Too seldom do we celebrate our strengths or study and perfect our successes. By mistakenly placing our faith in the Aristotelian notion that by attacking ideas we will strengthen them, we have perfected our mechanical skills of rational thinking and criticism. But imagine if every person and every organization devoted as much passion and time to building on their strengths: our souls would begin healing until we became awesome.

Psychologist James Loehr has helped to train, among others, tennis great, Martina Navratilova. Loehr has studied what the best tennis players do during the twenty-second break between points during a match. Loehr discovered that mediocre players use that time to react to the previous point — scolding themselves after a missed point, for example. The best players, however, spend the time preparing for the next point — relaxing, energizing themselves, planning their strategy, and tuning their minds.

5. *Love Before Competition, Hostility, and Fear.* Winning has come to mean defeating one's opponent — it seems there must always be a loser. Metaphors of war spike the vocabulary of modern leadership. One of the highest-paid speakers on the rubber-chicken circuit is "Stormin'" Norman Schwarzkopf, who earns $75,000 each time he tells business executives that leading a business team is the same as leading a war machine.

Aspiring leaders devour titles such as *The Art of War, Marketing Warfare, The Leadership Secrets of Attila the Hun* and *How to Swim with the Sharks.* The first of these books, which is based on the teachings of Sun Tzu, a Chinese military expert from 2,500 years ago, advises us that, "The secret of deception is knowing how to manipulate an enemy's perceptions" and "Fighting many is the same as fighting few."[1] Life has become an endless competition, in which we are all gladiators at some level, seeking to vanquish our opponents (who in truth are our colleagues) at school, work, home — even within our own country.

> Love seeks no cause beyond itself and no fruit;
> it is its own fruit, its own enjoyment.
> I love because I love;
> I love in order that I may love.
>
> SAINT BERNARD

Life is not a battleground — it's a playground. People are not motivated by war or by the fear of losing. Virtuoso performances are romanced from people, not beaten out of them. If we love what we do (*Mastery*), love the people with whom we do it (*Chemistry*), and love the reason for doing it (*Delivery*), would we still call it work? People are inspired to do what they do well by the love they feel for what they do (*Mastery*), by the people with whom they share tasks and relationships (*Chemistry*), and by their commitment to being of service to others (*Delivery*).

Our previous notions of leadership and management are being swept away. The Values Cycle is a model that enables *everyone* to become a missionary responsible for managing and leading, whether he or she sports a managerial title or not. The Values Cycle assumes that work is not war, but love. And the penny is just beginning to drop for a lot of people: we are on the customer's payroll; the organization is just a convenient way for the customer to get the money to us.

The more we decentralize, the more we will depend on the competence and human-relations skills of the individual. Airlines don't fail us, reservation clerks do. Automakers don't fail us, service staff at the dealership do. We all share the load, the opportunity, and the responsibility. It's the same for an organization, an orchestra, a hospital, a school, a government, or even a country. And it's the same for a family. *Building greatness is achieved one human being at a time.* Simply put, the difference between whether an organization is mediocre or superb is determined by whether *all* its individual members are mediocre or superb. The difference between organizations that are mediocre and those that are great is the attitude within each of us — our values and our culture. An inspired organization is simply the sum of inspired souls.

> **The need is not to amputate the ego but to transcend it.**
>
> NORMAN COUSINS

Few companies have pursued a Values-Centered Leadership more than Levi Strauss. Chairman and CEO, Robert D. Haas, says, "We are not doing this because it makes us feel good — although it does. We are doing it because we believe in the interconnection between liberating the talents of our people and business success."[2] And this is just as true in life as it is in work, because work doesn't stand apart from the rest of our lives; work is simply a part of life.

Gandhi said that he had only one standard: truth and non-violence. These two elements formed the standard for his life. Gandhi did not have one standard for home and another for work. Most people do not wake up saying, "I will tell the truth until I get to work and then I will start lying." And if we persist in trying to "kill" the competition at work, we may find that we are successful. This will result in hardship and tragedy for our customers, our friends, our families, and our communities. Worse still, another organization may be successful in "killing" us. We are part of a larger human family; we each possess a set of values that we practise throughout our lives — including work. It is therefore up to each of us to practise Values-Centered Leadership and embrace values that will ensure that we remain in good standing with our larger family.

And the paradox is, this is how we *all* become rich.

Love and Kaizen

To keep the lamp burning, we have to keep putting oil in it.

MOTHER TERESA

Combining two of the shifts from the front wheel — love and *kaizen* — is an elixir for the soul. More than any other, the question that the soul most wishes to hear from others is, "How can I love you better?" The greatest desire of the soul is the opportunity for partners to listen and be heard by each other on this subject and commit themselves to growing the love on which their relationship is based. Strong relationships, at home or at work, are based on the successful application of *kaizen*, or continuous improvement, to love.

The Vector

The Values Cycle			
The Vector			
	0-10		**0-10**
Mastery Undertaking whatever you do to the highest standards of which you are capable.	9	**Learning** Seeking and practicing knowledge and wisdom.	6
Chemistry Relating so well with others that they actively seek to associate themselves with you.	4	**Empathizing** Considering the thoughts, feelings, and perspectives of others.	7
Delivery Identifying the needs of others and meeting them.	7	**Listening** Hearing and understanding the communications of others.	7
Total	20	**Total**	20

Figure 12: The Values Cycle: The Vector

The Vector is a representation of the relationship between the Primary Values and the Accelerators. Figure 12. illustrates how the vector works. In the example shown, the rating for *Mastery* is an impressive 9, whereas the rating for learning (the Accelerator that drives *Mastery*) is a more modest 6. This suggests that the current high level of *Mastery* cannot be sustained indefinitely because there is insufficient learning present to maintain this pace.

In the case of *Chemistry*, the position is reversed. At 4, the level of *Chemistry* present is weak, but this is likely to improve because a significant level of empathizing is present.

Finally, *Delivery* is rated at a respectable level of 7 and is matched by a similar level for listening. This suggests that *Delivery* can be maintained at current levels, although no significant improvement is likely, because listening (the Accelerator for *Delivery*) is being maintained at a corresponding level.

As you can see, the Accelerators are predictors of future change in the Primary Values. A review of the totals of the vector in Figure 12 suggests that the person or situation to which it was applied is in relative balance. However, as the previous analysis indicates, it can be misleading to look at totals alone since this may obscure the variances within each Primary Value and Accelerator.

The Vector is a tool that helps in measuring the relationship between the Primary Values and the Accelerators. Hundreds of organizations and thousands of individuals have applied the Values Cycle to their everyday practice, using it to guide their decisions and navigate their journey to higher ground. All successful relationships and human actions depend on the routine practice of the *back-wheel values.* Friendships are built on these values; championship performance depends on them; customer service is defined by them; effective meetings and negotiations are guided by these values; marriages grow stronger through their daily use. Strong values sustain the spirit.

Before using the combination of the Primary Values and the Accelerators (called the Vector), practise the Primary Values alone by working through the exercises below.

Many other work-related processes can be designed using the Values Cycle model, such as business plans, customer feedback, service and quality standards, compensation plans, performance assessment, consensus building, leadership feedback, and project management.

One of the greatest benefits of the Values Cycle is that it is a life-model, not just a work-model, transferable to any situation and usable in any context. It has been effectively used in educational settings (teacher/student effectiveness), the home (parent/child communications), the political arena (elected official/constituent feedback), therapy (counselor/patient discussion), and among friends. It is an integrative, holistic process that works well in any condition where individuals or groups must interact with each other in order to be effective and fulfilled. With practice, you will find that the language and the values become second nature for you and a vital tool for renewing your soul. (See Chapter 6, *Blithe Spirit,* in which I have described how to develop a personal mission through the use of the Values Cycle model.)

Values drive all human interaction — not goals. In a spiritual organization, goals are derived from values. A life lived within a framework of sound values produces harmony, balance, and serenity for the soul.[3] Missionaries use Values-Centered Leadership to regenerate others and their organizations.

Before concluding a meeting, consider the decisions you have made and ask these three questions:

Mastery: Was it the best we could do?

Chemistry: Will it be good for people?

Delivery: Will it meet the needs of customers?

We call these the three gateways. If you can pass through each gateway by answering "yes" to each question, you have had a successful meeting. If you cannot answer "yes" to each question, your meeting is not over — you have more work to do.

Using the questions below, ask a colleague to rate you on a scale of zero to ten. Then do the same for him or her, discuss the results, and develop a plan that will help you both to strengthen your relationship and thrive together:

Mastery: How would you rate my skills and competencies?
   And my learning?
   What learning must I do to increase my Mastery in your eyes?

Chemistry: How would you rate my relationship and interpersonal effectiveness with you?
   And my empathy level?
   How can I empathize better (and with whom?) in order to increase my Chemistry with you?

Delivery: How well do I meet your needs?
   How well do I listen?
   How can I listen more effectively so that I increase my Delivery with you?

   (This format is equally effective when used by spouses who are committed to deepening their relationships.)

Create Employee Development Programs by dividing responsibilities and personal development objectives into three sections:

Mastery: What are the main tasks, skills, and competencies for which I am responsible?
   What continuous learning is required in order to achieve the desired levels of Mastery?

Chemistry: With whom must strong relationships be built and maintained?
   What are the opportunities for enhancing communications through empathy (truthfulness, trust, accountability, energy, honesty, integrity, respect, compassion, and love)?

Delivery: Who are the customers for this function? What are their needs?
   How will listening be most effectively undertaken in order to hear those needs?

3

Truth Telling and
Promise Keeping

We are suffering from truth decay. Corporate history is littered with the disasters of denial. Companies that know their products are defective, dangerous, or damaging, deny it; managers who intend to limit the potential of an employee promise unwarranted opportunities; executives declare that their employees are their most important asset, then fire 500 of them. Employees who are told they are the firm's most important asset but become the most expendable conclude that truth is an ephemeral thing and suffer a crisis of trust and morale.

Nothing instils a sense of betrayal more than a lie, and betrayal is the dominant experience in a workplace that lacks soul. This absence of honesty in the workplace has built an accumu-

A lie which is half a truth
is ever the blackest of lies.
ALFRED, LORD TENNYSON

lated corrosion that has now reached epidemic proportions — our souls have been betrayed over and over again and we are hurting. Reversing this will take time, but we know how to do it. And we know that we cannot heal the planet with damaged goods.

Thomas Jefferson said, "Advertisements contain the only truths to be relied on in a newspaper," and today, even that statement may be untrue. Why do we find it so hard to tell the truth? We fight wars to protect the truth and we defend the concept of truth in our churches, our literature, and our constitution, yet real truth is rarely practised in our everyday lives.

Even occupants of the highest office in the land set shameful examples. For example, during the 1980 U.S. presidential campaign, George Bush (whose final campaign slogan was "Who do you Trust?") ridiculed the supply-side theories espoused by Ronald Reagan with the famous phrase, "voodoo economics." Later he joined Reagan's staff and became a born-again supply-sider. Tired of being criticized for his change of heart, he sought to rearrange the record. According to *The Nation*'s Christopher Hitchins, Bush called his network contacts, including his nephew at NBC, to see whether a tape existed of him saying "voodoo economics." When they reported that there was not one, Bush announced on February 9, 1982, to a crowd in Houston, "I didn't say it. Every network has searched for it and none can find it. So I never said it." NBC aired his denial speech that night, alongside a hastily discovered "voodoo" tape.[1]

What we think and what we say are seldom congruent. In our work lives especially, we are surrounded by a lack of truth-telling. It is difficult to find the truth in labeling, marketing campaigns, contract negotiations, sales forecasts, or job applications. We have learned not to believe politicians, corporate leaders, union bosses, newspapers, or anyone else keen to promote their point of view. In the Bible, we find the ninth commandment: Thou shalt not bear false witness against thy neighbor, (Exodus 20:12–17). What have we done to the ninth commandment? I do not ask this question out of any sense of righteousness, but rather out of sadness and wonder. Why is truth-telling something we expect of others but fail to do ourselves?

> **I just got wonderful news from my real estate agent in Florida. They found land on my property.**
>
> MILTON BERLE

The strangest irony is that we have been teaching a myth about all this: the misguided notion that strong human relationships can be built on a flimsy footing of deceit. How can we build harmony, respect, integrity, honesty, inspiration, leadership, or love on a foundation of lies? What logic supports the idea that we are ready to embark on consensus-building, ethics, culture-change, customer service, or quality "programs" before we have even built the necessary foundation of integrity on which to place them? Why do we expect to reach higher ground from a base of dishonesty? After all, if we can't even trust or tell the truth to each other, what are the grounds for expecting employees, customers, or suppliers to do any better?

> **We despise all reverences and objects of reverence which are outside the pale of our list of sacred things. And yet, with strange inconsistency, we are shocked when other people despise and defile the things that are holy to us.**
>
> MARK TWAIN

In modern organizations, there is often a tendency to substitute denial for truth-telling. When products falter, markets shrivel, losses loom, or our leaders make disastrous decisions, we often do not tell the truth by owning up to the problem and dealing with it. Instead we disclaim it, sometimes even hiring lawyers to maintain the fiction. When we sense a loss of control, we become afraid, and sometimes when we are afraid, we resort to lying. Lying enables us to maintain the illusion of control. This is a classic clash between the personality and the soul.

Straying from the truth nearly always causes long-term damage. When a mathematician revealed that Intel's Pentium computer chip produced the wrong answer when 4,195,835 was divided by 3,145,727, it seemed like an arcane observation about arithmetic. This was a moment when Intel needed to tell the truth. If they had told the truth about the faulty Pentium chip, most people would have been impressed by their admission that, with average use, the chip might produce one error in every 9 billion calculations — or once every 27,000 years of running a spreadsheet. Many chips are flawed to some degree. The average software user would have remained unaffected by such an obscure possibility while being impressed with Intel's forthrightness.

But the company's first reaction was to maintain a stony silence. When this alerted the attention of the press, Intel simply denied the existence of the problem. As the pressure mounted, the company attempted to put a positive spin on the incident. By this time, even those who had no interest in the facts were outraged by the corporation's deliberate attempts to manipulate and mislead. Six weeks after the mathematician's discovery, IBM halted shipments of computers with the Pentium chip and Intel's stock dropped 6.5 percent.

Perhaps this comes down to a lack of willingness in all of us to admit to others that we are vulnerable. We confuse vulnerability with weakness, believing that heroic leaders do not display pain or ignorance. Fear, as Emerson observed, always springs from ignorance. So when we lack knowledge, we play for time or offer bogus information. When we hurt or are caught off guard, we pretend to be strong and in control. We are afraid that any admission and display of imperfection will convey an aura of incompetence and failure. So we deny any suspicion of failure in an attempt to create an image of invulnerability.

Recently the U.S. Supreme Court ruled that brokerage firms cannot deny investors punitive damages in securities arbitration cases. One might think that this is a statement of the obvious, but the securities industry has employed a cunning deceit buried in the small print of the agreement that their customers sign when opening an account. Until this decision, nearly all agreements stipulated that the laws of New York State would prevail in all cases of arbitration. On the face of it, this appeared to be a harmless undertaking for customers, but most investors did not realize that the State of New York prohibits arbitrators from

> **The big print giveth and the fine print taketh away.**
>
> J. FULTON SHEEN

awarding punitive damages. The Supreme Court ruled that because the agreements did not make this clear, investors were unknowingly giving up important rights.

Teams Depend on Trust

Deceit creates toxicity and destroys *Chemistry. Delivery,* the art of identifying and meeting the needs of others, is not even on the lawyer's agenda when he or she is devising methods to remove the civil rights of customers. People who work this way demean themselves and therefore erode their self-esteem. This creates a heaviness of the soul. Lying doesn't make sense in any part of our lives, and this is no less so at work. Greatness is achieved through harmony and great teams succeed through interdependence gained through the certain belief that all members are scrupulously truthful. The magic ingredient in teams is trust, which is earned through consistent truth-telling. We learn to trust someone because he or she can be consistently relied on to tell the truth. When the person lies, he or she betrays us, and betrayal is no foundation for a great team.

> I am still looking for the modern-day equivalent of those Quakers who ran successful businesses, made money because they offered honest products and treated their people decently, worked hard, spent honestly, saved honestly, gave honest value for money, put back more than they took out and told no lies. This business creed, sadly, seems long forgotten.
>
> ANITA RODDICK, CO-FOUNDER, THE BODY SHOP, IN *BODY AND SOUL*

We simply cannot achieve superior performance, individually or in teams, through untruthfulness. Indeed, if a group lies, they are not a team, and no human has yet learned how to erect the beautiful structure called a team on a foundation of lies. If the members of a symphony lie to each other, they will play awful music. If members of a sports team lie to each other, the team will be mediocre. Perhaps most importantly, we cannot *know* each other unless we tell the truth. There is no other way.

More than ever before in our history, organizations depend on intellectual capital. Organizations are not the things listed in their balance sheet; they are the brains, motivations, knowledge, character, and emotions of *all* the humans behind the balance sheet. To work together effectively, to enjoy each other and therefore our work, we must relate with each other beyond our phony facades. Impersonating Hollywood images of real people, rather than simply being ourselves, results in our trying to convey images of leadership that are somewhere between Queen Victoria, Lee Iacocca, and Moses. Before we can communicate effectively, we must communicate authentically. Only a coward lies.

One of my three daughters was born with a congenital heart condition. She was a "blue baby," and underwent four open-heart operations. At the age of nineteen, her strength finally gave out, and she died during a desperate attempt to alleviate her constant suffering. My wife and I returned from the hospital to console our other two daughters. For a long time, there was much crying in our home. Even in the midst of all this sadness, I could not cry. This was partly because I believed that crying was not manly behavior, but also because I believed that it was my responsibility to provide strength, not weakness. So I lied. I never cried in the presence of others, especially my wife and other daughters. I never showed my emotions — I saved my crying for the blessed moment when I was in my car. It was the only place where I could let down my guard, discard the need to hide my vulnerability and pain, and release my anguish without fear of being judged.

I have learned better since. I have learned, with much difficulty, that it takes real courage to declare one's emotions. Hiding one's pain and vulnerability is easy. It is an act of cowardice — and a lie. To reach others, we must be honest, tell them of our hurt, and ask for their help. In organizations it is the same. We need to remind ourselves that we are all human, with frailties and foibles. We must acquire the maturity to realize that asking for help is not a sign of weakness. It is an act of courage, capable of yielding considerable personal benefit, often creating greater trust, compassion, and friendship. Above all, it is truthful.

In our work, truth-telling can lead to sharing imminent danger and thus avoiding it. This, in turn, can provide the opportunity for us to conspire (from the Latin, "to breathe together") for the common good. Truth-telling leads to higher ground and greater *Chemistry*. The truth puts the soul at ease.

Lies Corrode the Soul

Lying and cheating will corrode even the highest ideals. The first Olympic Games were held in 776 B.C. in Olympia in honor of Zeus, ruler of the heavens and the father of all the Greek gods. In A.D. 394, emperor Theodosius I abolished the games because the level of cheating had become so extreme. They were not reinstated until 1896. One wonders, with the sham-amateurism evident at the modern Olympics, and the widespread use of performance-enhancing drugs, whether we may be unable, once again, to protect the integrity of the Olympic ideal. Could we be forced to suspend them until truth-telling becomes a guiding Olympic principle again?

False words are not only evil in themselves, but they infect the soul with evil.

SOCRATES

Removing trust by removing the truth results in corrosion of the soul. The soul writhes in the pain of betrayal caused by lying and yearns for the comforting warmth of the truth.

Truth-Telling and Bureaucracy

Truth-telling and promise-keeping are the essential preconditions for trust and the cornerstones of *Chemistry*. Not until a sustained pattern of truth-telling and promise-keeping has been established, can empowerment occur. As I have written elsewhere, empowerment is defined as, "Trusting people, and giving them all the information, training, encouragement and authority they need to make the right decision for the customer."[2]

So truth-telling is a character trait that I vigorously encourage among my clients. Not only does it lead to unprecedented levels of decency and civility, but it has another huge advantage — it is efficient. In the doing-more-with-less era, one of the things that severely limits further efficiencies in organizations is the bureaucratic sludge that flows through corporate veins. This includes all the controls, reports, permissions, mandatory procedures, and other frustrating "administrivia" that most people live with as a matter of course. These procedures exist because management doesn't trust employees. But what if a major part of this activity were eliminated because we chose to behave in a truthful way, so that we could trust each other? What if we could scrap the controls because we knew that we were each utterly reliable when we made commitments and could be counted on to tell the truth if we made a mistake? What if the time invested in preparing and checking this information was redirected into work that inspires the soul? How would organizations look then? How would people feel about their work?

Most controls are put in place because we don't trust people and cannot rely on them when they promise not to repeat past errors. But the paradox is that trust is destroyed when we assume people do not tell the truth and cannot keep their promises. This attitude becomes a self-fulfilling prophesy. If you trust people, they will often respect your faith in them by repaying you with trustworthy behavior. They recognize the covenant you have put in place and will honor it. However, if you make it clear that you do not trust them, they will feel insulted and alienated.

A story is told of IBM during their glory days of selling "big iron" — their mainframe computers. One day, a deranged driver accidentally drove his car into the main reception area of a regional office in the southern United States. IBM did what you might expect a company to do in such a situation: management wrote a new policy. The IBM administrative machinery moved swiftly, developing a series of procedures for all reception areas worldwide. IBM staff no longer were to greet visitors in the reception area — they were replaced by subcontract guards who worked for an outside security firm. The uniformed security staff were safely placed behind armor-plated glass and visitors received their identification passes after signing in. IBM staffers collected their guests personally from the ground floor since the reception area was sealed and the public could not gain access to any other areas of the building. Security cameras scanned all areas. Every office of IBM around the world looked the same — a little like Alcatraz. Visitors to IBM felt unwelcome and intimidated.

I first heard this story when I was invited years later to work with IBM's senior management in a program of culture change. I started by proposing that all the intimidating structures in the reception area be dismantled and that the area be completely redone, replacing office furniture with home furnishings so that visitors would again feel welcome. The security firm was replaced by a professional and highly skilled receptionist. Comfortable chairs and couches surrounded tables with fresh flowers, daily newspapers, and information about IBM. There were rugs on the floor, pictures on the wall, and often nice touches such as freshly baked muffins were evident. Telephones were available for local calls and the receptionist would also arrange long-distance calls. The washroom facility was first class, and coffee, tea, and juice were readily available.

We lie loudest when we lie to ourselves.

ERIC HOFFER

Redesigning the reception area was the easy part. The tough part was getting IBM staff to understand that not all customers lie, want to steal furniture or the company's secrets, or regularly drive their cars through the plate-glass windows. It required an entirely new mind-set and a clear understanding that the old policy was hurting IBM's image, customer perceptions, and employee morale. It took several attempts but the new style was finally adopted, contributing to a changed perception of IBM by employees, customers, and partners.

An attitude change of this kind must be brought about gradually because of the depth of inner work required by each individual to effect these personal changes in attitude. We are asking the personality, and then the soul, to restore earlier levels of trust, and this can only be achieved through repeated and consistent demonstrations of truth-telling and promise-keeping.

The Economics of Truth-Telling

Organizations are stunned when they realize the potential opportunities available from releasing unproductive energy and activity so that it can be channeled into productive work. I estimate that at least 20 to 40 percent of human activity in modern organizations and in our personal lives could be redirected if truth-telling and promise-keeping were a daily practice — first by everyone inside the organization, and then by everyone outside.

From a purely economic standpoint, truth-telling may yield the greatest single untapped opportunity for reducing costs in corporate history. There are enormous financial gains from reducing costs if we can remove the controls that become obsolete in a truth-telling environment. Furthermore, people who tell the truth build mutual *Chemistry*. This speeds communications and makes them authentic — the dream of the soul. As much as anything, our souls are crying for authenticity. With it, we can build relationships and inspire each other and our customers and suppliers. The implications for increased revenues are obvious. What a gift — a technique for inspiring the soul *and* gratifying the personality.

> **A memorandum is written not to inform the reader but to protect the writer.**
>
> DEAN ACHESON

Almost all disaffections of the soul are the result of disappointments with people and organizations. These disappointments are usually the result of betrayals that can be traced to broken promises and untruths. When someone lies to us, we are crushed and our souls, saddened. On the other hand, a culture of truth-telling and promise-keeping is exhilarating and inspiring: a weight seems to drop from our shoulders; toxicity gives way to healing; joyfulness and trust prevail; and our affection for our associates and our work grows in our hearts. Leaders who inspire the souls of others do not treat promise-keeping or truth-telling lightly. For them, trust is not a subject to be compromised. Their passion for the truth and keeping their promises builds great *Chemistry*, which leads to great organizations that are populated by inspired souls. Transforming the workplace into a Sanctuary of truth-telling — a safe place that is different from others — inspires a new sense of vigor that causes us to fall in love with our work again.

"Truth-Telling Is Everyone Else's Problem"

When I work with individuals to help them follow a path of truth-telling, they nearly always describe themselves as punctilious truth-tellers — it is everyone else they say, who has a problem with truth-telling. When we show them the results of internal surveys or personal profiles that clearly indicate low truth-telling scores, they say that the information is wrong. This is like noticing that the oil level in your car is low and disconnecting the oil-level indicator to solve the problem.

Generally speaking, we are not used to telling the truth. Most of us dispute this notion until all of the everyday examples in our lives are held up for us to see — the budgets, expense reports, press releases, curriculum vitae — even our feigned laughter at our client's shaggy dog stories.

We do not tell the truth in most areas of corporate life, largely because we have found that not telling the truth works. Let me give you another example. Many people build a little fat into the expense sections of their budgets, providing leeway in case the actual expenses turn out to be higher than forecast. This makes it easier and safer to meet expense targets, collect bonuses, and avoid punishment and potential cutbacks in next year's expense allocation. Similarly, after preparing a reasoned estimate of anticipated sales for the year ahead, the number is often arbitrarily reduced, in order to provide a cushion in case things don't go as well as planned. This makes quotas easier to meet, attracts less management attention, and improves the chances of keeping next year's quota within a reasonable range. This is known as "sandbagging" or "fudging" the budget.

> **There is no sickness worse for me than words that to be kind must lie.**
>
> AESCHYLUS

Of course, in our hearts, we are confident that expenses will be lower than those budgeted and sales will be above forecast, but we don't say so — we lie. Some would argue that it is just a little lie, but it is a lie all the same and by turning a blind eye to this practice, we teach others to lie. It sets the tone for every other human transaction. If we can lie in the budgets, why can't we do it in the annual report? To shareholders? To employees? To suppliers? To the government? Soon truth-telling is banished from our work and eventually from all aspects of our lives.

Choosing Truth

For this reason, a renewed commitment to truth-telling is worth pursuing. How do we begin changing to a truth-telling culture? Here is one possibility. Arrange to have a truth-telling session with the person responsible for approving your budget. The agenda might look like this:

- agree that truth-telling is not practised currently as strongly as it could be and describe the reasons why this is the case;
- agree that truth-telling is desirable, that there exists a mutual aspiration to reclaim this higher ground and develop a plan that will lead to change and regeneration;
- discuss how budgets are generally sandbagged and where the pay-off for this practice comes from; review how to remove the advantages of lying;
- determine whether it would be safe to submit a "truthful" budget, ensuring that no conditions or penalties will be attached;
- negotiate and agree on the outcomes for varying levels of performance compared to the "truthful" budget; and
- shake hands and celebrate your arrival together at higher ground; regeneration has begun!

It is unrealistic to expect that we can move from truthlessness to truthfulness in one step. Reversing an embedded pattern of truthlessness is difficult and it takes courage to go first, to be the missionary. The goal is not to change the entire world in one fell swoop, but to change our own organization by creating our own Sanctuary, in which we can feel safe and grow, knowing that our souls are being nourished and protected. So we must initially create awareness of a better way and then systematically work through all of the activities where truth-telling is absent and design the alternative approach. Then we must ensure truth-telling becomes a safe thing to do in every relationship. After each small success, we should plan ways to spread our achievement to other areas of our work, relationships, and the organization.

The place to start, of course, is with ourselves. If we are not prepared to assume personal responsibility for our role as spiritual guides by telling the truth and keeping promises with each other, it is unlikely that the rest of the organization will find their way to this higher ground — let alone those outside such as customers and suppliers.

It is easy to talk about truth-telling, but harder to introduce the practice and make it an everyday habit. In fact, the hardest part of truth-telling is getting started. I have included a simple exercise at the end of this chapter that is designed to encourage a team to start truth-telling so that they all eventually become comfortable with it as an everyday practice. It might be a team at work, a committee, or perhaps your family.

Set the rules of truth telling in your Sanctuary:

- We are the missionaries.
- It is safe to tell the truth.
- There will be no recriminations.
- We tell the truth in a helpful and positive way.
- This is the beginning of our permanent commitment to mutual truth-telling and regeneration.

Establish a plan to keep the initiative alive; promise to tell the truth to each other from now on. Celebrate successes. Never punish people for telling the truth. Once you have started truth-telling, it will become easier with each initiative, its practice will become more widespread and things will never be the same. This is the work of the missionary that leads to regeneration and Sanctuary-building.

Promise-Keeping

Promise-keeping is closely related to truth-telling. Often broken promises are the result of an unwillingness to tell the truth in the first place. As Max De Pree, the former chairman of Herman Miller put it, "We talk about quality of product and service. What about the quality of our relationships and the quality of our communications and the quality of our promises to each other?" Every transaction or communication in life is founded on a promise. This is no less the case in business than any other part of our lives. It may be explicit or implicit. We make promises to employees when we invite them to join our team and assure them of opportunities, rewards, and fun. We make promises to customers in our package labeling, in warranties, in sales pitches, advertising, and public relations. We make promises when we negotiate between management and unions. We make a promise each time we say, "The check's in the mail," "I'll call you right back," or "We are not going to lay anybody off." We make a promise when we tell our spouses we will be home at a certain time for dinner. When we fail to deliver on these commitments, we are breaking a promise and, therefore, a trust.

Imagine yourself standing on higher ground. This higher ground is built on trust and integrity. When we make a promise to someone, we must then make a conscious choice whether we plan to stay on this higher ground or not. Each time we break a promise, we take a step down, creating some distance from the higher ground of trust and integrity, and it is very hard, sometimes impossible, to climb back. After many steps have been taken down towards the valley, the results of many broken promises with many different people, we become discredited. People can see that we are now standing in the shadow of the valley where there is no trust or integrity. Because people who give up the higher ground find it so difficult to reclaim, they find it easier to move to a new team where they can safely start again on a new summit — unless somebody knows their history and has heard about how they abandoned higher ground at their former place of work. The new team may be a new employer, a new spouse, or even a new country.

Truth is the beginning of every good thing, both in Heaven and on earth; and he who would be blessed and happy should be from the first a partaker of the truth, for then he can be trusted.

PLATO

When I was a young member of the management team at Office Overload, we met annually in Las Vegas. Jim Shore, one of the founding partners of the company, was a passionate gambler and a big man who was well known in the casinos. But I was in my twenties, I'd never been to Las Vegas before and I was intimidated by the glitz and pace of the place, not to mention the risk. During my first visit, I told Jim that I was nervous.

"Don't worry," he said, "I'll look after you." I took that as a promise. Jim Shore had a habit of wandering around the gaming tables every now and then to see how his team was doing. On this first occasion, it didn't take long before I was cleaned out and wondering what to do next. Jim's hand silently reached over my shoulder, placing a $25 pile of chips beside my freshly dealt cards. A promise kept.

I worked hard for this man who became my mentor and whom I deeply respected and loved. He kept his promises. On another occasion, I earned an enormous monthly commission that later turned out to be an exaggeration by the accounting department. I had made a large commission, but not quite as large as the check I had now spent. "Don't worry," said Jim Shore, and he told me to repay the excess over any time period that was convenient for me. Another promise kept!

Every year, Jim Shore took six of his closest employees on a fishing trip to Northern Ontario. I was fortunate to always be included on this trip. He piloted his Widgeon plane equipped with floats, which enabled us to penetrate the wilderness where few had been before. During those trips I learned many lifelong lessons about truth-telling and promise-keeping — we were alone in the wilderness and our survival depended on mutual trust.

In the fall of 1966 I left Office Overload to head up Manpower Limited. The following May, the old fishing party went on their trip as usual, but this time they went without me. When Jim landed his plane on God's Lake, he encountered some lingering winter ice that punctured one of the pontoons. The plane tilted sideways and sank almost immediately. Some of the occupants could not escape because they were below the surface, others tried to swim ashore in the frigid waters, but all of them, including my dear friend Jim Shore, drowned. Jim Shore promised he would look after me. I still miss him and his dependable promise-keeping, but the legacy of a promise-keeper lives on.

Our personalities fall in love with truth-tellers and promise-keepers, and our souls are liberated by them. The pathfinders of human consciousness — Buddha, Christ, Lao-tzu, Mohammed — and more recently, Gandhi, Gurdjieff, Krishnamurti, and Yogananda, held two core beliefs: love and truth, which have propelled them onto a different plane from the rest of humanity. Their teachings have become a Sanctuary for millions: love combined with kept promises and the truth paves the way to higher ground.

It's OK, son, everybody does it

When Johnny was 6 years old, he was with his father when they were caught speeding. His father handed the officer a five dollar bill with his driver's license. "It's OK, son," his father said as they drove off. "Everybody does it."

When he was 8, he was permitted to sit in a family seminar, presided over by Uncle George, on how to shave points off an income tax return. "It's OK, kid," his uncle said. "Everybody does it."

When he was 9, his mother took him to his first theater production. The box office man couldn't find any seats until his mother discovered an extra $2 in her purse. "It's OK, son," she said. "Everybody does it."

When he was 12, he broke his glasses on the way to school. His Aunt Francine convinced the insurance company that they had been stolen and collected $27. "It's OK, kid," she said. "Everybody does it."

When he was 15, he was made right guard on the high school football team. His coach showed him how to block and at the same time grab the opposing end by the shirt so the official couldn't see it. "It's OK, kid," the coach said. "Everybody does it."

When he was 16, he took his first summer job at the neighborhood supermarket. His assignment was to put overripe tomatoes in the bottom of the boxes and the good ones on top where they would show. "It's OK," the manager said. "Everybody does it."

When he was 18, Johnny and a neighbor applied for a college scholarship. Johnny was a marginal student. His neighbor was in the upper 3 percent of his class, but he couldn't play right guard. Johnny got the scholarship. "It's OK," they told him. "Everybody does it."

When he was 19, he was approached by an upperclassman who offered the test answers for $3. "It's OK, kid," he said. "Everybody does it." Johnny was caught and sent home in disgrace. "How could you do this to your mother and me?" his father asked. "You never learned anything like this at home." His aunt and uncle were also shocked. If there's anything the adult world can't stand, it's a kid who cheats.

AUTHOR UNKNOWN

Team Truths

(Please complete the statements below for each member of your team.
Complete separate sheets for each person and give the appropriate sheets
to each one when they are completed. This exercise helps teams to start the
process of truth-telling.)

To: _____

From: _____

Subject: Some truths I have always wanted to say to you:

1 I would like you to do more of:

_____

_____

_____

2 I would like you to stop:

_____

_____

_____

3 I would like you to start:

_____

_____

_____

4

The Courage to Live
with Grace

Grace with Employees

We live in a world that is becoming increasingly graceless. The word "grace" is derived from the Latin, *gratus*, which means praiseworthy. The dictionary defines *grace** as "beauty or charm of form, composition, movement or expression; an attractive quality, feature, manner, etc.; a sense of what is right and proper, decency; thoughtfulness towards others; good will."

Our souls are inspired by those with grace. They are people who appreciate the natural elegance of human relationships and regenerate us with their grace. They turn every communication and human association into beautiful music. They use their considerable charm and integrity, neither of which is shallow, to maintain symmetry and elegance in their interactions with others. They take the extra time to create harmony in their associations, and when their graceful ways clash with a graceless situation, they draw on their reserves of love and courage to maintain their grace.

Think of your favorite aunt, who always made you feel like you were the only person in the world, and considered the destruction of her living-room window by your baseball as part of your character development. We love people with grace and are drawn to their company. A little white-haired, elderly lady once approached Mark Twain after an evening lecture to tell him how much she had enjoyed his talk. "I wanted to thank you personally," she explained, "because you said you loved old ladies." Mark Twain smiled at her and then replied, "I do love old ladies and I also like them your age." The grace of Mark Twain endeared him to millions.

> **All men who live with any degree of serenity live by some assurance of grace.**
>
> REINHOLD NIEBUHR

Grace is the North Star of all individuals and organizations. When we wander from our course, grace can guide us back. Gracelessness is darkness, alienation, loneliness, and confusion.

---

*A full definition of *Grace* may be found in *A Note on Terminology* at the end of this book.

Within organizations we find that from time to time, a lack of grace pervades:

- **employees** and fellow members of our team,
- **customers** — our real paymasters,
- **partners** who provide much of the wherewithal to make our organizations function.

Seeing Life as Sacred

Reverence is a vital component of grace. Reverence includes awe, respect, love, and veneration. I remember when I was young, my mother taught me not to complain about the weather. If I would say, "It's a horrible day today," she would comment, "It is God's weather. If you criticize it, you are criticizing Him. It is important that we show reverence to God's weather." This advice has stayed with me to this day, making a deep impression and causing me to look at things differently.

Presumably, everything belongs to God, and we should therefore hold everything in reverence. This includes employees, customers, partners — indeed all humans, our work, the products and services we create, the equipment and buildings we work in, and the impact and meaning of what we each do. Native North Americans believe that everything in nature is imbued with a spirit — trees, rocks, mammals, fish, birds — and of course, humans. All of life is sacred and seeing it that way encourages us to revere and respect it. None of us is mean-spirited enough to harm a sacred person or thing. *If it is sacred, we will revere it.*

A Return to Civility: Relationships, Etiquette, and Saying Sorry

When there is a decline in civility, the toxicity within organizations increases and the soul shrivels. Civility is one of the most effective antidotes to this toxicity; civilized behavior is soothing to the soul.

The holy terrors of corporate life — downsizing, re-engineering, de-layering, restructuring, and merging, (which I have heard described as "shrink till it clinks") — all spell job pressure, stress, and firings. Organizations under siege become characterized by a culture in which the main concern is to look out for number one — at any cost, including brotherly or sisterly love. In these conditions, the last thing on a corporate survivor's mind is the art of communicating with grace.

The toxification of the office results in anger, resentment, betrayal, and people whose fuses are so short that they resort to snarling at each other. Time is in such short supply that investing in considerate communications becomes a luxury. *Chemistry*, which includes such old-world niceties as respect, courtesy, trust, truth-telling, promise-keeping, good manners, and grace, is reminiscent of an earlier time, when life's supreme challenge was something greater than hanging on to your job.

In the toxic organization, the soul is trashed. Phone calls are not returned, memos not replied to, appointments not kept, and rude conduct is a way of life. Outside the office, a red traffic light is an excuse to hijack your car at gunpoint. Inside the office, similar hostility has now become acceptable.

In a survey conducted by the Society for Human Resource Management, one-third of the respondents stated that one or more violent acts had been committed in their offices during the last five years, with 80 percent of them occurring during the last three years. Three-quarters of these events were ugly, involving fist fights, physical struggles, and thrown objects. If unchecked, this behavior deteriorates into harassment, intimidation, confrontation, and litigation.

Will is to grace as the horse is to the rider.

SAINT AUGUSTINE

Accountemps, a New York City firm that provides temporary accounting staff, surveyed executives from the nation's 1,000 largest companies and found that in 1992 they spent 13 percent of their time resolving conflict between workers, up from 9 percent in 1989. In 1993, a man with a grudge against a San Francisco law firm walked into their offices and opened fire with an assortment of weapons — killing eight and wounding six. Delayering, re-engineering, or rightsizing will not address the angst of this man's soul or the thousands of other souls who are aching the same way. Between July 1992 and July 1993 in the United States alone, over 1,000 workers were killed in the workplace and two million were attacked. Between 1980 and 1988, 6,956 homicides occurred in the workplace. Our lack of grace is so extreme that it is creating stress and toxicity that spills from the workplace into society at large.

This is hardly the best foundation on which to build harmony or nourish the soul. As in families, abusive behavior eventually results in disintegration of the unit. Good manners is the art of making others feels at ease.

Creating Tactile Territory

To show their affection, Russian men embrace and kiss each other. The French and the Italians kiss everyone. North Americans call it sexual harassment.

Humans are so inherently tactile that we will die without oxygen, nutrition, information, caring interaction, and touch — these last two being expressions of love. Some jurisdictions have passed ordinances that prohibit any form of touching. In New York, it is illegal for a teacher to touch a student, yet teachers will tell you that their students yearn more for hugs than knowledge. In circumstances of grief — a cancer ward, a war zone, a car crash, a funeral — we do not check the policy and procedures manual to determine whether hugging, consoling, and holding hands is permissible.

It doesn't take much to remove the soulless rules that have denied our souls the warmth of physical contact: organizations simply need to declare, formally if necessary, that their workplace is a Sanctuary, zoned as tactile territory. Organizations are potential meeting places, where we can comfort each other in our sorrows and celebrate each other in our joys. They are organizations of humans who need to laugh, cry, and hug, together. It is vital for the soul.

Regaining the Courage to Be Intimate

Before we can even approach the issue of being more tactile however, we must make it safe to *discuss* the real issues that affect people. We are strangely reluctant to do this. Michael Novak, of the American Enterprise Institute offers this insight, "In the Victorian Period, people in polite company ... wouldn't dare dream of discussing sex, but they would talk freely about prayer, meditation and sermons they had heard. Today the inhibitions are reversed. You can say almost anything about sex, and people will just laugh. But if you begin to talk about prayer or meditation, there's a distinct discomfort. Talking about ethics makes a lot of people squirm, not because they are unethical, but because they think that's rather a private matter."[1]

Many words cause people to squirm at work — ethics, emotions, loneliness, illness, personal finances, spirituality, truth-telling, promise-keeping. In fact, most issues that are essentially human and much of what *Reclaiming Higher Ground* is about elicit this discomfort.

In our mistaken belief that machismo is the hallmark of strong leadership, we too often pretend that none of these human foibles affects us. Thus we appear distant, cold, and mechanical to others, which alienates their souls. Being human, not mechanical, is crucial to opening our souls at work, and permitting the whole person to be present and contribute. Avoiding these and other issues of the heart — issues that are at the core of what it means to be human — starves the soul of its most essential requirements and blocks our creative energy and productivity.

When you are a Bear of Very Little Brain, and you Think of Things, you find sometimes that a Thing that seemed very Thingish inside you is quite different when it gets out into the open and has other people looking at it.

WINNIE-THE-POOH (A. A. MILNE)

Denying our vulnerabilities and avoiding intimacy with others leads to the greatest poverty the soul must endure: loneliness. Revealing our vulnerabilities in intimate one-on-one conversations is vital for our survival, and virtual conversations, in which humans do not interact beyond the superficial level, sometimes not even meeting at all, cannot fill these primal requirements. When the communications are both shallow and virtual, toxicity builds at an alarming pace.

Organizations are teams who depend on their relationships to achieve shared goals. This *Chemistry* leads to friendship and the most successful teams are collections of successful friends. It is not enough just to respect other team members, because functional respect is based on the personality. Deep friendship is a human connection between souls. When the soul is troubled by an absence of *Chemistry* among employees, performance suffers and the spirit withers.

The Power of Thank You

Saying "thank you" is comfy food for the soul, yet it is a practice that is largely absent from our work and personal lives. A recent study by the Dale Carnegie Foundation reported that during the previous six months, fewer than 7 percent of people in the United States had received a thank-you note from the person they reported to, acknowledging them for working hard or achieving a team goal.

In mechanical organizations, saying thank you is often considered a frill. Some people consider those who appreciate recognition or acknowledgment of their success to be insecure or immature. Recall the old story about the wife who complained to her husband that he didn't tell her he loved her anymore. "Look," he said, "I told

Gratitude is a fruit of great cultivation; you do not find it among gross people.

SAMUEL JOHNSON

you I loved you when we got married. If anything changes, I'll let you know."

We think that if we don't complain, we send a signal that we are satisfied, but such arid and understated appreciation starves the soul. The insensitive leader often resorts to standard-form thank-you letters and preprinted thank-you cards. This results in the sorry spectacle of busy people trying to get their computers to act as surrogate friends. The golden rule applies here: don't do unto others what you wouldn't do to yourself—unless you enjoy receiving phony, computer-generated thank-you letters. The soul can tell the difference.

At Disney, cast members (Disney-speak for employees) have a secret signal to give to colleagues who deserve a thank you—a thumbs-up gesture. At Disney theme parks, when employ-

We are all dependent on one another, every soul of us on earth.

GEORGE BERNARD SHAW

ees notice a colleague displaying *Mastery*—calming a distraught youngster, helping an older guest up some steep stairs, picking up something a guest has dropped—they signal their appreciation with the visual thank you of the thumbs-up gesture, which is not obvious to outsiders, but is always appreciated by fellow cast members.

Never Leave Work Angry

Much toxicity within organizations is caused by careless and often graceless communications. The damage this causes is avoidable: a little reflection on the impact of these hurtful exchanges and an effort to repair the harm caused would be good for the soul.

When I was working with a very large hospital recently, I asked a nurse working on a cancer ward how often she witnessed death. She told me there were seven or eight deaths on her ward each month. This nurse worked closely with terminal patients, trying to reduce their suffering, making their last days as comfortable as possible, and dealing with the pain of the families. I was shocked to learn of these mortality rates and asked if this caused her great pain. She acknowledged that although it was very difficult, she was trained to deal with the emotional stress associated with her work.

She then asked if I could guess what part of her work produced the greatest stress. After listening to my inaccurate guesses, she said, "It is the cruel behavior of staff to each other on the job, their pettiness and lack of consideration." We talked about this some more and her reasons became clear. The work produces high levels of stress with which nurses are taught to cope. But they are not trained to handle the resulting backwash that this stress causes in their interpersonal relationships, at home and at work. What we needed was some time to coach the nurses—a program that I called "Who Heals the Healer?"

People under stress often unintentionally transfer their frustrations to their relationships with others. They tend to be under time pressures and suffering from exhaustion. They snap at each other and, though they almost immediately regret it, they are too depleted to muster the energy required to do the one thing that would make everyone feel better—apologize.

The wise, premarital advice we received from our parents, "Never go to sleep angry with your spouse," is still sound. It also applies beyond the conjugal bedroom. An argument or disagreement at work will fester unless repaired. We have the opportunity to apply the same practice at the office:

> # *Never Leave*
> # *the Office Angry with*
> # *Your Colleagues*

Of course, we are not talking about anything much more sophisticated here than old-fashioned good manners and etiquette. But civility in a high-speed world has become a virtual oxymoron. Civility requires space, time, and quiet reflection. Civility is built on empathy, the Accelerator that drives the value of *Chemistry* and it requires us to make all of the Values Shifts on the front wheel of the Values Cycle. If we are conscious that we have just insulted someone, or hurt their feelings, or been rude or abrupt— it takes little effort to say sorry. The power of a public, and immediate, apology can be immense, and its healing effect profound. At the end of each day we have a choice — to wound or to heal the personality and the soul.

Walking Our Talk with Grace

The level of grace within an organization is set by each of us — not by someone else. The standards for organizations are those practised by our role models — *and if it's going to be, it's up to me.* Civility will not occur unless someone sets a new standard. We all need role models. We follow the example of those we admire, because we assume that their behavior led to their success. If we see shabby behavior leading to achievement, it is natural for us to copy it. In sports we have the choice of celebrating and lionizing O. J. Simpson, Mike Tyson, and Tonya Harding for their toxic behavior or Roger Staubach, Joe DiMaggio, Joe Montana, and Wayne Gretzky for their inspiring examples. If we make heroes out of bad-tempered, overpaid, substance-abusing, immature sports personalities, we should not be surprised that their example is used as a template by millions of impressionable people.

The hardest job kids face today is learning good manners without seeing any.

FRED ASTAIRE

We have alternatives, and we need them. One example is Grant Hill, the rookie forward of the Detroit Pistons basketball team. Hill made history by being the first rookie to be voted onto the All-Star game. Fans gave him more votes than anyone else. Not even Michael Jordan was the top vote-getter during his first year. Hill is a good player, averaging eighteen points, five rebounds, and four assists a game. While the fans admire his skills, what really turns them on is his grace and charm, so rare among the egocentric superstars of professional sports. Hill's mentor and Pistons guard Joe Dumars sums up the situation, "It's a league of guys who are out of control. Fringe behavior is being recognized and accepted, sometimes even rewarded. It is probably not a healthy comment that Grant is being recognized for just being a good person, but it's time we got back to that."

After a long drought, fans, like the rest of us, are ready to reward civility — Hill will be paid $45 million over eight years. Hill is organizing a summer camp for kids and despite his new-found riches, he lives modestly in a three-bedroom condo in a suburb close to the Pistons arena. Says Pistons coach Don Chaney (whom Hill calls "Sir"), "Grant is headed for stardom. You can't talk it, and you can't teach it. The fans are hungry —

hungry—and are getting tired of immature athletes. They want something better." A universal change of sentiment is growing. We want our heroes to transcend civility, not trash it. It is the same in our offices, in our homes, and throughout our lives. It is time for us to practise amazing grace. And the first step is ours to take.

All brothers are to preach by their works.

SAINT FRANCIS OF ASSISI

It takes courage to go first in all soul-work. Every time I meet one of my favorite clients, he jokes as he gives me a hug, "Let's hug, in an arm-curl, let's-invade-a-country, kind of way!" Even today, his joke reveals his emotional insecurity and awkwardness. Like most of us, he has been raised in a world where we have been taught that men who hug are sissies, that gentleness will be interpreted as weakness instead of leadership strength. The role of the leader who wishes to inspire the souls of others—the missionary— is to model the behavior desired, which is done by going first.

Grace with Customers

Thanks in part to Tom Peters's fundamentalist preaching about the need for a customer-driven culture, there can be few organizations of any kind that have not yet accepted the primary role of the customer. Almost every leader has implemented some kind of customer service or quality program. But very few organizations have internalized this understanding sufficiently to make it a fundamental part of their belief systems. When times are tough, customer service is often one of the first expenses to be trimmed. We continue to believe in, and therefore invest in, the customer—*as long as we can afford to*. Our commitment to maintaining a state of grace with the customer is often superficial and too often wavers in the face of other priorities.

The Mother Teresa Theory

We get what we expect. One of my clients is an agricultural chemical company. At the beginning of each growing season, farmers have a very small window of opportunity to apply herbicides and fertilizers. Any snags resulting from their application must be fixed quickly. In these circumstances, conventional wisdom holds that the sales representatives will find themselves confronted by irate farmers: *so they were trained to deal with irate farmers.*

But these assumptions can be challenged. I asked my client to pretend that Mother Teresa had joined our sales team. After receiving a call from an irate farmer, Mother Teresa drives to his farm in her Ford F-150 pick-up. As she jumps out of the truck, the farmer strides across the field towards her and notices that the representative is Mother Teresa. Does he hurl expletives at her? Does he vent his anger? Of course not. Although the farmer is the same person, with the same problems, *we* have changed, and by doing so, we have changed the farmer's behavior.

The behavior of others is neither a given nor is it separate from our own. We can do more than merely react to the behavior of others: we can dramatically and positively change and influence it. We call this phenomenon motivation. My client no longer "trains" sales representatives to deal with irate farmers; they have changed *their* attitude by empowering their sales teams to make decisions that meet the customer's needs — on the spot. The resulting growth in motivation and corporate performance has been remarkable — this same team has tripled their sales in the last three years, with exactly the same team members.

Quality as Sacred Trust

Why do we have Customer Service Programs or Total Quality Programs? After all, the reason we develop them is to improve failing levels of service or quality. If we were already providing perfect levels of service and quality, we wouldn't need a "program" at all.

We have a sacred responsibility to provide quality and customer service to others — both inside and outside our organizations. This is not a matter of discretion, but a sacred trust. It is about promise-keeping — we have made a promise to meet an agreed performance standard. We have given our word, our bond. Total Quality and Customer Service Programs are our desperate attempts to repair these broken bonds and to recover the trust we have lost with customers, employees, and partners. If we live up to our responsibilities in the first place, we will not need these repair programs.

As we discussed in the previous chapter, just as quality and doing it right the first time have now been found to be less expensive than saving money and cutting corners, so will we find that truth-telling and promise-keeping the first time will also be more efficient in the long run. Rethinking our practice in this way will both transform our bottom line and invigorate the soul.

The Customer Comes Second

I define a customer as someone who comes to us with a need. In the work setting as well as our personal lives, this makes almost everyone a customer. For the last fifteen years, organizations have been redesigning their approaches to customers with an array of campaigns and programs, consultants have been writing and teaching, and a revolution of awareness has resulted. But until we meet the needs of the souls as well as the personalities of employees, we will be unable to meet the similar needs of customers.

Poor customer service and quality, defined as bad *Chemistry* (a poor relationship) between the customer and the service provider, begins with the absence of grace between the leader and the rest of the team providing customer service and among team members themselves. This lack of grace starts within each individual inside the organization. If we have not learned to treat each other with grace, how will we learn to be graceful with our customers? If we live with grace inside our organizations, it will show up in our relationships outside them. Our messianic focus on the customer, at the expense of the employee, has kept us looking through the wrong end of the telescope.

Hal Rosenbluth has built one of North America's most successful travel agency chains, and the title of his book describes my sentiments perfectly: *The Customer Comes Second and Other Secrets of Exceptional Service*[2]. For years we have been pushing employees to provide better customer service and higher quality, and we have been incredibly successful. By almost every yardstick, North America leads, or is level with Japan, in both customer service and quality. However, there has been a casualty along the way: a growing number of people now hate their work, and are afraid of and distrust business leaders. They look elsewhere to nourish their souls. *They may be married to work, but their real desire is to have an affair of the soul.* As we have been raising the standards of customer service and quality to levels that many naysayers believed were impossible, we have abandoned the souls of our employees, without whom our organizations would simply grind to a halt.

A Total Quality Program for People

A revolution is occurring. Growing numbers of people are no longer prepared to carry the torch of continuing improvements in customer service
and quality without a commensurate increase in service and quality for
themselves—a Total Quality Program for Employees. Their message is
that employees come first and customers come second, and if we get it
right, in that order, we will regenerate and build the greatest organizations
in the world by inspiring the souls within them. These will be Sanctuaries—places of deep inspiration—because leaders will have learned to
reconnect with the souls of their employees and customers.

Marriott Hotels, Resorts and Suites Division, not unlike many organizations, loses 60 percent of its front-line service staff every year, 40
percent of them within the first three months. Human resources vice
president Richard Bell-Irving estimates that it costs as much as $1,100
to recruit and train each replacement. He says, "When someone leaves,
it messes up your employee teams, messes up your productivity, and
messes up the service you provide to your guests."[3] Our choice of language indicates one attitude and this may offer a key to Marriott's staff
turnover: an employee's first three months with Marriott are called
"probation"—the same term used for felons who are on parole or serving a sentence outside in lieu of incarceration—hardly a description to
inspire the soul.

Yet this style is typical in mechanical organizations where people are
viewed as nothing more than parts or production units, instead of souls.
This example shows how our treatment of employees and our low levels
of respect for them can deaden the soul and therefore generate low standards of customer service and quality. In retailing, respect for people is so
low that one-fourth of retail workers have no health insurance, and 40
percent earn less than $14,764 per year, the official poverty level for a
family of four in the United States. No wonder they mumble "Have a nice
day" with about as much sincerity as a two-by-four.

Our levels of insensitivity to the soul can produce effects that would
be laughable if they were not so distressing. Some years ago, Kmart was
simultaneously downsizing and urging employees to tell shoppers, "Thank
you for shopping at Kmart." The sales staff, struggling to do more with
less, became so harried that they condensed this greeting into an acronym
and shouted "TYFSAK" as they frantically tried to move bewildered customers through the check-out.

Before organizations can connect with the souls of customers, major shifts in attitude will be required. Many leaders use their recent discovery of the customer as evidence of their sincerity and genuine dedication to service and quality. However, TQM, customer service, and the other trendy buzz-words of the recent past were more about survival than honoring the customer. After living in the shelter of import quotas for so long, if the auto industry hadn't cleaned up its quality act, it probably wouldn't exist today. Negative option marketing, misleading labeling and advertising, limited warranties, environmental abuse — all are actions undertaken by organizations that proclaim themselves to be "customer-driven."

Hal Rosenbluth puts it this way, "It's our people who provide service to our clients. The highest achievable level of service comes from the heart. So, the company that reaches its people's hearts will provide the very best service. It's the nicest thing we could possibly do for our clients. They have come to learn that by being second, they come out ahead.... If we put our people first, they'll put our clients first."[4]

Being Unique in a World of Sameness

The entire airline industry buys its planes from the same handful of manufacturers, uses the same types of computers, uses the same air traffic controllers and baggage handlers, flies to the same cities, and lands at the same terminals. So how do airlines distinguish themselves? The first strategy of differentiation was the frequent flyer program, invented by American Airlines. The company enjoyed its distinctive advantage for three weeks, before it was copied by another airline, and not long after that, by the rest of the industry. This caused them to become the same as all the others once again. The next strategy was deep discounts. This resulted in the greatest financial hemorrhaging in airline history, with losses in 1992 equal to all the profits earned by all the airlines in their entire cumulative history. This caused them all to look alike again, in more ways than one — they were all losing money.

We live in a time when we can all duplicate each other's technology within three weeks. Meeting the needs of our customers is no longer a mere matter of mind — it is now a matter of the heart — reverence for the sacredness of people and the planet — what we call love. Individuals and their organizations will no longer be distinguished by their technical excellence alone, but by the level of their spiritual commitment to those they serve. The financial recovery of the airline industry is underway and one or two companies are distinguishing themselves by doing something that they have never done before: managing their business from the soul instead of the personality. The day they make this an ongoing practice, the flying public will choose to do more business with them, at reasonable prices, thus making the industry viable once more. People are drawn to Sanctuaries. Being good to the soul is good for business.

Grace with Partners

Much of my life is spent traveling to cities where I address audiences. The arrangement is simple: for a fee, I will fly to a town, stay overnight if necessary, make my speech, and fly out again. I often fly coach, whether my clients ask me to or not; some are surprised and most are delighted. Some of my clients make me fly on "no-name" airlines, put me into "no-tell motels" and leave me to fend for myself with audiovisual equipment and facilities. Other clients will go out of their way to spoil me.

Not long ago, I arrived late at the hotel where I was due to give a speech the following morning. After being picked up at the airport, I arrived at the hotel where a VIP greeted me with a glass of champagne and took care of all my requirements as my bags were whisked to my room. When I reached my room, I opened the door and found a beautiful suite, where much effort had been expended to make it elegant and comfortable. There was a sumptuous bathroom with an oversized Jacuzzi whirlpool in the corner, a basket of fruit on the credenza and a vase of flowers to make me feel at home.

I thanked my client the next day and asked why she had taken so much trouble to fuss over me. She said, "You are the speaker and it is your special room. When I booked this hotel for our convention, I booked the best room in the hotel for you. We want you to be fresh, relaxed, and happy and to enjoy being with us. We want you to bring our audience to their feet, cheering." I guessed that my client had invested $150 above the normal room rate, or twenty-five cents for each of the 600 audience members. Did I give that audience twenty-five cents of extra value and passion? You bet I did!

The traditional relationship between partner and vendor is based on mechanical organization thinking. Each party views the other as separate, as an adversary trying to take advantage of the other. Each side is on guard, defending themselves against loopholes or careless oversight of detail. Traditional thinking pits a purchasing manager against a vendor, a graceless relationship in which both are seeking opposing goals. The purchasing agent seeks the best product, quality, and service for the lowest price, while the vendor looks for the best margins possible in order to survive and make a profit. A friend of mine told me, with barely concealed delight, how he had negotiated a contract with a client, for a price that was twice what my friend thought was fair value. The company signed the contract and two years later declared bankruptcy, partly as a result of being locked into this onerous agreement. As part of the refinancing package, the new owners asked my friend to renegotiate the contract to include terms that were more favorable to them, which he was forced to do. But when the contract expired, he was not invited to bid on their future business.

> **The role of the customer is to teach companies how to do business with them.**
>
> PETER BLOCK

Who got the best deal? In the end, a deal that's good for me but bad for you is bad for both of us. Contests where one party wins and the other loses, the so-called "zero-sum game," are graceless and noxious to the soul. How can the soul be nourished by the certain knowledge that a contract has been negotiated at an unfair price, which could lead to the supplier losing money, and perhaps to bankruptcy? How can the creation of so much human pain be considered "winning"? The theoretical winner — the customer who succeeds in extracting unrealistically low prices or unreasonable terms from a supplier — enjoys a hollow victory, savoring the short-term financial advantage but enduring the longer-term moral bankruptcy and spiritual loss. Meanwhile, the supplier feels cheated and demoralized and suffers a sickness of the soul. There is no winner; both are spiritual losers, because while it may appear that the customer is the victor in a win/lose deal, closer scrutiny reveals that there are no victors — it is a lose/lose deal. As Martin Luther King, Jr., observed, the old law about "an eye for an eye" leaves everybody blind.

In reality, partners are on your team; it's just that they are not on your payroll. Ideally, customers and their partners share a vision, bring different strengths to the party, and pool their respective *Mastery, Chemistry,* and *Delivery,* in order to reach a mutual objective. When a partner and a customer agree to negotiate terms that are in their mutual best interest before they work out the details, they will make magic together and a win/win deal will emerge.

There are few industries in which consumers are more price-conscious than in the field of computers. Finis Conner helped to launch two major disk drive manufacturers, Shugart Associates and later Seagate Technology, which grew to become the largest in the business. Eventually, Conner decided to strike out on his own, starting his own disk drive company. Unlike many other companies who make their own components, he decided to buy them from suppliers and instead of owning his plants he decided to lease them. At the beginning, Conner went to see Compaq, one of the largest PC makers, to learn how he could meet their needs for disk drives. In a true spirit of partnership, Compaq decided to bankroll the new company, thus ensuring a steady supply of disk drives. At the beginning, Compaq was Conner's only customer, but the symbiotic relationship helped him to make a profit in his first quarter. Conner continued to collaborate closely with his customers in order to achieve win/win deals in a business that is notoriously volatile. To avoid sudden bottlenecks, Conner lined up assembly space ahead of schedule. Said Conner President, William Almon, "We have two buildings in Singapore, complete with clean rooms but with no people in them, ready to go." This attention to partnering helped Conner become a leading supplier to the computer industry and the market leader in disk drives for laptop and notebook computers.[5] In 1995, Seagate and Conner merged.

Thomas T. Stallkamp, Chrysler Corp.'s chief of purchasing, credits Canadian auto-parts giant, Magna International Inc. with providing 148 different cost-cutting proposals over the last two years, which he believes could result in annual savings of $93-million. That's the potential of every partnership that is available to customers who invest in their relationships with their suppliers.

The employee, customer, and supplier all seek one thing—to become whole. After all, they are souls seeking a human experience first, and employees, customers, and partners second. In our quest to become whole, we frequently forget this. We all live in hope that in every relationship we will be able to reconcile the needs of our personality with our quest for spiritual meaning—what is intimate with what is infinite. Often, we mistakenly believe that as soon as we have succeeded in meeting the short-term needs of the personality, we will be able to turn our attention to meeting the needs of the soul—when we have fed our personality, we can feed our soul. But the two cannot be separated or compromised in this way. When graceless acts disappoint us, in whatever our role at the time—employee, customer, or supplier—the absence of grace intrudes into our lives and corrodes our souls.

Gracelessness foils our attempts to become whole. The resulting spiritual poverty ruins the health of both body and soul. Our challenge therefore, is to infuse all relationships at work with grace. Our work is made up of many small endeavors, which, if done with love, will be graceful, and consequently, inspire the soul. To quote Mother Teresa, "We can do no great things, only small things with great love." If we feel good about being employees, customers, and partners, we will regenerate ourselves and our organizations, and work will no longer be a four-letter word.

If you mean to profit, learn to please

WINSTON S. CHURCHILL

5

The Alchemy of the Soul

When speaking to a Bear of Very Little Brain, remember that long words may Bother him. It's more fun to talk with someone who doesn't use long, difficult words but rather short, easy words like "What about lunch?"

WINNIE-THE-POOH (A. A. MILNE).

I realize that the reader is not Winnie-the-Pooh, but I also realize that this chapter contains some long words. I apologize and urge the reader to persevere, because it is my hope that the value of the information will be more than worth the struggle.

Why Is Work Making Us Sick?

North America has the highest incidence of heart disease in the world, spending more of its GNP on health care and other health issues than any other nation on Earth. Last year, General Motors spent more on health care than on steel, adding $900 to the price of every car sold.

When we talk about corporate strategy or leadership in business, many people use the violent metaphors of war. In their book, *Marketing Warfare*, authors Al Reis and Jack Trout advise us that, "The true nature of marketing today is outwitting, outflanking, outfighting the competition. In short, marketing is war, where the enemy is your competitor and the ground to be won is the customer."[1]

> **Two things are bad for the heart – running uphill and running down people.**
>
> BERNARD GIMBEL

We frequently refer to business as war and "tell the troops" that the competition must be destroyed, killed, or murdered, and our territory defended. When things get tough, we complain that the competition is killing us and we react by developing offensive, aggressive strategies that will enable us to conquer and dominate markets. As we advance on the enemy, we design category killers and scorched earth policies, pledging to wipe out the enemy without taking prisoners. We thrill to the image of being dangerous and using our weapons to blow our competitors out of the water, assuring ourselves that when they are dead meat we will achieve victory and control.

We relish the language of war, believing that it inspires heroic performance. But in truth, when we use the images of war, we don't inspire people — we make them sick. The constant use of violent language creates toxicity within people. Organizations, because they are the sum of the people in them, succumb to this toxicity.

We use violence and aggression to communicate our ideas in advertising, the media, our entertainment, our strategies — even naming a golf club, the "Big Bertha," after a World War II gun. We have become so desensitized to violence as a metaphor, that all the big guns do it!

Our approach to violence might be typified by Vince Lombardi's famous quotation, "Winning isn't everything, it's the only thing," the implication being that, as long as you win, anything goes. So we mistakenly believe that the fearsome clichés of war, violence and intimidation, inspire and motivate. We have assumed that our role models should be heroic leaders: male, macho, tough, nail-spitting ass-kickers — like Rambo. But it doesn't work like that. The qualities of modern leadership are more likely to be found in the wisdom of saints, mystics, and gurus than Attila the Hun, and from our female as much as from our male energy.

War is the business of barbarians.

NAPOLEON BONAPARTE

We Are Alchemists

Though we seldom realize it, every one of us is an alchemist. Alchemy is a combination of chemistry, philosophy, and mysticism. It was practised in the Middle Ages by alchemists who often gave up their lives to search for the "Philosopher's Stone," reputed to be an elixir made from salt, sulfur, and mercury, which could change base metals into gold and lead to perpetual youth. A New Age of Alchemy has arrived and you and I are the alchemists. Today's philosophy is human motivation and the mysticism is an unswerving belief in individual greatness. Modern scientists call the chemistry, psychoneuroimmunology, or "PNI" for short.

Every day, we alter each other's biochemistry, and as a result, we create happiness or sadness, elation or depression, mediocrity or greatness in those with whom we communicate. We all have immense powers that can heal or wound each other's souls — with every word we utter.

The Body Is a Pharmacy

First, let's look at the human body. Our physical beings are really no more than an elaborate pharmacy. We are a complex chemical soup, being adapted and renewed every second by our environment, our emotions, our diets, and each human interaction. Our bodies are in a continuous process of renewal. We make a new skeleton for ourselves every ninety days, a new liver every six weeks (for some people, this is a major advantage), a new skin every five weeks, a new stomach lining every five days, and new stomach surface cells every five minutes.

Some changes in our biochemistry create human toxicity. Jon Franklin has pointed out that at any time nearly one-third of the population suffers from chemically caused illness. He writes, "... one out of every 100 of us

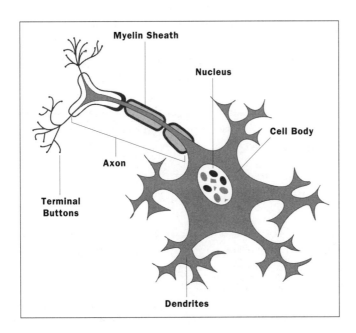

Figure 13: The Neuron

is schizophrenic, two more are schizoid, eight are phobic, seven are addicted, six are depressed, perhaps five are criminal. Perhaps another five are destructively irrational at any given moment..."[2] Each of these chemically caused sicknesses eventually festers in the soul.

The Neuron

The brain is composed of over 100 billion cells called neurons, each of which is capable of exchanging signals with tens of thousands of neighboring neurons. Each neuron is a tiny data processing center and although no two are identical, they share similar features: a cell body, several dendrites, and an axon. The dendrite is a tiny tendril trailing from the cell body through which each cell receives signals from others. The axon is a tail attached to the cell body, and a terminal button is located at its end. All human emotions and feelings, as well as our physiological well-being, are triggered by electrochemical communications between neurons.

The brain produces or activates over sixty different chemical secretions and is therefore able to prepare prescriptions that continually alter the emotional and physiological state of the body. There are many ways to alter this; diet is one of them. If you felt an urge to become happier, for example, you could achieve this by consuming milk, chicken, bananas, and leafy greens — foods known to stimulate the production of dopamine, one of the body's "uppers." If you feel depressed, this might be caused by eating sugars or fats, both of which stimulate acetylcholine, one of the body's "downers." Cuddling animals, playing with children, and engaging in humorous entertainment — all have the potential to alter our biochemistry and therefore boost our moods.

The Hand or the Fist

We can communicate in two ways: with the open hand or the clenched fist. Some leaders believe that fear is a powerful motivator. While this may be true in some circumstances for the personality, it is virtually never true for the soul. Though we may be grateful that we still have a job, and this gratitude may motivate us to put in the minimal effort necessary to keep it, our souls will still yearn to be set free at the end of the day.

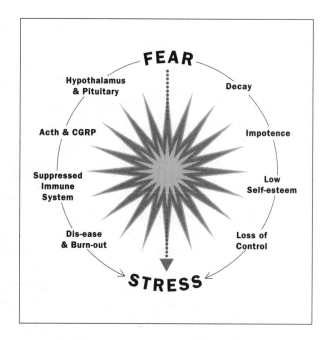

Figure 14: The Fear and Stress Cycle

The Biochemical Effects of the Fear and Stress Cycle

Figure 14 illustrates how intimidation and fear create stress. The left side of the Fear and Stress Cycle represents the biochemical or physiological effects of fear and the right side represents the emotional or psychological consequences. When we are afraid, the hypothalamus, the emotional center of the brain, and the pituitary gland are activated. The pituitary gland sends a message that releases a stress hormone called adrenocorticotropic hormone (ACTH) into the bloodstream. The ACTH arrives at the adrenal glands, which in fear or anger produce the hormone epinephrin. This triggers a quick boost of energy through the release of glucose, stimulating the heart and increasing the blood circulation to the muscles and causing the adrenal glands to produce more than thirty different hormones. Some change the body's metabolism, increasing the rate at which fats and proteins are converted into sugar, thereby increasing the available fuel for the body in action. Hydrocortisone, a natural form of cortisone, is released to reduce tissue inflammation.

As the adrenals discharge adrenaline and noradrenaline, the heart pumps faster to speed the passage of stress chemicals through the body's systems, blood pressure rises, and the pupils of the eyes dilate in order to improve vision. The combined surge of hormones relaxes the bronchial tubes in order to effect deeper, improved breathing, which generates greater supplies of oxygen. The increased hormones build up the blood sugar to maximize energy, slow down the digestive process to conserve muscular energy, and shift blood supplies so that the blood can clot more easily should the body sustain an open wound.

All of this happens in seconds, during which time the body becomes transformed into a tense configuration of immensely altered substances, geared to meet demands well beyond normal capacity. We call this condition stress. It is highly toxic to the body and extremely corrosive to the soul. As the body adapts to deal with the recent stress, it shuts down the immune system so that the biochemical resources can be diverted to maintaining its survival mechanisms. When the immune system is suppressed, the body becomes vulnerable to *dis-ease*. In its search for relief from the pain, the stressed population turns to the health-providing community. This is why the health bills of General Motors, and the nation, take off.

The evidence linking disease with stress is strong. Countless studies suggest that stress leads to diminished healthy cell growth and to depression. Depression is caused by the emission of biochemistry resulting in hyperactivity. Medical specialists have found that certain medications can alter this chemistry and alleviate depression. But these interventions deal with the symptoms of the pain, not its cause. *Prozac does not heal the soul.*

The Psychological Effects of the Fear and Stress Cycle

We've looked at the biochemical effects of stress, now let's look at the psychological and emotional effects — the right side of the Fear and Stress Cycle. When we are afraid, we become preoccupied with survival. In survival mode, the body cannot grow because it is dedicated to surviving the dangers presented. If we are not growing, we are dying and in these conditions, we cannot refurbish our skills, so they decline. Declining skills result in a reduction of *Mastery* and, therefore, a decline in self-esteem. This, in turn, leads to a loss of control and therefore increased stress. When we are out of control, we experience deep anxiety. Reflect on the last time a close relative was seriously ill: your anxiety was heightened whenever you were unable to exert a comforting level of control on any of the conditions.

The Biochemical Effects
of the Love and Exhilaration Cycle

Now let's look at the Love and Exhilaration Cycle shown in Figure 15. In my seminars, I often ask participants to reflect on the period in their careers when they were most highly motivated, exhilarated, and passionate about their work. Their first thoughts nearly always describe a relationship with an individual—a mentor, a caring leader, a teacher whom they loved and who loved them. In other words, the electrochemical reactions and therefore the emotional sensations that they found most pleasurable were those stimulated by a leader who communicated and taught with love—not fear. These were periods of deep spiritual nourishment and personal evolution in their lives. Mentoring, one of the essential components of learning, is a gift to oneself as well as to others. The act of mentoring is the act of self-healing.

Figure 15: The Love and Exhilaration Cycle

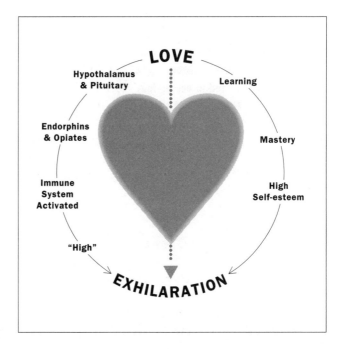

Anyone who has worked with someone they loved—a great teacher or mentor—can remember the wonderful feelings of passion and exhilaration. Note, we are using the term exhilaration—not stress. The biochemistries of stress and exhilaration are entirely different. The notion of "good stress" is a myth; there is no such thing as good stress anymore than there is good poison. When we do something because we are afraid, we become stressed. When we do something because we love the person for whom we are doing it (*Chemistry*), love the way we feel when we do it (*Mastery*), or love the reason for doing it (*Delivery*), exhilaration is the result. As the left side of the diagram shows, the hypothalamus becomes activated, not by ACTH this time, but instead by endorphins and opiates, including interleukin-2, the body's natural "uppers," which lead to the "high" or the "rush" that we experience when we do the things we love. The immune system is strengthened as a result—people who love what they do are rarely ill.

The Psychological Effects
of the Love and Exhilaration Cycle

On the other side of our diagram, the psychological and emotional impact of love, we see a remarkably different picture from the Fear and Stress Cycle. When we love what we are doing, such as playing the violin, what is the first thing we do? We take violin lessons. When we commit to learning, the result is greater *Mastery* and increased *Mastery* leads to improved self-esteem. When we develop greater self-esteem, we attain greater control, we feel in charge, and we feel good. These feelings lead to exhilaration and exhilaration illuminates the soul.

> **If you permit your thoughts to dwell on evil, you yourself will become ugly. Look only for the good in everything, that you absorb the quality of beauty.**
>
> PARAMAHANSA YOGANANDA

Lessons from a Mouse

Stress is deadly. Researchers have demonstrated the dramatic effects of stress in mice. Mice tend to live for about two years, but if a mouse is placed in a laboratory cage and a cat is released into the room every few hours, the mouse will die of natural causes in six weeks—a victim of burnout and stress. If another laboratory mouse is fed a low-cholesterol diet, caressed and shown affection, exercised regularly, and spoken to in a loving way, it will live for six years.

When all three mice — the stressed-out, six-week-old mouse; the ordinary, two-year-old mouse; and the cosseted, six-year-old mouse — are examined, researchers have found that their intestinal organs have all aged identically. As these experiments with mice demonstrate, we create burnout by producing toxicity. Our biochemistry is poisoned and our immune system compromised. In short, we kill each other with stress. Therefore, fear and stress are as deadly to the personality as they are to the soul.

The Biochemistry of Language

Let's look at what happens when we use violent language or are subjected to abuse by aggressive and hostile individuals. When a stressful situation occurs, such as a threat or an insult, the body's sensory network transmits information to the cortex, alerting it to danger. Signals are relayed to the rear of the hypothalamus (home of the stress or "fight-or-flight" response), which reacts by sending messages to the pituitary gland. Medical researchers have noted that depressed patients are unable to maintain appropriate levels of T-cells (thymus-affected, helper and suppressor cells that mitigate viral, fungal, and bacterial infection), B-cells (helpers that are manufactured in the bone marrow) and NK-cells (natural-killer cells that spontaneously recognize and remove tumor- and virus-infected cells). This leaves the body more vulnerable to illness and therefore greater depression.

> ... words are effective only insofar as they convey a meaning or have significance. It is their meaning which is effective. But "meaning" is sometimes mental or spiritual ... we can even influence the bio-chemical processes of the body with it ... (meaning) can make me ill or cure me.
>
> CARL GUSTAV JUNG

The effect on the electrochemical activity in our brains is determined as much by the way we communicate as by what we communicate — the words as much as the music. In his book *Head First*, the late Norman Cousins described the effects of receiving information in an insensitive way. He wrote about patients who, after receiving the news that they were suffering from multiple sclerosis, suddenly experienced acute depression. In one case, the father of a twenty-six-year-old patient walked his son home from the doctor, and later recounted, "By the time we got home I thought my son had aged twenty years. He was walking like an old man."

In another example, after a handful of spectators at a football stadium became ill, a doctor suspected a soft-drink vending machine. The public announcement to spectators that the vending machine was now off limits because someone had contracted food poisoning from the drinks was so insensitively handled that the stadium became a sea of people retching and clutching their stomachs. Over 100 persons had to be hospitalized, yet the soft drinks were later found to be innocent.[3]

As described earlier, signals that incorporate fear activate the hypothalamus and trigger our biochemistry. We may feel ill simply because the words used in the communication are toxic and the toxicity is transferred directly to us. Educational theorist Joseph Chilton Pearce suggests that the context as well as the content affect our learning. For example, even though a person may have a natural inclination for history, if he or she found their history teacher to be repellent, associating the teacher with the subject could cause unpleasant feelings towards history.

Recent studies have shown that exposure to humor or even a video about Mother Teresa can result in significant increases in immunoglobulin A (an antibody that protects outer surfaces of the body), spontaneous blastogenesis (immune cell proliferation), and cortisol, (a hormone with immune-suppressing capability). Other studies have shown that exposure to ugly or frightening material, such as a film about Nazis in World War II, which produced anger and fear, resulted in the opposite effects.

The evidence from holistic medical groups treating cancer patients is overwhelming: if you can reduce the depression of the patient, you will increase the number of immune cells being produced by the body and therefore available to resist the disease. The touch of a tarantula's legs on one's skin or the touch of a lover's hand set off entirely different electrochemical reactions in the limbic system, the hypothalamus, and therefore throughout the body. Reprimands, threats, and punishments stimulate different electrochemical reactions compared with encouragement, praise, saying thank you, and behaving with love and grace.

When the heart overflows, it comes out through the mouth.
ETHIOPIAN PROVERB

All human communications are transmitted and received on a continuum ranging between negative and positive, between fear and love. Which biochemicals are released by the brain depends on whether a person is experiencing pain and fear, which releases stress hormones, activates the limbic system and puts the body in "stress mode," or love and pleasure, releasing "uppers" that lower blood pressure, heart-rate, and oxygen consumption. Since the soul and the body are one, our experiences of love or fear directly influence us to the core of our being.

All this suggests that when we create hostile or aggressive relationships at work, or at home, we cause human depression, which compromises the immune system. This creates a dysfunctional environment in our bodies and ultimately within our organizations. The result in *dis-ease* and sickness of the soul.

During my seminars, I demonstrate the power of words to change our biochemistry with two experiments. First, I ask for a volunteer who is currently suffering from a headache, a migraine, or any other stress-related pain. Through a process of tactile healing techniques, visualization, autosuggestion, and loving energy, *we are always able to immediately ease, and usually remove, the pain.** To establish a contrast, I ask for another volunteer, and suggest that, at the count of three, we sing the national anthem together at the top of our lungs! Just before the count expires, I let the volunteer "off the hook." I then describe the changes they have just experienced in their biochemistry, better known as stress. I ask the volunteer to confirm my descriptions. *They always do.*

Of all base passions, fear is most accursed

WILLIAM SHAKESPEARE

Through these live demonstrations, I am able to show that we all have the capability to inspire or demotivate, to heal or wound each other, through the practice of modern alchemy. We are the controllers and conductors of much of the biochemical activity in ourselves and others. Since the cause of stress is conflict and the cause of conflict is fear, we are far too ready to choose fear as a motivator, when we know that love works so much better. Our choice is critical, because it will determine which biochemicals are set off and therefore which moods and reactions we experience. We each have the power to wound or inspire the soul.

Choosing Love instead of Fear

Those receiving the signals also have options. They can be intimidated by fear or they can rise above it, releasing the appropriate biochemistry necessary to reduce the emotional pain and respond with love. Only the mind

---

* Readers who would like a copy of a tape that includes a definition of the healing process and a do-it-yourself approach to healing headaches are invited to contact the author on the World Wide Web of the Internet at http://www.secretan.com

can manifest fear. The options chosen determine the biochemical reactions in the limbic system and therefore the quality of work and life.

It is usual to consider sources of inspiration solely in psychological or emotional terms — the language of personality. But an entirely new dimension of inspiration is added when we consider how every human communication triggers the limbic and endocrine systems and affects the soul. When we talk of killing the competition, we should be mindful of the old adage, "Be careful what you wish for, because it might happen."

What Vince Lombardi Really Said

We have been misled. Vince Lombardi never said, "Winning isn't everything; it's the only thing." Although this saying is often attributed to him, it was actually written by a newspaper reporter. What Lombardi really said was, "Winning isn't everything, but wanting to win is." This is a very different sentiment. We have been using the wrongly attributed quotation to justify something that Lombardi never intended, believed in, or practised. He was not a fan of fear and intimidation. He led with love, creating exhilaration within his team. The correct quotation continues, "Mental toughness is humility, simplicity, Spartanism, and one other, love. I don't necessarily have to like my employees, but as a person, I must love them. Love is loyalty. Love is teamwork. Love respects the dignity of the individual. Heartpower is the strength of your corporation." Vince Lombardi did not beat performance from others by using fear; he coached them to greatness with love.

The Power of Thought

The alchemy of the soul does not depend on being present. In 1987, Randolph Bird, a cardiologist from the University of California at San Francisco, undertook a research project. He conducted a double-blind study of 400 patients suffering from heart attacks and severe chest pains. Half of the patients were prayed for by a group outside the hospital and half were not. None of the persons praying knew or had met any of the patients, and none of the researchers, patients, nursing staff, or doctors knew who was in each group.

By the end of the controlled experiment, none of the prayed-for group had required assistance from mechanical ventilators, while twelve patients in the not-prayed-for group had. There were fewer deaths and better recovery rates in the prayed-for group than in the not-prayed-for group. Researchers have since replicated this experiment and many have tried unsuccessfully to disprove the findings. If the variable had been a new pharmaceutical, instead of prayer, it would have been hailed as a new miracle drug.

If our thoughts can positively alter the health of two hundred people from a distance, without foreknowledge or communication, is there any reason to doubt that we can negatively affect the well-being of others just as readily? It is even more obvious that when we are in the immediate company of others, we can directly influence their biochemistry — for better or worse. We are alchemists, creating changes in each other's biochemistry through our communications and, in the process, we hold the capacity to wound or heal souls. We are just beginning to realize the power of the human brain to alter almost everything on the planet. As Jon Franklin puts it, "A thousand years hence, when our descendants look back on this time, it will not be the name of Albert Einstein that comes to their lips. For while the forces contained within the nucleus of the atom are truly powerful, and though they may burn hot and bright, they pale when compared with the energy of the human mind."[4]

> **Heard melodies are sweet,**
> **but those unheard are sweeter.**
>
> JOHN KEATS

It is too early in the evolution of the science of PNI for us to understand the exact technology involved, although half-a-million research papers are devoted to the study of the brain each year. I am convinced, however, that in the years ahead, scientists will win the Nobel Prize for their discoveries in this field.

In the meantime we can all cultivate our communication and leadership skills by becoming aware of the principles involved, realizing that how and what we communicate, and the words we choose, is the new alchemy of our time. Our words are like biochemical surgical tools, with which we can mend or break the chemistry of others. Through our words, we have the capacity to raise or dash each other's spirits. We can make our organizations inviting or sickening to our souls. We can find soulmates or alienate others' spirits. We can help the souls of others to be joyful or sad, friendly or angry, inspired or dejected. Our words determine our biochemistry and therefore the state of grace for our souls.

> **How good is man's life, the**
> **mere living! How fit to employ**
> **all the heart and the soul**
> **and the senses forever in joy!**
>
> ROBERT BROWNING

We must choose our words with care.

6

Blithe Spirit

We have made work a four-letter word. We are doing it more and enjoying it less.

According to University of Maryland sociologist John P. Robinson, we have five more hours of free time per week than we did thirty years ago.[1] We're doing less housework, having fewer children, and retiring earlier (and richer) than ever. But what are we doing with this extra time? Are we playing, indulging our relationships and hobbies, or just goofing around? No, we are *working* more. As Stephan Rechtshaffen has put it, we are living in a time when, "If you can balance three spinning plates on three sticks, you are rewarded with a fourth. And then a fifth."[2]

Our average day starts with a rude get-up routine, a gut-wrenching commute to work, and a coffee and muffin before we hit the floor running.

> **The world is too much with us; late and soon,**
> **Getting and spending, we lay waste our powers;**
> **Little we see in nature that is ours; We have given our hearts away, a sordid boon.**
>
> WILLIAM WORDSWORTH

For ten hours, we maintain a video-arcade pace until it is time to be dragged through the commute knot-hole again — this time backwards. We even try to do several things at once — we drive, drink coffee, eat a doughnut, listen to tapes or radio, and talk on our cellular phones. As the day begins to close, we grab some exercise, pick up or make dinner, have staccato conversations with the kids, attend the municipal meeting and the school committee, read some business journals, call some friends, speed-read a novel, check the alarm and poof!... it's all over until we do it again tomorrow morning. We multiply the number of activities in our life without experiencing them. But life is not a drivethrough experience.

This busy-ness and over-commitment has become our religion, providing pseudo-spiritual meaning and a way to reinforce our self-esteem. Instead of gaining meaning from within (the domain of the soul), we attempt to do so from without (the domain of the personality) — through more achievements, accomplishments, and activity. But all this has one drawback: it isn't fun, and if it isn't fun, we shouldn't trust it. The Japanese have even given a special definition to this chronic work addiction that kills: *karoshi*, death from overwork, from which 10,000 people die each year. Work is meant to be spirit-lifting, not spirit-deadening. It's meant to give us life, not death.

An interesting phenomenon has occurred over the last few decades: as we have become less comfortable with our emotions, and especially about revealing them to each other, we have sought refuge in work. More than any time in history, we define ourselves by our work: "I am an executive," "I am a writer," "I sell cars." We ask each other "How are things at work?" when we mean, "How are you — are you fulfilled and happy?" It is as if there were no other defining patterns in our life, and for an increasing number of people this is true.

How We Made Work a Four-Letter Word

Work is a new word. When our ancestors worked the land, they didn't "go to work"; there was no separation between home and work. I have been interested in the origins of the word "work" for over thirty years and during that time I have not been able to find its use in the English language prior to 1599 — when Shakespeare first used it. Greeks and medieval Europeans had no word for work. Native North Americans have no equivalent word in their vocabulary. The classical Greeks and later the Romans considered work done with the hands, for income or trade, appropriate only for slaves.

Wage labor, as work has become today, was an emblem of penury in times past — and for many it is the same today. Today, our work is characterized by a manic stream of deadlines, meetings, expiry dates, renewals, press announcements, and new product launches, and we try to squish an hour of quality time with the kids into the diary between 7 and 8 p.m. We are each living a "life by Day-Timer" as we are whisked along by digital clocks, cellular phones, pagers, faxes, and computers that supervise everything from our cars to our security systems, all measured in nanoseconds.

> **Work is much more fun than fun.**
>
> NOEL COWARD

We celebrate these frenzied lifestyles, making heroes of our manic entrepreneurs, celebrating their brilliant appeal to the personality, even as they leave a trail of trashed souls in their wake. *We have become human doings instead of human beings.*

Seventy-year-old Pierre Péladeau's 58 percent equity stake in Quebecor Inc. is worth nearly $350 million. This $5-billion media printing, publishing, and forestry powerhouse is North America's second-largest printing company. Péladeau has been married three times and now has a companion. Reflecting on his entrepreneurial compulsion, he observed, "When I got married the first time, I had a wonderful woman, absolutely beautiful. One day — we had just bought a house — she asked me, 'Don't you think you've got enough?' I said, 'It's not a question of if I have enough or not. It is a question of can I stop or not?' And I cannot stop, that's it."[3]

Twenty years ago, Michael Cowpland, the hard-driving founder and CEO of software giant Corel Corp., hired his tennis pro, Ed Hladkowicz, who eventually rose to become sales manager of Corel's Systems Division. For twenty years, Cowpland and Hladkowicz played tennis matches, until November 1991 when Hladkowicz was fired. Cowpland neither warned him that the division was being shuttered nor called him personally. "It was a total shock to me," said Hladkowicz. Cowpland did call a week later — to ask his shocked tennis partner when their next game of tennis was going to be. This was the defining moment when his old friend and tennis partner became his *former* tennis partner.[4]

Peter Newman, author and former editor of *Maclean's*, used to rise at 4 a.m. and write until 9 a.m. when he went to his office to edit *Maclean's* for the day. He says that his schedule would be thrown off if his elevator stopped a couple of times on the way up to or down from his seventh-floor office.[5]

Ted Rogers, CEO of Rogers Cable, schedules every moment of his day from 7 a.m. to 11 p.m., seven days a week, one year ahead, and in less detail for the following two years. His goal, as it is for so many of us, is to use his time ever more efficiently. *As a result, we have learned to be productive, but we have forgotten how to just be.*

The time-driven, goal-oriented, macho pattern of work eventually spills into our personal lives. Merrily Orsini, a single mother of two boys and founder of an elder-care company in Louisville, Kentucky, remembers the pattern well. She posted charts and graphs on the refrigerator door, specifying schedules for dish-washing, garbage, and other household chores. There were deadlines too: "Walk dog by 5 p.m." But "life by Day-Timer" doesn't inspire all teenagers. Merrily Orsini ended up walking the dog.[6] As Lily Tomlin has put it, "The trouble with the rat race is that even if you win, you're still a rat."

Our personalities generate much of the joy and fun in our lives, appealing to this side of us. Our personality is inspired by our toys, entertainment, holidays, status, acceptance, and personal worth. But a blithe spirit can also be gained through laughter, love, giving, sharing, conversation, learning, faith, beauty, peace — these are gifts of joy to the soul. We can derive happiness from the *things* in our lives, from *life* in general, or from *within*. The choice is ours; we have only to consider our personality and our soul and ask, "Whom does it serve?"

The Loss of Community

Doing things better has become synonymous with doing things faster. In this pressure-cooker existence of continuous acceleration, people notice that something is missing in their lives. They describe a yearning for more time, but, deep down, what they really yearn for is their lost sense of community. The people with whom we spend most of our waking lives — our colleagues at work — have been reduced to memos, titles, telephone conversations, and E-mail messages. Busy people arrive at their succession of meetings late and leave early, rubber-stamp items in overcrowded agendas and defer others until the next time. Their knowledge of each other, let alone the issues, is bizarre in its superficiality. Then they fly off to their next appointment or to beat a pending deadline. The resulting shallowness of these personal relationships creates an emptiness inside us all.

Rolling Back the Information Overload

One of my clients, the president of a medium-sized company, told me that he spends between four and five hours every day initiating and responding to E-mail. This leaves a mere three to five hours each day for him to attend to the rest of his presidential activities. An overachieving, senior bank executive, who used to keep his children waiting as long as two hours in his office as he finished up paperwork in the evening, recently died at his desk — he was fifty-one years old. These examples are not atypical in an era in which we are all dancing as fast as we can while being asked to do more with less. Executives everywhere are crying for relief from information overload.

Technology has created a near miracle in the growth in speed and volume of information, but there has been no matching improvement in the quality of data produced. The rise of technical *Mastery* has not been matched by a sensitivity to *Delivery* — the needs of the user. Desktop computers have empowered almost everyone to produce data, yet there have been few guidelines for users. The result is

I hold in my hand 1,379 pages that modern organizations are choking
of tax simplification. with information and in their endless quest
DELBERT L. LATTA for an edge, executives feel compelled to review everything for fear of overlooking an obscure, but possibly vital, detail. The soul is left with no time for contemplation. Some simple disciplines would restore quality to the communication of information in organizations and bring the runaway production of data under control. Brevity, executive summaries, smaller circulation lists, composing off-line, editing, more frequent stale-dating of messages, and, most important, greater consideration for the recipient — a front-wheel Values shift from *me to you* — would all help. If originators imagined that their messages were being chiseled in stone, they might use fewer words, string them together coherently, or not bother at all.

There are two problems with E-mail. The first is its superficiality — it conveys the words, but seldom the music. It often requires extended ping-pong exchanges to tease out the subtleties and the essence of the communications. We confuse frequency for depth. The president of one company believes that he has "meaningful" personal communications with his son, a senior vice president, through E-mail. Sadly, this is almost their sole means of interaction.

"High tech, high touch" works best when we use more "touch" and learn how to use the "tech" more effectively. This means taking the trouble to visit with people, listening to them, and discussing the issues in a way that includes the personal relationships. There is not much listening or discussion associated with E-mail. Elevating the "touch" and modulating the "tech" in organizations results in more personal contact and greater *Chemistry*, during which deeper levels of communication occur. The soul has no chance of getting past "control/delete" until this happens.

The second problem is the way we use E-mail (and the majority of other data tools) to promote political agendas — cyber-ego. Many executives clog the E-mail with their personal agendas, spinning reams of data to support their positions, budgets, new product ideas, hiring decisions, expansion plans, and self-advancement objectives. This clutter becomes everyone else's time-trap.

What has been said for E-mail can be said for voice-mail and all other forms of data production. The new missionaries must respond quickly to the data overload crisis because although it is designed to improve all the problems it creates, its misuse does not eradicate them — it amplifies them. The misuse of communications technology impairs personal and organizational effectiveness and productivity, wastes resources, confuses people, muddles communications, complicates the decision-making process, generates stress, and weakens the soul. When the souls of people are weakened in this way, their organizations are weakened as a consequence.

The current data deluge is making people's lives miserable. Organizations need to develop an active and rigorously disciplined program leading to a dramatic reduction in the volume of data with a commensurate increase in its quality. This will enable people to return to higher ground again where they can achieve the three Primary Values: *Mastery*, *Chemistry*, and *Delivery*.

Careers of Random Chance — or Life Purpose

One of the reasons for such a wide-scale disenchantment with work is that surprisingly few of us purposefully chose the work we do today — we drifted into it ("I answered an ad"), gravitated into it ("the company transferred me") or graduated into it ("I took accounting as it seemed like a good idea at the time"), or were intimidated into it (I wanted to be an artist, but my Dad's a doctor). We may like to think that we chose our work, but it is more likely that only our personalities (and not our souls), chose our work. Later, we learn how much we hate our work, causing many of us, as Thoreau put it, to lead lives of quiet desperation. By the time this realization occurs, we have become trapped by the lifestyle our work affords — victims of personality. Few of us muster the courage to take time out to redirect our lives, as we must if we wish to be "on purpose," and give ourselves a chance to redress the opportunity we missed to decide on our life's purpose. The second time around represents an opportunity for the soul to express its voice.

> **Did you ever hear of a kid playing accountant – even if he wanted to be one?**
>
> JACKIE MASON

I am constantly amazed by the number of people I meet at my seminars or workshops who tell me they have waited for over half their lives before deciding to reassess the priorities and direction of their lives. Having fun at work depends on loving our work. This means doing something we love. There is no point in slaving in a hell-hole until the age of 65, only to be able to say, "Phew, glad that's over!"

Personal Mission

One way of defining our life purpose is to prepare a personal mission. A lack of purpose in our lives may result in a joyless person at work. When we work without connecting our activities to a sense of meaning and life purpose, we starve the soul. Work cannot be fun until we align our passion with our task. Work will be just a job until we close the gap between what our heart is calling us to do, and what we are actually doing. This is accomplished by completing deep inner work, in which we review our personal Mastery, Chemistry, and Delivery, and then use these insights to prepare a Personal Mission.

Is my work smaller than my soul?

MATTHEW FOX

Each of us has different talents and values. We each have unique motivations or reasons for why and how we act, make decisions, and live our lives. These motivations, influenced by our talents and values, provide the touchstone for our decisions, behavior, and priorities, helping us to focus and fully *live the moment* while helping others, directly and indirectly, to do the same.

When our lives are aligned with our Personal Mission, we will be doing what we love, with our developed skills and talents — and our actions will be consistent with our values. The result is an opportunity to build our future, as we choose. The soul will come alive if we can offer positive answers to the following questions:

- Is there joy in my work?
- Does my work give joy to others?

To know what we want to do and how we want to do it provides us with our focus. This focus helps us to make the right decisions that will keep us on course. It will help us to envisage our future and this, in turn, will cause us to change our present actions. If North is the place we want to be, we must choose a path that will lead us there. If we change our minds and decide to travel South, this decision has the automatic effect of causing us to change our current direction. Our Personal Mission is our map for maintaining our balance and sense of direction in challenging and changing situations.

A Personal Mission has two parts: first, what we call the Higher Mission; and second, the Life Mission. First we must determine our Higher

Mission which, though expressed in many different ways, is universal. The Higher Mission of our lives is...

- to serve others through *Mastery, Chemistry,* and *Delivery*
- to *"live every moment nobly, passionately and with love"*[7] in order to make our planet a better place for all its inhabitants
- to bring more kindness, compassion, honesty, truth, and love into the world
- to not only **do** something but also **be** something

Take a moment to reflect on this question:

What is Your Higher Mission?

_____

_____

_____

_____

_____

_____

_____

Our Life Mission serves our Higher Mission. If our Higher Mission is the end, our Life Mission is the means. Our Life Mission is a very personal matter and is uniquely fitted to each soul. Defining your Life Mission will help you to answer the question:

To what are You willing to commit Your life in service to this planet and all its creatures?

These are some examples of Life Missions from our Life Mission workshops:

- Providing patient care that brings love, wellness, and happiness into the lives of others (a nurse)
- Coaching others to greatness with energy and love (a business consultant)
- Writing and performing beautiful music so that the spirits of people will soar and their lives will become enchanted (a musician)
- Creating ideas that achieve positive results for others (the president of an advertising agency)
- Helping others to build their self-esteem (a dental surgeon)
- Coaching leaders to higher ground (mine)

To find out where your passion lies, first take stock of your life. This can be done by answering the following questions based on the three Primary Values:

Mission-Building—Step I
The Primary Values

Mastery: What are the tasks that you enjoy doing, and the skills you enjoy practising so much that, when you do them, you are in a state of flow, losing all sense of time?

Chemistry: In your life, who are the people (friends, family, clubs, associations, employees at work, acquaintances) that create positive energy for you, bring joy to your life, and lift your heart?

Delivery: Think of customers as "all those who come to you with a need." First list them. Then identify their needs. Which of these needs do you best meet?

The exercise above will help you to identify the things you love to do well (*Mastery*), the people you love to be with (*Chemistry*), and the needs of others you most love meeting (*Delivery*). When you do these things, your life will become seamless; you will not, as Yeats put it, "know the dancer from the dance."

This exercise will also help you identify the *Mastery* you wish to gain, the *Chemistry* you wish to build, and the *Delivery* you plan to meet.

As you will recall from chapter 2, Culture and Values, the Primary Values are driven by Accelerators. So the next step is to identify the Accelerators that will lead to the Primary Values as follows:

Mission-Building—Step 2
The Accelerators

Learning leads to **Mastery:** What *learning* must you undertake in order to achieve your desired *Mastery*?

Empathizing leads to **Chemistry:** How will you *empathize* and therefore build your relationships with those who create positive energy in your life and lift your heart?

Listening leads to **Delivery:** How will you *listen* to the needs of all of your customers so that you meet their needs with elegance and grace?

Every day we are faced with dozens of decisions. We may choose to make these decisions using alternative styles. We can choose to act in the best interests of the soul, by bringing more *Mastery*, *Chemistry*, and *Delivery* as well as kindness, compassion, honesty, truth, and love into the world — or we can act from personality, by being competitive, ego-driven, even hostile and angry. These choices are found on the front wheel of the Values Cycle. It is from here that we may derive the alignment needed for our life journey: the Values Shifts that foster our ideals, principles, behavior, standards — our moral manifesto. The front wheel provides our direction, representing those Values Shifts that provide alignment for our bicycle. These are Values Shifts from personality to soul. The front wheel teaches us how to Shift our Values, permitting us to do the following:

Mission-Building—Step 3 The Values Shifts	
Choose	**Instead of**
to focus on **YOU** and your needs	me and mine
to lead **PEOPLE**	managing things
to be competent at **KAIZEN** (doing the same things better)	relying solely on achieving break throughs (doing things differently)
to celebrate and build on our **STRENGTHS**	dwelling on our weaknesses
models based on **LOVE** and compassion	models based on competition and fear

Select from these Values Shifts and add your own to them. Then personalize and fine-tune them to create a list of those values most important to you. Select the key values that will guide you in your commitment to realigning your life.

You are now in a position to weave this information into a plan that will define your Life Mission. As you follow your new Life Mission, you will gain a renewed sense of fun and joy. Though your journey will never be completed because each new destination along the way will cause your path to broaden and offer new choices, you will never again have "just a job." You will be embarking on a journey that gives your life purpose. You will have the inner knowledge that you are serving with meaningful intent on this planet — giving joy a chance to return to your life. You will be on purpose.

> **I am like a little pencil in the hand of a writing God who is sending a love letter to the world.**
>
> MOTHER TERESA

Stress Busting

Stress is one of the most alarming issues I see in my work. Contemporary employees are stretched so thin, I wonder how much more they can take. I expect them to throw open the windows, like the characters in Paddy

Chayevsky's *Network*, and scream to the world, "I'm mad as hell, and I'm not going to take it anymore!" I often wonder if there is a mathematical formula at work here: one unit of stress cancels ten units of fun.

According to psychotherapist and former monk, Thomas Moore, the complaints he most frequently sees in his practice are:

* emptiness
* meaninglessness
* vague depression
* disillusionment about marriage, family, relationship
* loss of values
* yearning for personal fulfilment
* hunger for spirituality[8]

In my work, I too see the same symptoms. I also notice that people are aware of the problem but are often unwilling or unable to remove the causes. In her 1991 best-seller, *The Overworked American: The Unexpected Decline of Leisure*, Juliet Schorr described this syndrome as a work-and-spend trap. Yet we know that stress is not caused by events or people; it is caused by our reaction to them.

I don't claim to have discovered the answer to a stress-free life, but here are some ideas that I have collected over the years that I have found to be helpful in reducing stress:

* Meditation is a powerful force. Adopt the daily practice of meditation and use it to teach yourself the art of relaxation and regain control of yourself and your emotions. At the end of your meditation, consider your options. Your life is about the choices you make.

> **And if God cares so wonderfully for flowers that are here today and gone tomorrow, won't he more surely care for you?**
>
> THE GOSPEL ACCORDING TO SAINT MATTHEW

* Reflect. Pause to consider the alternatives and to filter out the trivia. Remember that you always have options. What you do is the result of what you choose to do. Think about lifestyle and work options — there is an endless variety of choices and it may be time for you to pursue them.
* Try not to sweat the small stuff in life. Perfectionism at work is a major source of stress. I am forever trying to override my tendency to be a clean desk freak. Even though my office is at one end of my house, I like to leave

my desk free of litter at the end of the day. I always try to return any out-standing telephone messages and clear up the mess before the day's end. But when I was recovering from a serious ski accident, I found that I just didn't have the energy to keep on top of my messages. In a few cases, I would not be able to get back to a caller for as long as two weeks, but my clients didn't seem to mind. When I told them why I had not called, they understood and we got our business done somehow. It just didn't seem to be a big deal. I am not inferring telephone rudeness — just balance.

> **One of the symptoms of an approaching nervous breakdown is the belief that one's work is terribly important.**
>
> BERTRAND RUSSELL

- Fulminating about a problem yields few answers but lots of stress. Teach yourself to think in terms of solutions rather than problems. Think winning, not whining. We have enough global whining.
- Irate or abusive bosses thrive on intimidation, bullying, and fear. But think for a moment: it is likely that you are overestimating the damage they can inflict because they need you at least as much as you need them. Remember that *Fear* is really *False Evidence Appearing Real*. So just smile at their bilious rhetoric and hope they feel better soon.
- Focus on the moment. Make it sacred. Do whatever you are doing at this moment as well as you can. I have called this *Mastery* and it is the source of self-esteem; focusing on the now leads to *Mastery*; focusing on time and goals leads to speed, anxiety, and stress. Attempting to do too many things at once results in superficiality, mediocrity, and error, the opposite of *Mastery*, which leads to a loss of self-esteem.
- Live for the moment, not the past or the future. The past is gone and can't be altered. The future is filled with crises, and pleasure and possibilities — some real and some imaginary. If you worry about them all, you may stress yourself into a puddle. Besides, life is too short to be used speculating about and planning for every potential disaster.
- Focus on one thing at a time. It is a recipe for excellence. When people try to intimidate you by imposing their priorities and deadlines, gently remind them that you use a "one-at-a-time" approach and they are next in line. You are not the cartoon road-runner.
- There are two kinds of energy in life: positive and negative. Our time on this planet is precious, so try not to waste a moment of it generating negative energy. It takes the same amount of effort to initiate negative energy as it does positive, but only the positive kind can build and

grow successful events and people. Competition is negative. Ease up on trying to beat the other person. Think win/win. Concentrate on the Accelerator of learning, which will increase your *Mastery* and self-esteem. Then the concept of "competition" will become irrelevant.

- Seek peace not war.
- If you do not like something or someone's action, attempt to change it or learn to live with it — just once. After that, move on and don't fret over it. The past is over; it is this moment that we are living for.

> **I can feel guilty about the past, apprehensive about the future, but only in the present can I act. The ability to be in the present moment is a major component of mental wellness.**
>
> ABRAHAM MASLOW 1908–1970

- Tell it "like it is." This way you won't get knotted-up inside. This does not mean being cruel — just honest. If other people don't like it when you tell the truth, realize that this is just as much their problem as it is yours.
- Eventually, your children will become responsible adults. When this point arrives, declare to them that you can no longer accept responsibility for their hang-ups, crises, trials, or tribulations. Tell them that although you love them dearly and you will always be ready to help them in any way you can, you will not credit or blame yourself, for all of the current, or future, events in their lives.

> **Having a family is like having a bowling alley installed in your brain.**
>
> MARTIN MULL

- If you are not happy at the moment, visualize happiness, and become authentic about it. Be an optimist: expect the best. It will have a wonderful effect on others and reflect back on you. Happiness is not about getting what you want but about wanting what you have. Leo Buscaglia once asked a stranger in New York how they were. "Terrific!" came the reply, to which Leo Buscaglia responded, "Then why don't you tell your face?" As Leonard Cohen sings, "There is a crack in everything, that's how the light gets in."
- Lateness is a stress-builder. We are never late, we just don't start soon enough. Resolve not to be under the pressure of lateness anymore — start earlier.
- Choose to be well. Diet, exercise, rest, lifestyle, communications, and relationships are all important factors in your wellness. Even when we create a Sanctuary, the contemporary pace of life is easier to handle with a body and soul that are fit.

- Some people are better suited to certain tasks than others and, though it may pain you to admit it, you may not perform at world-class levels in every skill. Do the things that you are good at and a*sk others to help you* with the rest. And once you get a dog, try not to bark any more.
- Speaking of dogs...get one.
  As my wife and I sat in front of a roaring fire one evening, with our dog Spirit asleep in my lap (although far too big to be there), I twirled my wine glass and wondered aloud if a loving animal helps to strengthen the immune system. I don't know if it does (although there is much scientific evidence to support this theory) and I don't know if it doesn't either. But my inclination is to think that Spirit is good for the soul, if you see what I mean. The sense of peace that comes from a deep and loving connection with another human being and a living breathing canine offering unconditional love is good for the soul. So my recipe, in addition to getting a dog is to...
- Let go, give yourself permission to fall in love.

Work as Art, Not Machine

In working with my clients I try to encourage them to design their organizations artistically, rather than mechanically — in a way that is soulful rather than Newtonian. This requires them to change their thinking in a fundamental way. It is uncomfortable for many traditional managers to abandon their commitment to goal-setting because they depend on personal and corporate goals to navigate through life. These navigational beacons take the form of strategic plans, marketing plans, sales objectives, budgets, quotas, targets, product development plans, and so on. While most of these are invested with enormous energy and thought, they tend to fall into one of two categories. They are either tribal rituals ignored as soon as they are completed, or they become the reason for the organization's existence. Both create stress, the former through cynicism and hypocrisy, the latter through fear and intimidation. In either case, corrosion of the soul results.

Without these navigational aids, many traditional managers would lose their bearings altogether and become hopelessly lost. Quantified goals and plans, in Newtonian organizations, guide us to each goal, where we pause briefly before defining the next one. There is no grace in a squirrel cage.

In the 1960s, Tom Chappell and his wife, Kate, moved to Kennebunk, Maine where they founded Tom's of Maine, a company that sells organic shampoos, soaps, deodorants, and toothpastes. Chappell left a sales position at Aetna Insurance, and recalls, "In my darkest days, I was working for aims that were too narrow for me. I was working for market share, sales growth, and profits. It was a sense of emptiness. I was to some degree depressed, undirected, unconnected to myself. I felt like an actor because what I was doing was not authentic. I was a phony to myself because I wasn't living up to what I cared about."[9]

Living a goal-directed life is modern but unnatural. Even though there is no shortage of experts who urge us to plan, no other part of our lives is managed this way. It isn't fun; it is graceless and it is not fulfilling.

After spending a decade building a business from scratch to $100 million in annual sales, I asked myself the same question others ask in similar situations, "Is this all there is? What's next? $200 million? Isn't there anything more liberating, more meaningful?" A plan is an artless way to appreciate life, like interpreting da Vinci's *Mona Lisa* by analyzing its paint chemistry, or using an oscillograph to appreciate Beethoven's Fifth Symphony. Using *Cartesian reductionism* in this way to understand our bodies, for example, leads us to divide them into the smallest understandable parts, until we are studying the cell. Of course, understanding the cell does not mean that we understand the body, any more than understanding the body means we understand the cell.

It is the same in organizations. Using Cartesian reductionism to produce departmental, and even personal, plans, does not help us to understand the organization, let alone inspire the soul. Quantum physics has shown us that this mechanical approach only works when we think of the world as parts in a Newtonian machine. If we want to address the soul, these tools are useless — the soul cannot be subjected to the rigorous analysis of mechanical science.

I am not arguing for the abandonment of goal-setting, but to change the nature of the goals and how we set and measure them. Here is my alternative. Think of the activities of life — personal and organizational — as art. Why do we create art? To inspire the soul. Imagine that your work is art, not a machine.

> **Avoid a negative approach to life. Why gaze down the sewers when there is loveliness all around us? One may find some fault in even the greatest masterpieces of art, music, and literature. But isn't it better to enjoy their charm and glory?**
>
> PARAMAHANSA YOGANANDA

The creation of art is not undertaken in order to achieve another work of art. Only investors measure art by dollars, or square meters, or weight, or quantities of colors. For those who love the intrinsic value of art, it is designed to inspire the soul, and to keep on doing so for as long as possible. Isn't our work the same? Isn't the point of our work to inspire the soul? Should we not ask, "How does this task inspire my soul and the souls of others?" each time we embark on a work activity? Is it not just as important to ask "How can I make this a soulful task?" as it is to ask, "How do I make my budget?" This takes us back to the Primary Values. Think of some critical aspect of your life, and ask these three simple questions:

	Yes	No
Mastery: Is this the best I can do?		
Chemistry: Will it be good for people?		
Delivery: Will it meet the customer's* need?		

If we ask these three questions, and measure our aspirations and effectiveness this way, we will eventually augment, and in some case replace our mechanical approach to goal-setting with the approach that characterizes the Sanctuary — measuring the quality of our work by the degree to which it inspires the soul. If we are sincere in our attempts to inspire the soul as well as the personality, to create blithe spirits, then we must add another dimension: joy. When our work becomes art, we will create grace, experience joy, and invigorate our souls with freedom and fulfilment — some of the essential components of regeneration.

> **The moral flabbiness born of the exclusive worship of the bitch-goddess SUCCESS. That – with the squalid cash interpretation put on the word success – is our national disease.**
>
> LETTER FROM WILLIAM JAMES TO H. G. WELLS

---

*The concept of *customer* being used here is anyone who comes to you with a need.

7

Soul Provider

Traditional compensation programs are designed to manipulate and control the personality, not the soul. If we wish to inspire the soul, we must first speak to it. If we reward the personality and ignore the soul, should we be surprised if we are ineffective? For more than a century, we have paid attention to rewarding the personality. What magic could we create if we deliberately began to reward the soul?

The Dogtrine

Let me tell you how I obtained my *dogtorate*. As I mentioned earlier, I have a wonder dog called Spirit. Her name is well earned — she is energetic, spirited, and loves life. When she was a puppy, I soon learned (notice I'm the one doing the learning!) that when I wanted her to sit or come to me, some techniques worked better than others. Today I know that if I try scolding, intimidating, or frightening her, I am wasting my energy. When she was a four-month-old puppy, I learned that if I really wanted her to come immediately, I had to make myself totally irresistible. This usually meant bribing her with a biscuit. Today, I find that love is the key motivator. Since it works, I use it. I have abandoned scolding, intimidating, and screaming because they do not inspire her, but instead cause her to be afraid and stubborn. Besides, it creates toxic tension in me. Love works.

Every dogma has its day.

ABRAHAM ROTSTEIN

I have thoroughly studied this phenomenon and concluded that it deserves the status of a universal law, which I have called *The Dogtrine*:

Others will meet your needs if you first meet theirs.

Similarly, others will ignore your needs if you ignore theirs. And fear is the most effective demotivator. The last piece of my research is ongoing: I am trying to understand why so many humans have yet to learn this lesson or to apply it to each other. Although we now know that intimidating, threatening, or frightening are ineffective when attempting to inspire dogs, many people still believe that these are effective techniques for inspiring humans. Why do we persist in using motivational techniques with humans that are not even effective with dogs?

It is time to throw out negative incentives, penalties, and punishment as techniques to encourage high-performance teams. We are all yearning for more love in our lives — not more fear. It is the deepest yearning in our hearts. If we replace these negative ways with encouragement, compassion, trust, patience, *empathy*, and love — we will release the untapped potential of humans. Any dog could tell you that.

> **Dogs come when they're called; cats take a message and get back to you.**
>
> MARY BLY

One Size Does Not Fit All

Many leaders whose awareness is still limited to personality continue to design reward systems that bully, intimidate, punish, or ostracize the individual whose soul they are trying to inspire. The diversity of their personality-based reward schemes and compensation plans is matched only by their bleak understanding of the workings of the soul. Their calculating, anxiety-causing incentives achieve the exact opposite effect they intend, causing the soul to cower in a cheerless corner of the heart.

No two souls are alike. There has never been, there is not now, and there never will be another soul like yours. Yet in classical Newtonian form, we persist in mass-producing compensation programs designed for *generic people*. For those fortunate souls who are unfamiliar with the "Hay Guide Chart-Profile Method" — one of the most extreme examples of soulless compensation design — I will explain it. The Hay System rates jobs (not people) according to their know-how, problem-solving, and accountability content. The goal is to achieve parity among jobs where the tasks are dissimilar but the intellectual effort is not. This provides a *salary level* that places each individual in hierarchical clusters, such as "level 5" for example. By determining the plateau, one is also able to determine one's pecking order.

Suppose for a moment that we establish a new organization. To help us create our management team, we retain the William Shakespeare

Employment Agency. The agency finds several talented candidates and we offer positions to a number of individuals including Richard II and III, Henry IV and V, King Lear, Macbeth, King John, and Richard the Lion-Hearted. Do we reward all of these people with the same compensation plan? As senior managers, will they all be happy with the levels determined by the "Hay Plan"? Will both Richards receive similar value from the disability insurance program, or would Richard III prefer a horse in exchange for his kingdom? Henry IV felt that, "If all the year were playing holidays, to sport would be as tedious as to work." So should both Henries get two weeks' annual vacation or three? Will King Lear and Macbeth respond to the same psychotherapy or will Macbeth alone be tormented by the damned spot? Will King John and Richard the Lion-Hearted gain equally from the seminar on "Building Interpersonal Skills with Your Brother"?

Salary grading systems that convert individuals into "levels" dehumanize the personality and offend the soul. They represent the triumph of me and my requirements (the payroll, accounting, and human resources functions) over you (the beneficiary) and your unique motivational needs—the opposite of the Values Shift on the front wheel, *from me to you*. The administrative goal of simplicity is achieved by converting people into numbers and making them as homogeneous as possible—good for the administrators but deadly for the soul.

Selfish and spirit-deadening approaches such as these seek a lazy solution over an authentic engagement with the soul. Such mechanical behavior, in which we treat people like machines, regarding them as no better than production units, is a spiritual affront. Our failure to recognize the uniqueness of each soul conveys a very obvious insult.

Only one reason prevents us from designing as many reward systems and compensation plans as there are souls: we lack the missionaries who are prepared to invest the time and money to develop the infrastructure and technology needed for a total custom design. While made-to-measure manufacturing to meet the specific requirements of each customer is commonplace in leading-edge production companies, we have yet to show the same empathy to employees. If two employees each earn $100, and one prefers the cash while the other prefers time off in lieu of the money, what is preventing us from meeting their simple requests—beyond lack of conviction and our administrative hang-ups and inflexibility?

The Total Quality Program for People

While TQM and customer-driven practices have raised the awareness of quality to unprecedented heights in North America, employees are still waiting for a matching Total Quality Initiative. The breakpoint is near. An age of light is dawning. As remarkable as the results of Total Quality have been over the last twenty years, they pale compared to the people-power that awaits release as soon as we apply the same philosophy to the soul. Then people will believe that leaders, at last, are genuine in their claims that employees are their organization's most important asset.

If this breakthrough is accompanied by a radical overhaul of reward systems, offering an infinite array of material and non-material rewards appealing to the personality as well as the soul, that are limited only by the imagination and not the structure, then a tidal wave of inspiration in the workplace will follow. When these rewards are perfectly tailored to fit the needs of each soul as well as the needs of the organization, a radical transformation of workplace dynamics will occur. Custom-designing rewards to the unique requirements of each soul is a fundamental component of regeneration and of building a Sanctuary.

Intrex

Our desire to contribute and serve is directly correlated with the intrinsic and extrinsic rewards that we can expect for doing so. Reward systems that inspire the soul are usually a combination of intrinsic and extrinsic

Figure 16:
The Intrex Inspiration
Model

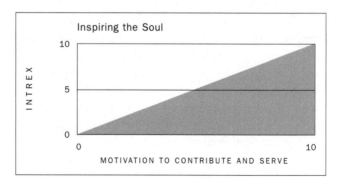

pay-offs. The formula shown in Figure 16 demonstrates that the greater the appropriate mix of intrinsic and extrinsic reward, which I call *Intrex*, the greater the motivation to contribute and serve. One of the most powerful intrinsic rewards is meaning.

Meaning and the Soul

I learned a wonderful lesson about the intrinsic reward of meaning from one of my clients, Medtronic, the world's leading manufacturer of pacemakers. For a retreat that I organized in Bermuda, the company invited a guest luncheon speaker. He introduced himself as Arne Larsen, and, as he held a pacemaker over his head, he said, "When you are making one of these, you may think you are simply making a sophisticated piece of equipment, crammed with technological wizardry, manufactured under very demanding conditions, using highly trained and expensive people. All of this is true. But I want to tell you something: I have had nineteen of these during the last twenty-nine years. And it is because you make them so well, every time, that I am able to stand here today and speak to you. Furthermore, in my engineering company in Sweden, there are 400 employees who depend on me, and therefore on this pacemaker, every day. So when you make a pacemaker, please understand the *meaning* of what you are doing." There was not a dry eye in the room.

We each yearn for meaning. We need to connect what we do with its utility and value for people and the planet. Meaning is one of the most powerful of all intrinsic rewards and it sings to the soul. We all have a responsibility to help each other understand the deeper meaning of what we are doing. None of us just makes pacemakers — we are helping someone to stay alive so they, in turn, can touch the spirits of hundreds of others and provide meaning to them in their lives — at home and work. This is true meaning and it inspires the soul.

Listening to the Soul

Each year I work with an advanced group of teachers at the University of Toronto. The student teachers study one of my books, *The Way of the Tiger*, which is a story about a teacher, who is a white tiger called Moose, and his student, who is a chipmunk called Tamias. Teachers like the book because it demonstrates the ideal relationship between teacher and student.

One day, a seasoned and expert teacher in the class told me that she had unsuccessfully tried to motivate her students to complete their class assignments. She was frustrated and disappointed. She wondered if I had any suggestions. I asked if she had difficulty with all or just some of her students and she said she had difficulties with about a third of them. I asked several questions about special characteristics and differences, hoping that this would yield a clue that could explain their attitude. This probing eventually revealed that all the poor performers seemed to be from the Caribbean. I asked her what she felt inspired their souls. She thought for a long time before answering, "Music." This was the clue that provided the basis for a solution. "Why don't you offer to help organize a reggae day at your school so that all of these students can form a band to display their musical skills. Then invite all of their classmates to celebrate their successful grades — providing they complete their class assignments on time?" It was simple, she tried it, and it worked. When you think about it, what is so unusual about rewarding with music, recognition, applause, fun, joyfulness, and techniques that speak, or even sing, to the soul?

> **I now perceive one immense omission in my psychology – the deepest principle of human nature is the craving to be appreciated.**
>
> WILLIAM JAMES

American Express conducted an internal survey that found that, more than anything else, employees wanted free time. American Express therefore arranged for some of their customer service agents and credit analysts to set their own hours and to work from dusk to dawn if they so chose. Many Amex travel agents are now encouraged to work at home, using computer terminals to answer calls from customers, who have no idea where the Amex employee is based. The Amex survey also found that employees were hungry for career advice, so the company set up career resource centers at several facilities, enabling employees to inquire about learning opportunities. Employees at Intel get an eleven-week sabbatical every seven years to meet the need to refresh and remove the toxins of burnout.[1]

It doesn't take much imagination to realize that employees who can sit in their own homes, drink their own coffee, pause to walk the dog or to have lunch with the family will be more soulful and therefore more productive. Others are turned on by the opportunity to develop and learn. These motivators of the soul, *Intrex* at work, are a long way from the cookie-cutter approach to rewarding employees that we have been using. The dollars and sense of changing our approach are overwhelming.

Some years ago, the *Harvard Business Review* published an article entitled, "The Dangers of Rewarding 'A' and Expecting 'B.'" The title said it all. Insanity has been defined as the repeated tendency to do the same things while expecting different results. We get the results we reward, so we must fit reward systems not only to the results we seek, but more importantly, to the needs of the soul receiving the reward. The reward may be material or non-material, since one or both may be appropriate, but the option should be with the recipient. In this sense, the employee, and in particular his or her soul, is our customer. We need to meet the needs of each of these souls, not our own. Of course, the sweet paradox is that by meeting the soulful needs of others, we meet our own.

Think Pink

Since Mary Kay established her now-famous cosmetics empire, her philosophy has been the same: that every person in the company, from newest recruit to chairman of the board, should live by the golden rule, "Do unto others as you would have them do unto you," and three priorities: God first, family second, and career third. She has called these the "go-give" spirit. Mary Kay believes that the go-give spirit is the true foundation of her company's success. "By giving of oneself and being sincerely interested in the total person, you are able not only to bring out the best in others, but also the best in yourself. One of the remarkable benefits is the positive impression it leaves with customers. Moreover, this giving attitude is passed on to your family and friends."[2]

The most prestigious award at Mary Kay Cosmetics is the "Miss Go-give Award," the purpose of which is to "promote the continuing practice of the go-give spirit and to recognize those who have exemplified this spirit through their loving actions." Each quarter, across the entire company, directors vote for a "Miss Go-give" and from the quarterly winners, they select the annual winner, who is awarded the Sue Z. Vickers Memorial Award. Says Mary Kay, "Sue Z. was without a doubt, one of the most outgoing, helpful persons I've ever had the pleasure of knowing. She was willing to give you the shirt off her back...our annual Miss Go-give Award has become the most desired of all the awards we give—better than a pink Cadillac."

Many large and successful companies like Mary Kay are built on intrinsic rewards because often these rewards are even more effective than extrinsic ones—they speak to the soul. Although hundreds of sales and achievement awards are given annually at Mary Kay, the most prestigious is the Go-give Award. As Mary Kay has proven, the key to achieving desired results is to reward them. This is how Mary Kay created a world-wide Sanctuary.

Intrinsic rewards are achieved by nourishing and appreciating the grace in our work. I work extensively with companies in the insurance industry. Life insurance, as much as any other product or service, is a gift of love. When someone insures their life, they are sending a message to the beneficiary: "I love you so much that I want to shield you from any financial pain that may be caused by my disability or death." We encourage life insurance salespeople to measure their work by the number of people they have helped to give these gifts of love. Property and casualty insurance can be viewed the same way: bad things happen to good people, and insurance is the means by which insurers help these good people to recover from a raw deal. The intrinsic rewards can come from the grace inherent in the work we do. Indeed, if we are not able to see grace or meaning in our work, we may need to ask ourselves why we are still doing it.

Designing Reward Systems for the Soul

We behave in response to rewards, avoiding behavior that attracts negative outcomes and adopting behavior that is positively reinforced. Many leaders wrongly assume that everyone will respond in the same way to material or extrinsic benefits alone. Most organizations challenge their salespeople, top producers, innovators, managers, and profit-generators with tangible rewards, such as travel, gadgets, money, and assorted hardware like desk-sets, clocks, or employee-of-the-month plaques.

This approach causes us to overlook two opportunities. First, it only presses a few of our personality buttons, the buttons of the soul being largely unaffected by a soapstone carving with the company's logo stamped on the front. Second, it does nothing to reinforce the self-esteem or reward the souls of the average producers and the administrative support staff, maintenance people, technicians, suppliers, and customers— even the steady, if unspectacular, salespeople, who, though not accorded heroic status, are just as critical to their organization's success.

At issue too is the logic of traditional thinking about incentives. Do people strive for excellence in order to win the employee-of-the-month plaque? Or do they strive for *Mastery*, and, as a result, achieve rewards? Does Monica Seles play great tennis in order to become rich or because she loves the game and equates *Mastery* with spiritual Nirvana?

Traditional reward systems often gratify the mind but insult the soul. *Delivery* is the secret of crafting a reward system that inspires the soul.

First, we need to understand the person we are seeking to inspire, and whether he or she is moved by the personality, the soul, or both. Then we should try to design the reward system so that it specifically meets the intrinsic as well as the extrinsic needs of each individual. We achieve this by using one of the Values Shifts on the front wheel — *from me to you.*

Mastery never seeks reward; rewards always find Mastery.

THE WAY OF THE TIGER: GENTLE WISDOM FOR TURBULENT TIMES

A travel incentive program may be simple and efficient to design (an emphasis on *me*), but until we shift to *you*, and ensure that it is appropriate, we have merely met *our* needs to design a program. Before we can do this wisely, we must set aside our impulse to design answers in favor of some deep questioning: What would make it good for you? How can we develop a win/win result? What do you need from me or the company right now? What are the concerns in your life and how can we help to dispel them? What would relieve stress, tension, anger, pain, fear, or insecurity in your life and can we design a reward together that would help? How can we help you grow? What would inspire your soul?

As a result of asking an employee such questions, for example, we might receive the following response: "You know, one of my greatest disappointments, which is a dark corner of my soul, is my relationship with my kids. I would dearly love to build our relationship together and to get along better with them." Isn't it perfectly legitimate for us to respond, "We are a large and successful organization, with talent, influence, and assets. We have a network of connections and contacts. Let us use these resources on your behalf to help you to rebuild your relationship with your children. In what way would you like to see us use the organization's resources to help heal your soul?" Applying *Intrex* in this way can transform individual and team performance.

Or suppose another employee wanted to learn a musical instrument. Traditional managers would usually reject paying for this activity on the grounds that music is not work-related, and therefore is outside the organization's mandate. But why wouldn't we arrange and pay for music lessons? Wouldn't our employee be moved at the deepest level and produce outstanding work as a result? If we cast generosity and consideration across the waters of our employee's souls, it will come back to us, again and again, in a tide of appreciation and high performance.

Are we getting personal? You bet we are. Reward systems that identify and successfully answer these kinds of questions, and many more, can lift the spirits of people because they show that the leader cares and recognizes each person as a unique soul. This is called *Delivery*. Individual-specific reward systems contrast starkly with the vanilla, off-the-shelf, merit programs, such as the notorious Hay Plan, that are widely used in organizations today. Anyone who still believes that employees become excited by hearing that they have been elevated to *level 5* status has probably yet to learn the subtleties involved in fanning the flames of passion that lead to inspired souls and therefore extraordinary performance.

One Soul, One Reward

All this has profound organizational implications. First, because every one of us is unique, we cannot expect to inspire each individual soul until we design programs that separately fit each one of us. Often when I first suggest this to my clients, the accounting, information systems, human resource, and payroll professionals, and often the president too, throw up their hands in sheer dismay and horror, convinced that I am not bolted together properly. One president recently responded, "Not seriously?" Yes, seriously!

Inspiring each special soul requires single soul systems. We mistakenly believe that being fair means *leveling down* to the mediocrity of the valley floor, where life is the same for everyone and where reward systems are designed for the convenience of the traditional managers. In reality, fairness is achieved by listening to the needs of souls and then meeting them. This Primary Value we call *Delivery* is to be found on the higher ground. Great organizations are built one person, one inspired soul, at a time, and our one-size-fits-all approach crushes the potential and our ambitions for personal and organizational greatness.

8

Soulspace

If you were to seek an environment that would encourage you to produce the most inspired work of your life, where would you go? Would your office or factory spring immediately to mind? Or would you choose a verdant forest, a rocky mountain, or an ocean at sunset? Or perhaps a beautiful temple, an art gallery or museum, a fine hotel, or a concert hall? It is a tragedy that the soul is not enraptured by the contemporary office tower. Yet if we intend to inspire the soul, why don't we create beautiful environments that are physical Sanctuaries too, where our spirits can soar? How can people produce inspired thinking while they are incarcerated in such an uninspiring environment?

Much of this book explores the relationship between our work and our inner environment—the soul—which I have called a Sanctuary—but we must also consider another environment, our physical surroundings, which I call a soulspace. A soulspace is an environment that engages the soul, encourages it to sing, and inspires greatness. The soul has a love affair with a soulspace. The soul's response to its immediate surroundings can vary dramatically depending on the relationship between the body and its setting. If our physical surroundings are not friendly or sympathetic to our senses, a negative reaction will be caused that adversely affects our biochemistry. From our senses these signals then travel to our immune system, and then rapidly to our soul.

> **A day spent without the sight or sound of beauty, the contemplation of mystery, or the search for truth and perfection, is a poverty-stricken day; and a succession of such days is fatal to human life.**
>
> LEWIS MUMFORD

For years I have been telling audiences about a case study concerning Canada's largest bank. It is a sorry example of large-scale demotivation and inspirational myopia. Over time, the bank has made several attempts to adjust my perception of them. Recently I was invited to visit one of their flagship locations and was indeed impressed by their world-class facilities and cutting-edge, automated banking services. Pausing by the automated teller machines (ATMs) on our tour, I was told how much money and effort the bank had invested in creating an environment that was friendly and pleasing to customers.

At this point, I asked the bankers to describe the friendliest physical environment in their lives. After some thought, they talked about their homes. Our homes are a good benchmark, because most of us go out of our way to make them friendly and pleasing. Often they are expressions of our souls as much as our personalities. I asked the bankers what elements would make a home friendly and pleasing to them. Among other things, they described soft furnishings, comfortable tables and chairs, cut flowers and plants, a fireplace, carpets, art, music, subdued lighting — a warm, inviting ambiance. Then I asked them to describe the automated teller area: chrome, glass, polished granite, industrial-grade floor coverings, suspended ceilings, strip lights, plastic, an uninspiring picture screwed to the wall, no windows, and aggressive advertising.

> **Banking may well be a career from which no man really recovers.**
>
> JOHN KENNETH GALBRAITH

Is this environment pleasing and friendly to customers? I think not. These are traditional managers pretending to be evolved. This is egocentric office design — functional, low-cost, vandal- and hazard-proof, and designed to withstand wear-and-tear for a commercially feasible period. This is not even considerate to the mind and body, let alone to the soul. In our working environments, we need to shift from attitudes that are mechanical and Newtonian to those that are artful.

> **Beauty is truth, truth beauty.**
>
> JOHN KEATS

If we say that we have designed an environment that meets the needs of customers and employees, while the evidence is a stark lack of beauty in those surroundings, we are being untruthful. *The environment tells the truth directly to the soul, regardless of what the personalities are saying.* When pictures are screwed onto walls, the message is, "I don't trust you." No matter how fine the words, the fastened picture tells no lies.

I don't mean to imply that one should not screw pictures onto the wall in high-traffic, unsupervised areas. But it is simply not truthful to say that when we screw pictures onto the walls, we are deliberately creating soulspaces for customers and employees. If we really want to inspire the souls that visit the ATM, why not assemble a group of creative, iconoclastic thinkers and ask them to design an automated teller soulspace? Although we might not choose to hang pictures on the wall, instead we might hang framed sections of the daily newspaper, for people to read while waiting to access the ATM; create a graffiti wall or a finger-painting wall; or a bank of personal compact disk players; or an "honor-system" paperback library; or sell coffee and donuts; or, since the customers have their credit cards in their hands anyway, install swipe-machines for placing orders for dinner that would be ready by the time the customers arrived home. Or perhaps we should accelerate the trend to home banking because home is where the customer would rather be. All we have to do is consider things from the soul's perspective.

My comments are not directed specifically at banks, since they apply equally to most organizations — although the government and not-for-profit organizations usually win the prize for creating the most miserable, spirit-deadening locations. We delude ourselves in two ways: we discount the importance of the physical environment to human performance and potential, and we rationalize our poor design with the spurious argument that mediocrity is acceptable in a work setting.

Beauty captivates the flesh in order to obtain permission to pass right through to the soul.

SIMONE WEIL

But imagine the extraordinary, liberating impact and the magical work that could flow from sacred workplaces designed for the soul. Think how designing with the soul in mind could transform airports, department stores, schools and universities, hospitals, and medical and public buildings, to name a few. If these places were sacred, would we be more likely to love and respect them? If these were beautiful places and we loved them, how might the human performance within them be transformed?

Soulless workplace design, based on the flimsy reasoning of "commercial reality," is simply not justified. There are too many examples that disprove the argument. Consider Wegmans, Singapore Airlines, or Herman Miller's ergonomically designed offices. Consider how some industries carefully and lovingly create a beautiful ambiance for employees and customers, knowing that establishing a connection with the soul is critical to their business. We all have our favorite places that fit into this category — neighborhood restaurants, friendly bookstores, welcoming hotels, the village store, the head office of ServiceMaster in Downers Grove, Illinois, and The Body Shop.

The Body Shop

The Body Shop was founded by Anita Roddick in Brighton, England, in 1976. It has since grown to more than 1,300 shops trading in forty-five countries, in twenty-three languages. It is more than a company that makes and sells naturally inspired cosmetics and skin and hair products. Led by a visionary, it is a company on a mission to change the world. Cosmetics are simply the commercial vehicle that supports the cause. Anita Roddick recently observed, "I have been part of a different, smaller business movement, one that has tried to put idealism back on the agenda. We want a new paradigm, a whole new framework, for seeing and understanding that business can and must be a force for positive social change. It must not only avoid hideous evil, it must actively do good."[1]

More than anything else in life, Roddick is a missionary who values passion, and this is evident in everything the company does. It is especially evident in the company's attitude to the global environment and its local environment — the stores, offices, and factories where people work and visit with The Body Shop. From its beginning, The Body Shop has been against animal testing of cosmetics, campaigned for human rights and environmental protection, promoted "Trade Not Aid," developed trading relationships with indigenous people, supported numerous causes including Amnesty International, and campaigned to stop violence against women. The store window of The Body Shop is more a political statement than a showcase for products. The company, whose strategy is driven by its values, embraced my company's corporate theme, "The Heart, Mind, and Bottom Line," (and the layout for this book) as their own during their 1993 annual conference in Canada.

When I describe the extraordinary uniqueness and remarkable achievements of The Body Shop, people often dismiss the company as a "new age," trendy organization that is not typical of the mainstream. They think it is easy for such an organization to show flair, adopt causes, take political stands and treat employees, suppliers, and customers with grace. But The Body Shop is no different from any other organization. It is a manufacturer, distributor, and marketer of cosmetics and skin care products — not dissimilar from Revlon, Lancôme, Estée Lauder, or Avon. It simply behaves differently from all of them because it chooses to — a choice that is available to any organization.

A thing of beauty is a joy forever.

JOHN KEATS

The Body Shop ethos is embodied in one of its companies, Soapworks. The company sells nearly 30 million bars of soap each year, which used to be purchased from a German supplier. The Body Shop decided to build their own soap factory in Easterhouse, on the outskirts of Glasgow, Scotland, an area of high unemployment, urban decay, and demoralization. Soapworks started with a handful of employees. In building Soapworks, Anita Roddick made a moral decision first and a commercial decision second. "I would rather employ the unemployable than the already employed. The soaps are up to 30 percent more expensive, and we will be putting 25 percent of the net profits back into the community. But it is better for my company. It is an example of what keeps the soul of the company alive."

The Body Shop started in Canada in 1980 and by 1992, the Home Office, production, distribution, and training facilities had grown into four separate buildings. From the start, the vision for the new headquarters was of a soulspace. First, in keeping with the company's commitment to recycling, a decision was made to recycle an entire building. Instead of demolishing an existing building or constructing a new one, the firm purchased and recycled a thirty-five-year-old printing warehouse in an industrial zone of Toronto. Said Margot Franssen, The Body Shop's Canadian president and partner, "We wanted the building to reflect The Body Shop's culture and values, by minimizing its environmental impact...we also wanted to make it an open, fun and functional place to work."

Franssen's first step in creating a soulspace was hosting a "charette"— an intensive brainstorming session attended by fifteen professionals, including building and landscape architects, engineers, environmental geologists, waste reduction and recycling experts, energy conservationists, day-care facilitators, and horticulturalists, as well as ten employees. This team reviewed the conceptual ideals of every aspect of the building, with the goal of maximizing the benefits for future inhabitants and minimizing environmental impact. They brainstormed for twenty-four hours with a goal of transforming the building into an example of extraordinary innovation in design, renovation, engineering, energy conservation, landscaping, and waste management.

Conservation was an important goal. All of the drywall and most of the paint used in the renovation were derived from recycled materials. Reclaimed furniture was refinished for use in the offices. Sinks and toilets discarded by Toronto's Prince Hotel were installed in the washrooms. Floors were covered with carpets made from post-consumer nylon and laid with solvent-free adhesives. Glass destined for a landfill was used for the windows.

The Body Shop's other goal was to engage the soul of visitors. The production facility is located off one side of the reception area. One factory wall is made of glass and joins the "bored room," enabling members at board meetings and production staff to see each other as they work. On the other side of the reception area is The Body Shop minishop, used for training and developing merchandise displays. In this way, as one stands in the front lobby, the beginning and end result of the business can be seen at the same time. With one glance, a visitor gains a perspective of the whole company.

The team of designers sought to encourage a sense of community within the building. Interior offices are laid out along "streets," with names such as "Dewberry Drive" and "White Musk Way," based on The Body Shop's products. These converge at a "town square," bathed by a huge skylight, which is called "Inspiration Intersection" and serves as the spiritual center and meeting place of the building. Numerous skylights conserve energy and bring sunlight to the rest of the building. Unlike many office buildings, most areas have individual light switches, so that employees can regulate their lights, and the office is divided into twenty-two zones, each with its own heat pump.

The interior is bright and natural-feeling, splashed with colors such as wheat, lemon, and grass green. Walls are decorated with hand-drawn pictures and colorful posters depicting The Body Shop products and environmental and social campaigns. A two-storey mural of the Amazon rain forest enhances the day-care center (called the Department of the Future), and thought-provoking and amusing quotations are written on walls and bulletin boards throughout the building. The office layout gives the best views to desk-bound staff, by locating them near exterior windows, while private offices are located in the center of the building. The most picturesque views are on the southwest side of the building, so the Department of the Future and the staff lounge are both located there.

Beauty is truth's smile.

RABINDRANATH TRAGORE

A 4,000-square-foot greenhouse has been built along the southern exterior wall. Called "The Living Machine," it is a Canadian-invented, self-contained, biological waste-water treatment system. Waste water flows from the building into several pretreatment tanks and, from these, into a pond containing free-swimming creatures such as clams, snails, fish, and aquatic plants. Water is drawn up from the pond into a series of large plant- and moss-filled pots hanging overhead. The waste water cascades from the pots back into the pond, which in turn, drains into a series of marshes populated by water-purifying plants. After the water is "polished" by this process, it passes through an ultraviolet filter, finally returning to holding tanks, where it is ready for reuse. The goal is to treat waste water on site, so that it can be reused, rather than discharging it into the municipal sewage system. The Living Machine also doubles as a peaceful greenspace in which employees can rest and relax.

The missionaries at The Body Shop have created a Sanctuary in what they refer to as "urban-pavement-with-power-lines." This formerly desolate area has been transformed into a natural habitat with meadows, hedgerows, wooded areas, and a natural wetland. A "Physic Garden" has been built, which borrows from the traditions of medieval monasteries.

The Body Shop's Home Office is a place where employees work, students tour, franchisees shop and do business, customers visit, and retail staff are trained. Above all, it is an island of regeneration. The physical environment sends a message, to employees and visitors, of passion, openness, lack of hierarchy, sensitivity to employee's needs, social and environmental awareness, commitment, fun, and professionalism. The Body Shop management believes that instead of taking work home, the workplace should be a soulspace that becomes a little more like home.

Environments That Make the Soul Soar

When I describe The Body Shop to others, I am often told that it is easy for them and difficult for others. This is not the case. The Body Shop, to the outside observer, is simply a manufacturer and retailer and, in that sense, is no different from thousands of other companies. If we needed a lesson, the example of The Body Shop teaches us that there is no excuse for creating ugliness in the workplace, or anywhere else for that matter. Ugliness corrodes the soul and its growing presence produces an ever-increasing threat to human fulfilment. It is hard to achieve Olympian performance while laboring in the devil's stables.

Business has a unique opportunity to create Sanctuaries that connect directly with the soul by fashioning islands of community, friendship, warmth, and beauty, in a larger environment where these qualities may be less evident. Our opportunity is to create sacred soulspaces so engaging to people's spirits, that we are as irresistibly drawn to them as we are to any place of outstanding beauty.

If the workplace is a Sanctuary, it can and should be a welcome contrast to less sacred and inviting places. A lovingly designed Sanctuary has the same capacity to draw people as a place of worship, an art gallery, or a park. These are places to which we are drawn because their ambiance encourages us to recharge and invigorate ourselves — to regenerate. In these settings, our thoughts turn to creativity, inspiration, reflection, integrity, friendship, and love.

Our Sanctuaries should enthral and create awe, drawing human perfection through our very souls. The world's greatest poetry is not about ugliness; it is beauty that inspires great poetry. In the same way, a Sanctuary that is sacred has the capacity to become the

Things are beautiful if you love them.

JEAN ANOUILH

crucible for human potential. With its treasure chest of human and capital assets, why should business not rival the impact on our souls that is routinely achieved by often impoverished churches, art galleries, and public parks? It is difficult to understand the logic of workplace designers who expect the soul to shine in the hideous darkness of a budget-strapped, unimaginative environment. In the design of a Sanctuary, the Values Shift *from me to you* directs us to place the interests of the soul first, because, by doing so, we will harness its energy — and that is good for business. Our goal is not to make the spirit cringe, but to make it soar.

9

Competitive Spirit

At the end of World War II, researchers from the Japanese Imperial army conducted a study to determine the final words uttered by fatally wounded soldiers. They anticipated hearing such things as "Long live the Emperor!" or "Banzai!" but they were surprised. Most soldiers did not give tributes to the Japanese Emperor, but instead could be heard crying, "Oka-san, Oka-san," — Japanese for "Mom!" *These soldiers were crying for their mothers.* When these young warriors realized that this was their last hurrah, their image as a strong, aggressive, and fearless hero fell away, no longer seeming important to them. Their egos were eclipsed by their souls, and they simply wanted their mothers.

Deep inside, we are all exactly like this. We are vulnerable, hungry for love and intimacy, yearning to restore our female energy, filled with more questions than answers, and, above all, very human. At our core, personality gives way to soul. Meanwhile, on the outside, the phony macho hero that we strive to project—the swaggering Arnold Schwarzeneggers and Sylvester Stallones we bring to work and life—yearn to step aside for the real human within. The more we incorporate Hollywood into our self-image, the greater the distance between our personality and our soul. It is only when we begin to communicate authentically from the soul that we meet real people. Real communication in work and life cannot take place while two actors are talking to each other through their personalities. When we each learn to replace our macho charade with consistently genuine communication from the soul, we will transform ourselves, detoxify the organizations in which we work, and inspire all of the souls affected.

> **Strong men can always afford to be gentle.**
> **Only the weak are intent on "giving as good as they get".**
>
> ELBERT HUBBARD

After presenting this idea at a conference recently, an elderly man approached me. He said that he was Russian and had been a member of the liberating armies at the end of the war. He then went on to describe some of the events during that time. According to his account, Hitler had forced young boys to strap anti-tank bombs on their bodies before hurling themselves in front of the advancing allied tanks. As they did so, horrified onlookers could hear them screaming, "Mutti!, Mutti!" — German for "Mom." The resistance of the soul to aggression and violence seems to be present at all ages, in all languages, and in every corner of the universe.

I referred earlier to my serious skiing accident a couple of years ago, in which I broke my leg in nine places. The mountain descent, followed by the ambulance ride from Sugarloaf USA to Franklin, Maine, would have seemed interminable without the merciful presence of morphine. During the hours that I was in the operating room, my wife talked with the owner of the ambulance company. She asked him what people discussed with him while they were grievously injured and in great pain, during their ride to the hospital. He replied that a surprising number talked of their parents, especially their mothers. So this pattern seems to be universal. When our personalities let our guard down for any reason, our souls reclaim a voice and the personality-driven image we project to others suddenly seems irrelevant; we do not talk aggressively about killing the competition, avenging loss of market share, or blowing away another candidate for promotion. Instead, we talk about our families, our loves and fears, and our passions and dreams — the matters that inspire our souls.

The Dysfunctional Effect of Competition

In a 1994 address to the beverage industry in Atlanta, Georgia, Coca-Cola President, M. Douglas Ivester, said, "I'd like to earn your friendship, but that's not really my priority. And I want to earn your respect, but that's not really my priority either. I want your customers. I want your space on your shelves. I want your share of the customer's stomach. I want every single bit of beverage growth potential that exists out there."[1] When we reject friendship and respect in favor of market share, we reject the soul in favor of the personality. Is this approach a civilized way to live? Is this good for the soul? How can we propose that we eliminate the competition, put their employees out of work, so that they can no longer pay their mortgages and food bills, and then claim our commitment to high moral and ethical standards? Is it feasible to leave home in the morning as individu-

> **I object to violence because when it appears to do good, the good is only temporary; the evil it does is permanent.**
>
> MOHANDAS K. GANDHI

als of integrity, put in a day at the office killing our competitors, and then return to our civilized family values and go to church on Sunday? When we spew these violent wishes, aren't we kidding ourselves that we live sacred lives that nourish the soul? Violence is a continuum. At its mildest, it is characterized by rudeness, selfishness, and irritability and at its extreme, it manifests itself as war. It is simply a matter of degree.

In reviewing the strategic plans of a very large multinational company recently, I came across this statement: "I know I can count on you to aggressively embrace these plans and make them happen." What does an aggressive embrace actually feel like? Is it nice? How do we *make* people make things happen — don't they have to *want* to? These phrases seem to have the ring of a "tin man" approach to motivating the soul.

We have come to use the term "competition" in a very negative and unfriendly way. The word "compete" is derived from the Latin, *com*, which means together, and *petere*, which means to seek, hence to *strive together, be qualified*. The more colloquial dictionary definition is "rivalry, seeking or striving for something in opposition to others." Usually the term carries lethal force, literally or metaphorically, implying rivalry, unfriendliness, even hostility. It pits people against others in a power struggle designed to create a winner and a loser. Repeated victories by one side eventually eliminate the other. Competition creates personal stress, weakens physical and mental health, causes low self-esteem, demotivates, toxifies organizations, damages personal relationships, and is an ineffective way to build teams. It focuses on the negative energy of destroying an opponent instead of the positive energy of enhancing value for employees, suppliers, or customers by meeting their needs. It plays to the base appeals of the personality instead of the humblest yet strongest force in the universe — the love within our souls.

> I wonder what our world would be like if men always had sacrificed as freely to prevent wars as to win them.
>
> FRANK A. CLARK

In a word, the concept of competition is highly dysfunctional. Zero-sum competition, in which one side wins all the time, eventually wipes out all the other players. Then what shall we do? Our "competitors" are consumers and fellow residents of this planet, each with families, friends, mortgages, food bills, and credit cards. Regular human beings, just like us, work for our competitors and when we have put them all out of business and bankrupted their companies, what will be our next move? Is that all there is?

If Charles Dutoit, the leader of the Montreal Symphony, were to wake up each morning and bellow, "Let's destroy Seiji Ozawa, and the Boston Symphony," would he and his orchestra make rapturous music? If he and his musicians developed a strategic plan to compete with all theaters and restaurants in Montreal because they vie for the same disposable income, would this lead to the creation of one of the finest international reputations in classical music? I don't think so, yet he has created a world-class orchestra. Like Charles Dutoit, we have all been blessed with individual gifts; it is up to each of us to use them to support each other, not to create fear in the hearts of others and pursue their destruction.

Tom Chappell, the founder of Tom's of Maine, says, "It's not winning at all costs. It's challenging yourself to win according to who you are. So now I'm trying to engender more kindness. I'm trying to link what I'm doing more to the environment and the community...we take market share and shelf space away from P&G and Colgate on a daily basis, and we don't do it with money and muscle, which they have plenty of. We take it away with a product that meets the expectations and aspirations of a particular customer who shares the same values as we

> **Hillel said: What is hateful to you, do not do to your neighbor: that is the whole Torah; the rest is commentary; go, study.**
>
> BABYLONIAN TALMUD

do."[2] It is becoming clear that despite the near-deafening levels of talk about global competition, competing weakens rather than strengthens us as individuals and as organizations and, as I suggested in Chapter 5, it is making us ill. Perhaps it is time to reconsider whether competition, and the notion of being red in tooth and claw, is the appropriate basis for our relationship with others.

Winning without Competition

Phil Jackson, coach of the three-time NBA-Championship-winning Chicago Bulls conjures up a much more wholesome, inspiring, and positive image of competition, the original definition in the dictionary: *striving together*. He says, "It is not winning or losing that's important...it's the dance between you and your teammates, between you and your competitors. Don't even think of them as your opponents; they're your partners in the dance." Thinking of competition this way shows the negative version for what it is: a dark, poisonous, and irrelevant attitude. Yet competition is the dominant paradigm of our time and anyone who questions it will probably be considered flaky or idealistic.

I work with missionaries in companies where vendors share accounts with their customers, where competitors collaborate to meet customer needs, where vendors specify competitors' products in order to meet customers' orders, where departments ditch their turf-oriented thinking to pursue a shared vision, where unions and management conspire (from the Latin *to breath together*) to create breakthroughs in the market, where customers and suppliers develop strategic plans together and collaborate to determine the compensation plans of employees. I work with associations where technology is shared with other companies in the same industry, where learning opportunities are considered a vital part of ensuring that individuals and their organizations remain relevant and therefore thrive in the future. I even work with one large organization that invited a smaller company to sell its product under the larger company's own brand name — with breathtaking results. I work with organizations where individuals are *not* serving a life sentence of beating the competition. These are inspired and enlightened places — Sanctuaries from competition — where the soul soars along with performance because competition is an anachronism.

> ... my value system says I don't have to get everything to win, and I can win without someone else losing.
>
> SANDRA KURTZIG, FOUNDER, ASK COMPUTER SERVICES

Mastery: Playing to Win

As we have seen, the Latin roots of the word competition mean *striving together*, specifically to contend for a prize, which implies winning. Winning is an important life goal for most of us. But it is important to understand what "winning" really means. Winning is "doing what you do as well as you can"—another way of describing what we have earlier referred to as *Mastery*. It has nothing to do with competing with or destroying someone else. Competition with others is fueled by negative energy, fear, and stress, while winning through personal *Mastery* is achieved through positive energy, leading to exhilaration. Winning the respect, trust, affection, friendship, and loyalty of others, especially customers, partners, employees, and even "competitors," is the path to soulful profitability. This is the true definition of winning and it renders competition based on negative energy an arid concept that is irrelevant to the soul.

As we saw in Chapter 5, all human action takes place on a continuum between fear and love. We either do things because we love the people and experiences associated with them, *Chemistry*, or because of the fear they instil in us. Our lives are stalked with fears: death, poverty, illness, rejection; and enriched by what we love: family, friends, good health, success, and wealth.

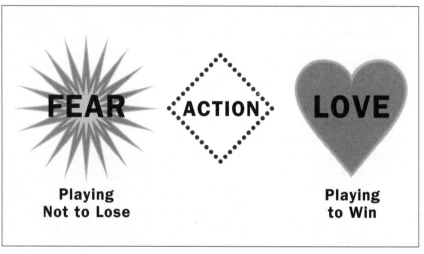

Figure 17: Playing Not to Lose and Playing to Win

We have the option to choose: we can either defend ourselves from our fears — *Playing Not to Lose* (meeting the needs of the personality) or we can seek to fill our lives with love — *Playing to Win* (meeting the needs of the soul).

Playing-to-Win Agreements

Contracts provide us with a very real and frequent example of our choices. Agreements between two parties can be developed from either of these two differing philosophies: agreements in which we play not to lose, or agreements in which we play to win. The playing-not-to-lose agreement tends to be one-sided and heavily slanted in favor of the party responsible for drafting the agreement. This is usually the party that perceives itself to possess the greater "power." Such an agreement is couched in win/lose language that seeks to gain advantage over the other party. It expects the other people to cheat and assumes that they cannot be trusted. It plans for the worst, covering all negative eventualities and provides penalties and negative incentives for breaches, non-compliance, and non-performance. It usually includes extensive language covering the interests of the "more powerful" party, and shows little consideration or accommodation of the legitimate interests of the other party. It demands what it is not prepared to give.

The playing-to-win agreement, on the other hand, is both fair and compassionate. It does not seek to assert power, but instead seeks to encourage mutual opportunities and benefit. It invites the advantages of synergy and partnership. It does not try to enforce terms on one party that the other refuses to match, but instead gives equal consideration to the interests of both parties, summoning the best, rather than assuming the worst. A good agreement based on playing-to-win principles is based on shared values and assumes that both parties will become one, in pursuit of a common goal. A playing-to-win agreement is signed by both parties together, because they both *want* to. It aims to become an agreement between two souls.

An example of such an agreement, drawing from the philosophy of Playing to Win and using the Values Cycle is outlined below:

The Playing-to-Win Contract—Our Commitment to Each Other

The Primary Values

1. Mastery   **What are the critical tasks, skills, and competencies required to successfully implement our agreement?**
What overall standards are expected? What constitutes excellence? What will it take to reach the very highest standards? What will it take for both parties to be the best? What skills, competencies, and practices are required? What expert knowledge is required? What is the core knowledge, professional development, learning, teaching and expertise, information systems, technology and science, technique, efficiency, sophistication, artistry, and accomplishment required to execute our agreement successfully? What are the opportunities for *kaizen*, or continuous improvement?

---

2. Chemistry   **With whom must we build and maintain strong relationships?** How and with whom will these harmonious relationships be established? What current relationships must be repaired, maintained, or built? What are the necessary characteristics and attitudes for building strong relationships? How will relationships be developed beyond the superficial? How will we continuously develop opportunities that will lead to stronger friendships and bonds based on trust, mutual respect, integrity, improved communication, and truth-telling? How will we build more win/win partnerships? In what situations will teamwork be critical? When will a gregarious style be an asset? Are there situations where it is essential to be easy to get along with? How will we develop the necessary conditions for creating and deepening mutually satisfying and rewarding relationships — with employees (and their partners), customers, partners and industry colleagues?

3. Delivery   **Who are the internal and external customers* for this function or activity? What are their needs?** How will focus be brought to bear on their needs, motivated by enlightened self-interest and altruism? How will we foster a passion that is matched by both parties for meeting the needs of others? How will we develop respect for their needs? How will we achieve a balance between meeting the needs of customers and making a profit, knowing that profit is the result of a successful customer-focused philosophy? How will we maintain a philosophy of "win/win" deals and relationships? How will we ensure that customers are treated as partners rather than adversaries? What is the clear mechanism for distinguishing between doing the right thing and doing things right? What mechanisms will be established for defining clear standards of performance for both internal and external customers?

The Accelerators

4. Learning   How "does the bar get raised"? What will it take to reach and exceed the agreed standards of *Mastery*? What continuous learning will be needed to exceed the agreed levels of *Mastery*? Where? When? Why?

5. Empathizing   How will opportunities be created for enhancing communication through *Empathy* (truth-telling, promise-keeping, trust, accountability, energy, honesty, integrity, respect, compassion, and love)?

*The reader will recall that the term *Customer* has been given a wide meaning which includes *anyone who comes to us with a need*. For a more detailed definition, see *A Note on Terminology*.

6. Listening   How will *listening* be achieved in order to meet the needs of others? How will we develop a high level of attentiveness in order to maximize the understanding of our communications with others? What are the means by which we will shut down "mental chatter" so that we can give undivided attention to others when communicating with them? What skills and practices will be drawn upon to look for other signals when *listening*, besides words, such as body language, intonation, and expression? How will we develop the skill of "hearing the words as well as the music"? How will we *listen* openly, and in the most effective way possible, in order to understand, without being defensive or manipulative?

The Shifts

7. From ME to YOU

What steps are being undertaken to appreciate the real value of the other party to this agreement? How will we ensure the right balance in favor of meeting their needs more than our own? How will we meet the needs of their soul? How will we create opportunities for both of us to develop and learn?

8. From THINGS to PEOPLE

How will we show a higher concern for the innate value and sacredness of **PEOPLE** than for the acquisition and stewardship of material things? How will we design our agreement so that it encourages us to continue doing so?

9. From BREAKTHROUGH to KAIZEN

Are there incentives and plans for practising **KAIZEN** (helping others to continuously improve and do the same things better) as diligently as seeking breakthroughs (doing things differently)? What are the incentives that encourage us to do both?

10. From WEAKNESSES to STRENGTHS

What are the mechanisms for applying a spiritual practice of celebrating and building on **STRENGTHS**, rather than dwelling on weaknesses? What is the incentive to continue doing so?

11. From COMPETITION and FEAR to LOVE

What encouragement does our agreement hold for **LOVING-KINDNESS**, in every aspect of our relationship, that calls on us to show compassion and generosity instead of competition, fear, and conflict; does our agreement embrace the language of LOVE, rather than the hostile and adversarial language of war?

Getting What You Expect

If we expect fear and competition, we may find them. A legend from the Middle East tells how a merchant's servant in Baghdad came to his master one day in great consternation.

"Master," he cried, "Someone bumped into me in the crowded marketplace this morning. When I turned around I saw it was Death. I caught his eye and he gave me such a strange and terrifying look that I am now in fear of my life. Master, please lend me your horse so that I may flee... with your help I can be far away in Samarra by nightfall."

The merchant was a generous man and, leading the servant to one of his fine horses, he sent him away. Later, as the merchant was strolling through the marketplace, he noticed Death standing in the crowd.

"Why did you frighten my servant this morning and give him such a threatening stare?"

"I did not threaten him," said Death. "It was a look of surprise...I was astounded to see a man this morning in Baghdad when I have an appointment with him tonight in Samarra."

Playing not to lose is a negative, energy-draining style of living that tends to be self-fulfilling. It has no upside — one cannot score goals when defending one's own goalmouth. When we are playing not to lose, the best that we can hope for is to minimize the number of fears that turn into reality. Playing to win, on the other hand, has a limited downside and an unlimited upside — the right kind of odds, as any gambler would agree. It is therefore in our best interests to fill our lives with grace and love, and take every step we can to remove the toxicity and dysfunctionality of competition from our daily practice.

Giving Before Taking

Jack Kornfield tells a story about two young children, an eight-year-old girl with a rare blood disease and her six-year-old brother. The family learned that the little girl required a blood transfusion, but because she had a rare blood type, their search for compatible blood was unsuccessful. The mother and doctor asked the little boy if he would donate his blood to save his sister's life. He replied that he would have to think about it. After a couple of days, he said, "OK, I'll do it." They went to the hospital and laid down beside each other while the blood was successfully transferred. After a few minutes, the little boy called over the doctor and, with great composure, whispered, "Will I start to die right away?"

Already in his young life, this little boy was playing to win. He had nothing to win by playing not to lose. He created the circumstances in which he couldn't lose. Even in death he would be a winner. If he survived, he would create a win/win result—for himself, his sister, and his family. By playing to win, he ensured that his self-esteem would be reinforced for the rest of his life and a constant flow of positive biochemistry would shield him for years ahead. This little boy demonstrated the positive definition of competition, to strive to make great efforts to do one's best, a constant process of moving towards *Mastery*.

This type of competition seeks excellence and distinctive performance and leads to exhilaration. As we have seen, it heals the immune system and nourishes the soul. Competition as rivalry, on the other hand, leads to stress and burnout and is a primary cause of the malaise afflicting people and their organizations today. Antagonistic competition causes anxiety, poisons relationships, and is inherently toxic. There is no healthy destructive competition—in the end, it kills the victim as well as the perpetrator. *How can we become well, by wishing others ill?*

Internal Competition

We have been referring to competition between organizations, but the damage caused by competition within organizations is just as corrosive to the soul. Some traditional managers believe that their careers are best advanced by gladiatorial competition with employees over the scarce resources within, instead of by cooperation, which enlarges the size of the entire cake. Thus it is common for executives to be locked in dangerous conflict over budget allocations, capital expenditure approvals, and the favors of those with power.

Paradoxically, cooperation tends not only to be more effective, but also more healthy. According to one researcher, the evidence shows that cooperation surely brings out the "best" in us. This finding has been held in virtually every occupation, skill, or behavior tested. For instance, scientists who consider themselves cooperative tend to have more published articles than their competitive colleagues. Cooperative business people have higher salaries. From elementary grades to college, cooperative students have higher grade-point averages. Personnel directors who work together have fewer job vacancies to fill. And not surprisingly, cooperation increases creativity.[3]

Competition is contrary to the natural wishes of the soul. The soul seeks to be whole, while competition seeks to divide—between winners and losers. We will be prevented from healing the pain afflicting the souls of millions in modern organizations until we embrace wholeness in everything we do. Wholeness embodies grace and draws us inevitably to cooperation. The soul naturally withdraws from competition, and is drawn towards cooperation. The soul is simply a part of a larger universe and it cannot achieve wholeness until we pursue it at every level.

In a system of democratic capitalism, we should be realistic in our expectations—we are not likely to witness an overnight conversion from competition to cooperation. However, there are bright prospects for at least distinguishing between the two types of competition:

- *striving together* for excellence to achieve *Mastery*, and
- hostile rivalry in opposition to others.

The first will heal us; the second will kill us.

PART TWO

THE MIND

10

Head First

There is a lot of walnut-shell management in mechanical organizations. Remember the old magic trick of hiding a pea under one of three walnut shells, shuffling them, and then asking someone to guess which one it was under? The pea had a hair attached to it, so if you knew this secret, you could tell the pea's location every time. The first few times were a novelty, but it soon became boring. Just like walnut-shell management.

As I mentioned in Chapter 5, the human brain will die if it is deprived of information, but the soul becomes impaired first. When we are starved of information, the soul becomes anxious, because it is naturally curious, questing, and restless. Yet managers in mechanical organizations invariably confuse the hoarding of information with the acquisition of personal power — and power has always been a tormentor of the soul.

Life seeks balance. When yin and yang, the female and male energies, are out of balance in organizations, the soul is forced to deal with the lack of symmetry, because it too seeks balance and wholeness. Information and answers represent male energy while questions represent female energy. When employees are deprived of the male energy of information, their souls naturally seek balance. This is disruptive for organizations because, paradoxically, the search for balance creates its own turbulence. The solution is to provide information — the missing male energy.

Open the Books to Inspire the Soul

The general myth is that the more information one can monopolize, the greater the power one can wield. This epitomizes the insecure, macho manager, without a guiding beacon of values or a commitment to grace. These are traditional managers ruled by personality, not by soul like Margaret Thatcher who is purported to have observed, "I don't mind how much my ministers talk — as long as they do what I say." Deprivation of information causes more than the brain to wither: it is a condition that makes the personality insecure and emaciates the soul.

Traditional managers also hoard corporate intelligence because they believe that if "sensitive information" should fall into the wrong hands, it will be used against them. The hubris and paranoia behind this notion is frightening. It infers that employees are so immature or untrustworthy that their treachery will lead to careless talk about "sensitive issues," causing "a competitor" to take advantage of the organization.

This thinking comes from another era, when a few heroic, well-educated (usually male) leaders possessed all the information and were uniquely qualified to make all corporate decisions. The downsizing of organizations, the removal of management layers, the advantages of technology, a more educated work force, the need for speedy decision-making in contemporary markets, and the growing specialization of tasks have all created a new context for decision-making, information, and power.

Today, there is an urgent need to place the maximum amount of information and authority necessary with those who are most suited to make a decision in the best interests of employees, customers, and suppliers. That usually means as close to the action as possible. Enlightened organizations like Levi Strauss have incorporated such objectives into their corporate philosophy. The corporate "Aspiration Statement" of Levi Strauss includes the following:

> EMPOWERMENT: Management must increase the authority and responsibility of those closest to our products and customers. By actively pushing the responsibility, trust, and recognition into the organization, we can harness and release the capabilities of all our people.

We are no longer living in an age of serfs and nobility, strongboxes and citadels. We are in the cyber-age, in which two souls — customer and service provider — seek to communicate and create meaning, and they want to do it now. Withholding information is just one of many ways traditional managers interfere with this natural phenomenon. In these mechanical organizations, the absence of meaningful information results in an escalating measure of personal angst for the souls within. Consider for a moment, the Indianapolis 500 pit crew for Team Penske. During the 1994 race, Penske's winning driver, Al Unser Jr., screeched to his pit stop, where six team members leaped over a three-foot wall, gave him a drink, changed four tires, refueled and made minor repairs, and returned him to his 200-mile-per-hour circuits, in less time than it takes you to read this sentence. Imagine how group performance would be diminished if every member of this team did not have all the information they needed to win?

The soul craves both information *and* the authority to use it wisely. The soul seeks to be free — to know and to do. The soul requires more, not less, information.

Jack Stack, Chairman and CEO of Springfield Remanufacturing Corp. (SRC) has built a remarkably successful company on the belief that "the best, most efficient, most profitable way to run a business is to give everyone in the company a voice in how the company is run and a stake in the financial outcome, good or bad." Since Stack took over SRC in 1983 from International Harvester and invented the annual planning process, revenues have grown from $16 million to $105 million and the number of employees has increased from 119 to over 750.

Stack has developed an open-book management style that involves all employees in the planning process, providing free access to financial information and corporate performance at any time. Every employee is involved in both the planning process and a bonus system based on meeting the plan's targets. Stack's real goal has been to encourage employees to think like owners. While SRC committed 11,200 hours to job-skill training in 1993, business and financial education took over 31,300 hours. "It's not like you have just one meeting and learn everything on the financial statement," says Kevin Dotson, who works in the Heavy Duty warehouse at SRC. "I learn more every time I go to a meeting. But you do understand the lines on the statement that you actually affect. That's how you see how you can be more efficient or how we as a small team can improve so the next group can take the hand-off more smoothly. We all have different jobs, but we're all pulling for the same goals."

> **This is the bitterest pain among men, to have much knowledge but no power.**
>
> HERODOTUS

In 1992, Stack put his ideas together in *The Great Game of Business,* which became a publishing phenomenon. Stack had hit a nerve. The response from readers, who knew there was a better way and who were hungry to learn a more inclusive and open management style, was overwhelming. Stack and his staff responded by developing a two-day course describing their approach, which he has since taught to more than 1,000 people who have visited his company in southwestern Missouri, to learn what he calls, "the only sensible way to run a company."[1]

An important step in creating open-book management is to share the numbers. Percy Barnevik, former CEO and president of Asea Brown Boveri (ABB), did just this by creating ABACUS — the ABB Accounting and Communicating System. It provides people at all levels in the organization with the same information, drawn from a single database. This communicates trust and produces a single set of data, enabling ABB employees to use the data in deciding on appropriate action rather than debating the validity of the numbers.

Based on my experience as a consultant to corporate teams, the secrecy surrounding information is unwarranted. It really wouldn't make much difference if the information did get into the wrong hands; our self-importance, driven by personality, just causes us to believe that this is so.

All men naturally desire knowledge.

ARISTOTLE

Some of the information that gives managers in mechanical organizations the biggest jitters is information dealing with compensation, structural changes, mergers and acquisitions, pricing, new products, or divestiture. The most sensitive information, of course, is information dealing with the personality: salaries, bonuses, promotions, performance, and the like. But this paranoia of the personality is really built on fear, which is the engine of power and control. Having achieved a measure of success, traditional managers become afraid of losing it so they consolidate their power by hoarding information. Power is the response of the personality that relieves the pain of fear, and so it is the opium of the fearful.

By restricting the free flow of information, power-seekers remove contextual meaning and thus cause fear of the unknown in the hearts of their victims. The power-seeker, measuring personality alone, finds the short-term successes achieved through fear to be intoxicating and becomes hooked. One power fix requires another. Giving up control of information becomes increasingly difficult and reasons for not doing so become more imaginative and paranoid every day. Traditional managers maintain their power bases through fear — by withholding information. We have come to know this style as mushroom management: keeping everyone in the dark and covering them frequently with manure.

If we pause to reflect on the need for classifying information, viewing the subject through the lens of our values, surely we must question our motives for secrecy. If we truly mean to apply the Values Shift *from fear and competition to love,* why don't we see information-hoarding as a fear-inducing practice and take the necessary steps to remove it? Don't we trust the people upon whom we depend to achieve our vision for the organization? If we have to choose sides at all, aren't our employees on *our* side? If the leaders of an organization don't trust and respect their own people enough to share information about the organization upon which they depend for their livelihood, why would those people treat their leaders any differently? Distrust breeds distrust.

Think about the messages that secrecy sends: "We don't trust you with this information," "You are not important enough to receive these reports." Although we are not usually as explicit as this, our implicit message is just as clear. Reflect for a moment on these messages and how they sound to your ears. How do they resonate with your soul? If they were spoken to you, would you find them wounding, hurtful, and insulting? They are messages that demoralize and demotivate people. They raise the ugly specter of class consciousness in organizations (those with the information being of a higher caste), and therefore encourage resentment, jealousy, and diminished self-esteem — all poisons for the soul. These affronts to both personality and soul cause people to leave their hearts at home. In other words, the damage caused by secrecy is by far greater than the possible risks to an organization through an open philosophy.

We live by information, not by sight.

BALTASAR GRACIAN

In mechanical organizations, the practice of walnut-shell management demotivates the personality and devastates the soul. In Sanctuaries, information is freely shared, and by doing so, we send a signal of respect and trust that engages the personality and inspires the soul. Equipped with the relevant information and freed from guesswork, rumor, and gossip, employees can contribute fully and their souls feel safe. Leaders who are open about information are frequently surprised at the innovative ways information is used and the dramatic results that can be achieved. The downside of secrecy is worth sacrificing for the upside of openness.

Walnut-shell management is equally insidious when applied to customers or suppliers. One imagines that large public corporations maintain departments of obfuscation, where the raw data for the annual report are sent to be sanitized, censored, hyped, and made ambiguous. This has created a parallel industry of truth-seekers, most of whom work on Wall Street, and busy themselves unraveling the disingenuous data in corporate financial statements in order to find out what is really going on. It has become a toxic game.

The practice of withholding vital information from suppliers is equally toxic. In both cases, we are sending the same message: we don't trust you, we don't respect you, and we are going to mislead you. This, of course, causes suppliers and customers to reflect back the same attitude to the organization. That we condone this practice is not surprising when we consider that the creators of this misleading or incomplete information experience the same insult every day from their own leaders. This phenomenon is often rudely referred to as "monkey see, monkey do."

George Gendron, editor-in-chief of *Inc.*, has long been a fan of open-book management, viewing it as a sign that a new breed of evolved leader is emerging in modern organizations. In a passionate editorial in June 1995, he wrote, "The open-book revolution is part of a broader and deeper change occurring around us, a change that will alter the environment in which everybody does business. I'm not saying that every company will open its books. Far from it. But I do think that every company will be affected by this new environment of increased economic literacy and financial accountability. How can companies adapt without going the open-book route? I couldn't say. But if I were running one of them, I'd sure try to figure it out soon."[2]

When leaders reappraise their attitude and release information to all employees, to involve them in the *mind* of the business, then, as Jack Stack has taught us, the employees will pick up on this signal and treat others with the same respect and integrity. Absence of information is like an autoimmune disease of the soul. The soul struggles to correct the damage, and nothing will deflect this effort, no matter how long the soul suffers, until it attains its goal, which is to become whole.

> **Ignorance is the curse of God,**
> **Knowledge the wing**
> **wherewith we fly to heaven.**
> WILLIAM SHAKESPEARE,
> *HENRY V, 1, 2*

Decision-Making — A Song for the Soul

The soul is a perennial questioner, but even if the quest for information is successful, the soul will not cease questioning and searching until it achieves another imperative: freedom. This is true in every aspect of life, not just at work. Two of the needs of the soul are simple and straightforward. They include adequate information and the freedom to participate in and make decisions — humble enough requirements for the everyday soul. Without these two, the soul remains frustrated in its pursuit of wholeness and balance. Meeting these needs is therefore a prerequisite for inspiring the soul.

This seems easier said than done. Those missionaries who have created Sanctuaries have already learned this, but in mechanical organizations, where people continue to be seen as parts, the use of power and fear causes information and decision-making to be unevenly distributed. Information and decision-making are frequently used to divide, manipulate, and control people — practices that are highly repugnant to the soul. In defending the habit of secrecy and autocracy, traditional managers frequently assert that their employees do not have the capabilities to make decisions. They are probably correct. After all, if employees are deprived of access to information and shut out of the decision-making process, they will have no practice or experience in these matters. In mechanical organizations, this self-serving argument is used to maintain the status quo.

A 1994 study by Gordon Group Inc., for the California Public Employees' Retirement System (CalPERS), showed that companies that involve employees frequently in decision-making enjoy stronger market valuations than those that do not. Says Richard S. Koppes, CalPERS' general counsel, "This is one of the screens we'll use in looking for what companies we target."[3] Tandem Computers has established a tradition of decision-making by consensus. Most departments meet frequently, and often an entire department interviews job candidates to see if they get along well with the team. "Town Meetings" are held regularly for employees to discuss new developments. Tandem nurtures the spirit of community and communication among employees in many ways from consensus meetings to "weekly popcorn parties."[4]

All work is sacred and all work is soulwork. If certain essential elements are missing from our work, such as information or the opportunity to contribute to the decisions that affect the organization and therefore our own life and livelihood, our work will deprive our souls. Since we are living in the information age, it is plainly absurd to withhold information and decision-making power from the people who need it and can use it well — those doing the work. Without information and decision-making authority, what other work will knowledge workers do in the information age?

Information and the ability and authority to use it wisely is a song for the soul. Almost everyone has experienced the bliss that comes from tapping into relevant data and using them effectively to achieve *Mastery* and make a difference. Great moments in school or college, creating a winning strategy in sport, delivering a bravura musical performance, achieving a personal epiphany through learning or travel — these are events that combine information and action and bless the soul with freedom and completeness. For many people, the opportunity to create similar magic in modern organizations is still waiting to be discovered and understood. We can help the soul to become whole by supplying the missing essence — information and action — and if we do, the release of untapped potential will so transform individuals and their organizations that existing rules of productivity, overhead ratios, leadership, and communication will be consigned to the dustbin of history.

The more decisions you are forced to make alone, the more you are aware of your freedom to choose.

THORNTON WILDER

11

The Invisible Code

The Myth of Empowerment

Like many people, I am a fan of empowerment, but I despair how the word has been debased. I feel the same way about empowerment as I imagine Bertrand Russell must have felt about Christianity, when he observed, "The problem with Christianity is that it has never been tried." Banks will tell us that their employees are empowered, which isn't obvious when a teller is asked to bend the rules. Oil company executives will say the same thing, but don't try to negotiate a volume discount at your local gas station. In fact, as soon as one invites the average North American retail or service worker to compromise, make a deal, or break the rules, one quickly realizes that empowerment is a victim of stunted development. It's a myth. It never happened. *Rules rule.*

Margaret Thatcher, Britain's former prime minister, often touted the importance of empowerment, but her practice was different. An apocryphal story is told of Maggie Thatcher taking her Tory cabinet to dinner. "Roast beef," she told the waiter. "And the vegetables?" he inquired. "Oh, they'll have the same," Maggie replied.

The difference between proclaiming and actually practising empowerment is about the same among most traditional managers. Talking about empowerment and not doing it is one of the greatest lies of modern organizations. And it is also one of the most destructive — to the personality as well as the soul. In 1995, Seagram CEO, Edgar Bronfman Jr., bought MCA for $5.7 billion. At the time some analysts believed that the company was worth more than $7 billion. Why was this? Matsushita, the former owners of MCA, refused to empower MCA executives, demanding that the prodigious cash flow they generated should be remitted to the parent company. Rather than lose these dollars to a parent that was unwilling to reinvest in its subsidiary, MCA executives spent them. This depressed profits and there were no inducements to former chairman Lew Wasserman and President Sidney Sheinberg to increase them, nor were they inspired to increase the cash flow.

One example was the television group, which had revenues of $700 million that produced a feeble profit of $5 million. This was despite being able to generate revenues of $100 million from syndicating a television library that had mostly been written off in earlier years.[1] The failure to empower employees may have cost Matsushita shareholders as much as $2 billion. This loss may pain their personalities, but their souls will ache more when they see the magic released that the former owners would not let out of the bottle. This example will also show how the personality also gains from the reward to the soul.

There exists a wide difference in understanding about leadership among leaders and those they lead. In research undertaken by my company, leaders tell us that the characteristics of good leadership include providing strong direction, having a vision and mission, and defining a clear strategy. But when we ask employees to describe the qualities they look for in good leaders they talk about compassion, truth-telling, respect, integrity, wisdom, fairness, listening, good communications, and heart.

Relinquishing control with grace is more easily achieved by the soul than the personality. The personality seeks to enhance the ego, and gaining power over others is the way the personality measures success in this regard. Those who seek positions of power, rather than leadership, frequently consolidate their authority by increasing their control over others. Only when the soul is invited to share the responsibility of leadership does an invisible code of trust, love, and respect replace the edicts, policies, and rules of the mechanical organization.

I do not mean to propose that order should give way to anarchy. Rather, I believe, we should remove, reduce, and replace the rules that smother souls in organizations — what we might call the three R's of the office environment — so that the code of trust, love and respect can take hold.

The Tangled Web We Weave

Walter Scott wrote, "Oh, what a tangled web we weave, when first we practise to deceive." The soul is oppressed by overdirection — at work, in society and throughout our lives — and in its eternal quest for freedom, unity, and wholeness, the soul struggles to escape from this tangled web of tyranny. Yet we strive to weave an ever-greater tangle of deceit and counterdeceit.

In the last three decades, the number of journalists in Washington has soared from 1,500 to 12,000 and they are kept company by 91,000 lobbyists. In 1960 there were 365 paid political lobbyists registered with the senate. Today there are 40,111, or 400 for each senator. The staff of congress has doubled since 1970.

The management of modern organizations has become similarly tangled with the yang of the personality, which is the "How to," instead of addressing the yin of the soul, which is the "Why?" We have become resigned to the staggering growth in bureaucracy because traditional managers keep telling us that it is part of managing the deceit that is engulfing organizations in the complicated and litigious society in the 1990s. Our personalities may have become inured to all this red tape, but our souls keep searching for the light, fleeing from constraint and regulation, finding bliss only when rules are replaced with vision and values.

Values Replace Rules

The inspired soul is grateful for guidance, coaching, or technical teaching, because it takes these gifts and uses them for graceful purposes. Rules describe what *cannot* be done, but the soul yearns to be enabled, to know what *can* be done. Rules are limiting; values are liberating. The soul welcomes the opportunity to say "yes" instead of "no" and the soul finds the boredom and insensitivity of excessive regulation to be demeaning. When we are working from soul, instead of personality, there is much less need for rules.

As I suggested in Chapter 2, culture and values become the guidelines, and when we are called upon to make a decision, we will use our values to screen our judgment. An inspired soul knows what to do, because it follows an invisible code that is based on values. When people or assets are considered sacred, the inspired soul seeks to protect and enhance them.

At Hewlett-Packard, there is a strong commitment to doing things "the H-P Way." Says CEO Lewis Platt, "If employees understand the core values of the company are the anchor they can hang on to, it gives you a fair amount of freedom to change."[2] Intel's CEO, Andy Grove, says, "It's impossible for us to have formal management systems that keep track of every commitment and action that has to be taken in the rapidly changing environment we live in. Instead, there is an implicit understanding that if we nod our head in a discussion, we're going to do it."[3] He should know — Intel has grown from $3 billion to $12 billion in five years.

Using the template of the Primary Values of the Values Cycle, we can develop our screen for decision-making:

Mastery Undertaking whatever you do to the highest standards of which you are capable.	**Am I doing it as well as I possibly can?**
Chemistry Relating so well with others that they actively seek to associate themselves with you.	**Will it be good for people?**
Delivery Identifying the needs of others and meeting them.	**Will it meet the needs of the customer?**

If we ask ourselves these three questions, and we are able to answer "yes" with passion and conviction, what additional benefit will be served by rules? After all, if we truly believe that we have used all the resources available to us to make the best decision we can at that moment, and if it will be of significant benefit to people, and if it will gracefully meet the needs of others' personalities and souls, what rule can be relevant in these circumstances? What has been left unsaid that could inspire the soul? Surely, anything more is merely redundant, perhaps demotivating?

Trust Replaces Control

The late Wilbert L. "Bill" Gore left DuPont after seventeen years as a research chemist to start W. L. Gore and Associates in the basement of his house with his wife, Genevieve. From the start, Bill Gore was a true missionary, plowing his own innovative leadership furrow. His style was original, empowering, and creative. The results of his unique leadership style included brilliant innovations such as Gore-Tex, a synthetic fiber used in fabrics and many medical, electronic, and industrial products. Gore's real genius, though, was his appreciation of the soul's need for freedom, which he recognized as an essential component of individual and therefore organizational success. This led him to develop the concept of the "waterline." An internal company memorandum describes the concept:

> Security and success of the Enterprise require that we be discreet in the exercise of our freedom if the reputation, financial security, or future opportunities of the enterprise are at risk. Consultation with the appropriate associates is necessary before actions taken that may involve these risks.[4]

Gore used the analogy that the Enterprise, as he called his company, can be likened to a ship, and all the people employed are, in effect, the ship's crew members. Because the crew members are interdependent, no one may drill holes below the waterline. They may drill holes above it but not below. Thus employees use the waterline as a self-imposed limit on their decision-making: "Is this decision above or below the waterline?" That is, will it materially affect others? If the answer is yes, they must consult further with more senior colleagues. If the answer is no, the decision can safely be made without referral. A combination of the waterline and the Values Cycle template described above is immensely liberating, because it replaces control with trust.

Who determines the waterline? No one does — it is a perfect example of true empowerment. If we are actually on a boat, we tend to know the location of the waterline. And if we do not know, our natural reaction is to find out by asking someone who does, or by taking a look. If we remain in doubt, we practise the value of *empathy*, and consider how our actions may affect others. If we lack full information and drilling below the waterline poses a risk, we pause. When we are sure of ourselves, we press ahead. In short, we are empowered. The soul can tell the difference between phony empowerment and the real thing — between confinement and freedom.

The soul keeps searching and hoping that freedom will be found one day, and until that day comes, the soul suffers. It is this suffering of the soul, caused by overmanagement, too many rules and not enough trust, that has propelled entrepreneurial spirits out of bureaucracies and into their own ventures. The research into entrepreneurship is consistent in this regard: it describes the yearning to be free, the stifling effects of bureaucracy, and the passion to throw off the shackles of standard operating procedures. Bill Gore was a shining example of just such a refugee — he found his time at DuPont educational but suffocating.

The word "capitalism" is derived from the Latin *caput*, which means head. Democratic capitalism is uniquely intellectual — we create wealth with our heads. No institution on Earth has equaled democratic capitalism in its accomplishments for humanity and none holds such promise as capitalism in its ideal form, for meeting and enhancing the expectations of ordinary people. This is the higher ground that beckons and it is time for us to reclaim it. First, however, we must give people room to use their heads by unshackling them from thoughtless and unnecessary overmanagement. When people are given permission to use their heads at work, their souls will want to join them. When we consider bureaucracy, rules, and hierarchy, we must ask, "Whom does it serve?" The answer must be, "All of the souls that comprise our team." Like Perceval, all people know the value of asking the right questions. We must make it safe and worthwhile for them to do so.

12

Form Follows Function

The Energy of the Organization

Organizations produce energy flows, which consist of positive and negative fields. The soul screens and absorbs these energies, attempting to convert them all into positive action. The soul uses the positive energy it receives as a complement to its own reserves, applying the combination to step up the surrounding positive energy in the system. The soul has limited use for negative energy, which simply slows it down. Therefore, an excess of negative energy in an organization results in atrophy of the soul, caused by the external demand for the soul's positive energy. The organization, and the souls within it, are constantly releasing and absorbing energy and amplifying the positive or negative energy fields in the system.

Energy is eternal delight.

WILLIAM BLAKE

This dynamic ebb and flow greatly affects the condition of the soul, determining to a major degree whether the soul thrives or languishes. This is why one can experience the *tone* of an organization almost immediately when one steps inside its walls. This is a mystical sensation, familiar to almost everyone. Somewhere, deep within us, we experience a sudden surge of energy being transmitted to us by the souls of others and the entire organization.

A bad attitude is the worst thing that can happen to a group of people. It's infectious.

ROGER ALLEN RABY

On the other hand, some organizations emanate a sense of emptiness, loneliness, disorder, and melancholy that can be felt somewhere in the pit of the stomach. None of these sensations is easy to explain, but they are very recognizable and real. What we are experiencing is the soul's commentary on the energy it finds in a given environment.

The Silo Stifles the Soul

In the mechanical organization, people tend to think in bits and pieces. Instead of considering organizations as whole systems, traditional managers break them into parts so that they can be analyzed more easily. Most of Newtonian science uses this process of Cartesian reductionism in the same way. For example, we tend to equate the mind with the brain, thinking of it as a sophisticated computer that delivers instructions to the rest of the body. But this is an incorrect model that is only popular because it is a simple metaphor. In truth, every cell in the body has its own mind—and memory—with unique knowledge that it transmits as instructions throughout the entire system. The "mind" of the human, therefore, is not the brain but the sum of every cell in our bodies—about 100 billion of them. This model produces complexities that are very difficult for most non-specialists to appreciate. Yet this is the reality and our attempt to fragment everything into manageable pieces, while simple, is misleading and wrong.

It is the same in organizations. To understand whole organizational systems, we break them down into manageable pieces. This causes us to define the "parts" as functions and to label these as departments such as marketing, finance, and human resources. This is the business equivalent of dividing the human body into functions by establishing separate departments for blood, hearing, breathing, and touch. The body is a whole system and these activities are conducted by the whole body, not parts of it. Organizations are the same. Processes, not tasks, achieve goals.

Continuing to use the body as a metaphor, on its own, a single cell can achieve nothing meaningful. Nor, in isolation, can anything useful be achieved by a single function undertaken by a group of cells. Rather, processes involving entire systems result in action and change. Maintaining adequate blood supply, hearing, breathing, or touch is a systems process, not a collection of tasks, and none of these, on their own, can maintain life. Yet since the beginning of the Industrial Revolution, we have continued to analyze organizations by dividing them into functions and tasks and creating structure to match this view. Functional structures are not designed to inspire and fulfil the soul; they are designed to make life easier for a few senior traditional managers who wish to keep organizational power and control in their hands.

A friend of mine is an outstanding executive search consultant. After I introduced him to one of my reinsurance clients, the president gave him an assignment to locate a senior divisional executive. High-level searches are complex processes and this one was no exception. My friend conducted a continent-wide search to identify all the suitable candidates and their current locations. This search required a deep understanding of the organization, the candidate, and the people with whom he or she would eventually work.

Everything went well until the human resources department became involved. For them, the assignment raised issues of turf and professional specialization. The human resources staff believed that their professional training gave them an advantage not possessed by the president. They were keenly interested in the manner in which the search was to be completed, how the screening was to be done, how the short-list of candidates was to be developed, the psychological profiling, and so on. Although the human resources department had never handled a search assignment of this complexity or seniority before, they needed to feel comfortable with each step in the assignment and held lengthy meetings at each stage of the process. In order to maintain their authority, the human resources group asked the search consultant to channel all communications through them and to refrain from any further communication with the president. These concerns slowed the assignment considerably and introduced additional layers of communications clutter. When this happens, key candidates can be lost to another firm or can simply become frustrated or disenchanted and withdraw their candidacy.

My friend's energy was suddenly diverted from his mission into the resolution of these interdepartmental politics. In desperation, he called me to determine a strategy. Should he play along with the bureaucratic process of this human resource department? Or should he call the president to explain his dilemma and how these interferences were diminishing his effectiveness? How could he avoid appearing unprofessional and sloppy in the eyes of the president and re-create the original smooth communications he had enjoyed with him? Either approach ran the risk of creating ill-will, jeopardizing the success of the assignment, and possibly ruining his chances of future work. Nor did he want to become caught in a power play with the human resources function as a result of going over their heads and putting their noses out of joint. I urged truth-telling. The assignment was saved and completed successfully through direct contact between the president and my friend, with support from human resources.

Though the immediate damage to this assignment was averted, it wasted time and energy and lost commitment from the soul. The human resource bureaucracy survived another day, learning how to better justify their position for the next occasion. This sort of thing occurs every day in millions of organizations, bewildering the soul with the fog of competing agendas.

Departments like Quality or Customer Service are typical examples of the anachronism that functions have become. As I argued earlier, the only logical reason for establishing a Quality Department is to deal with a quality problem. If there is no quality problem, why should there be a department responsible for it? By establishing a Quality Department, poor quality becomes institutionalized and we fail to address its causes. This is like establishing a Department of Employment when a serious unemployment problem arises. The department is not the solution. The solution rests within an entire change in attitudes — a systems solution that is far more complex than the banal reaction of creating a department or function.

> The real test is whether we are going to have an efficient, program-oriented department or just another federal bureaucracy run by a group of people with their feet caught in their underwear.
>
> JOHN PHILLIPS

Everyone knows how to provide good customer service, but not everyone wants to provide it. The solution is not to develop a department or a new level of bureaucracy that monitors, controls, and trains good customer service into the organization. It is to give people a sense of "ownership" in the entire process so that they get up in the morning so inspired that they *want* to improve service levels and provide the finest service *their* customer could ask for. The passion behind their *Delivery* is so strong, it leads to innovation in the form of *kaizen* and breakthrough — a front wheel values shift.

Organizations waste enormous amounts of energy and talent channeling information around their hierarchies. The soul invests energy in these tasks but remains unfulfilled because it becomes detached, and often excluded, from the process. Organizations that create business units, or divisions, and that have undergone restructuring during the last few years, now find they have used up all their cost-cutting options. More important, because these organizations are driven by personality, they are incapable of devising approaches that will lead to personal evolution, motivation, and inspiration. As a result, the soul struggles in a confused and bureaucratic environment.

Sanctuaries are places where functional departments and structures have been replaced by values and personal relationships. Although there is a valuable contribution to be made by internal consultants, such as human resources, legal, marketing, and engineering, for example, their new role is advisory and facilitative, not operational. The knowledge and responsibility for these functions now rests within the hearts and minds of teams responsible for the entire systems processes that lead to end results. To use the example of purchasing, the objective is not to buy the cheapest component, but to ensure that we buy the appropriate widget that will help the team to meet the customer's service, quality, and price needs — *Mastery, Chemistry,* and *Delivery.* To do this, a team may decide that it is necessary to shore up their specialized knowledge with additional expertise by calling on internal or external consultants — but the system works best when the team itself makes the decision to seek further consultation.

Shortly after being appointed vice chairman of PepsiCo, Robert Enrico decided to commit half his time to coaching the next generation of Pepsi-Co leaders. He considered, and then abandoned, various ideas, including expanding the executive development budget, using inside functional departments or outside facilitators and gurus. Instead, Enrico conducted all the five-day sessions himself, scheduled the follow-up session ninety days later, and tailored the retreats to the development needs of each individual. Through this process, Enrico built a strong relationship with his team leaders and experienced a deep learning about their businesses and their philosophies as individuals. The retreats enabled Enrico to be intimately involved with the strategic thinking of his team members and to play a highly supportive role in shaping the company's direction.[1]

Even though Home Depot now employs 70,000 people, founders Bernard Marcus and Arthur Blank still lead coaching and development sessions for all employees. The leaders in these high-performing organizations are the head coaches — not the training departments.

The conventional strategic planning and human resource or executive development departments are no longer relevant to the flattened organization where speed and effectiveness are essential. More important, the soul becomes bowed by the structural burden that frustrates its quest for autonomy and wholeness. To the soul, structure is an impediment, not a means, to fulfilment.

In order to purchase a vehicle for lease to a customer, Ryder Systems, a national vehicle-leasing firm, previously required fourteen to seventeen approvals from different national and local functions. The company viewed each task as a separate activity that required the approval of a corresponding department. When the company changed its approach to these activities by seeing them as a single systems process — purchasing a vehicle to be provided to a customer — they eliminated unnecessary work, allowed the people directly involved to make the necessary decisions, and removed redundant approvals. Today this process can be completed with as few as two approvals and never more than five. As a result, the purchasing cycle has been reduced by one-third — from six to four months.[2]

Enlightened organizations all over the world are recognizing that removing the hindrances of functional departments creates organizational magic that inspires the soul — of employees as well as customers and suppliers. Chrysler Corp. used a non-functional, process approach to produce its Neon car much faster and cheaper than working the traditional way through separate specialized departments. Before spinning it off, Eastman Kodak's chemical subsidiary developed over 1,000 teams, scrapped the administration, manufacturing, and research and development functions and replaced the senior vice president of manufacturing with a team composed of all the plant managers. The vertical structure of General Electric's lighting business has been replaced with a horizontal design consisting of more than 100 processes and programs.

Owning the Process

Excessive structure creates negative energy and functional "silos" create energy blocks, preventing the free flow of positive energy that is so essential to the soul. Functional departments create competition and conflict, both of which are abhorrent to the soul. Negative energy creates a negative field, which translates into a deterioration of the soul as well as the personality.

There are literally hundreds of examples of this sad condition. A recent instance is Westinghouse Electric Corporation. In the late 1980s, the strategic planning department of Westinghouse was touted as the most sophisticated in the United States. Its role was to micro-manage the company's portfolio of products. Over time, the managers of the strategic planning department began to devote much of their time to justifying the existence of their function. They extended projections, exaggerated estimates, and camouflaged data — often with catastrophic results. Eventually bad loans and poor operating and investment decisions resulted in write-offs that cost $5 billion.[3]

The soul requires fluidity in which to flourish, and finds rigidity to be stultifying. This free flow is essential if the soul is to survive and grow. The soul doesn't want to be caught in battles between marketing and manufacturing or to spend interminable hours in meetings devoted to functional conflicts. Great organizations have recognized this and are creating new freedoms by tearing away both hierarchical and departmental structure, redesigning the organizations and looking at systems and processes rather than functions as the main organizing principle. Allied Signal, Boeing, British Telecom, Chrysler, General Electric, and Motorola are just some of the organizations committed to what Frank Ostroff and Douglas Smith of McKinsey & Co. define as "the horizontal organization." These new structures — free of functional departments — focus almost all of the organization's resources on *Delivery:* meeting the needs of its customers.

In the end, this is what inspires the soul — service to another. The question associated with the Holy Grail remains, "Whom does it serve?" If the soul can dedicate itself, not to functional activity or tasks, but to the process of meeting the needs of another — *Delivery* — it will find work to be inspiring and fulfilling.

Newtonian organizations favor the organizational structure based on little boxes connected to other little boxes because it is a simple system. If one looks at things superficially, superficial tools of observation will suffice. This is like looking at the brain and declaring it to be the seat of all human emotion, knowledge, and action, even though we know that this is not the case and that a vastly more complex reality exists. We prefer the Newtonian system for its simplicity; the new one takes time and energy to understand, and besides, we're busy running our lives with the old model and cannot take the time to learn a new paradigm. But the Sanctuaries of tomorrow will not be functionally or structurally designed. They will consist of teams that own the entire systems process, whether this is designing a car, developing the next generation of corporate leaders, buying a truck for a customer, or leading a lighting business.

The Internet is a good example of such a self-organizing system; one does not think it abnormal that in a system used by millions of people no one is "in charge," or that it is not divided into a hierarchical structure. In a Sanctuary, form follows function. These teams will "own" the entire systems process. They will be responsible for building their own learning models, systems, processes, rewards, benchmarks, assessment, communications, and fun. They will be responsible for integrating what they are doing with the objectives and activities of the rest of their organizations, as well as with their suppliers and customers. These will be teams of inspired souls that have been set free, unfettered by structure, but guided by systems, learning, and values and, above all, they will be mutually responsible for their own souls. This will require unbridled trust, which is one of the hallmarks of the Sanctuary.

13

The Soul and the Muse

The Roman goddess of grain, agriculture, and the harvest, Ceres, derived her name from the ancient word, *ker*, meaning "to cause to grow." To the Greeks, she was named Demeter, the daughter of Rhea and Cronus and mother of Persephone. The story of Demeter and her daughter, Persephone, explains the cycle of the seasons. When Persephone was carried off to the underworld by Hades, Demeter was so forlorn that she did not tend the crops, and the first winter came to the earth. Eventually, Zeus allowed Persephone to rejoin her mother for two-thirds of every year, and thus the cycle of the seasons began. The word "cereal" is derived from Ceres, and so is "creativity." Creativity fertilizes the soul, by encouraging personal development so that we may reap our harvest. Creativity nourishes everything in life.

Work is too often repetitive, boring, and meaningless, yet humans are born to create. Organizations are designed, as the word suggests, to organize: to manage, control, and restrain. True to her irreverent style, Anita Roddick, at The Body Shop, has bucked this trend by introducing a suggestion program that she calls the Department of Damned-Good Ideas.

The act of creating something is a soulful practice but when the creative spirit is restrained, it rebels. Organizations are therefore populated by rebellious souls struggling to be free — hardly a basis for personal development, discovery, or *Mastery*. The individual spirit yearns to be reawakened and released, but the organization seeks to suppress this independence and spontaneity. This contest of wills is not limited to the soul, or the personality of a few individuals, but implicates *all* of the souls and personalities in an organization. This is the antithesis of personal evolution and leads to corporate toxicity. This corporate-wide misalignment of soul and personality is highly corrosive to both. Breaking through to our muse in these conditions is never easy. In the eastern traditions, the universal life force is moderated within each of us through the body's seven centers of spiritual and emotional power. These are called *chakras* and link our emotional and spiritual energies and stresses. For example, the second chakra, located in the lower abdomen area, is the source of much of our creative energy. Because so much of our creative potential is smothered at work, and in the rest of our lives, this creative energy is often suppressed. Since it cannot find a focus it releases toxicity into the nearby organs. Thus, relief from our current epidemic of prostate and ovarian cancer and lower back pain might be achieved by nourishing the muse within our souls.

The Soul Transcends

Our work produces nothing lasting except what we contribute to the soul. Even the greatest accomplishments will crumble in the end; only our souls endure forever. Great corporations, factories, and every other material asset will mean nothing if they are not Sanctuaries in which the soul can make a lasting contribution. Our houses, cars, jewelry, and other trappings are destined to decompose — we must ask ourselves, "After our material entities have gone, will the contributions of our soul remain?" Our lives, and our work, are empty of meaning when we are uncreative. Without creativity we can exist, but can we be truly alive? What legacy are we creating for the soul?

The conditions that encourage creativity in modern organizations are extremely rare. Creativity requires the removal of pressure and judgment, two constants in mechanical organizations — and for that matter, society as a whole. Pressure and judgment accompany deadlines, budgets, committees, sign-offs, hierarchy, and rules, all of which, among other things, constrain the imagination.

Removing the Speed-Bumps to Creativity

Once upon a time, a number of creatures who were disenchanted with the current school system decided to start a new school. They overhauled the old curriculum and replaced it with running, climbing, swimming, and flying. To make it easier to administer and write the management information software, students were required to take every subject.

The duck was a champion swimmer, even surpassing his instructor, and was also highly proficient in flying. He displayed a weakness in running, however, and try as he might, *Mastery* in running eluded him. So the duck's instructor persuaded him to drop his swimming course in order to take a crammer in running. He studied hard, but his webbed feet became blistered and sore, which interfered with his prowess in swimming. He became an average swimmer, but since average was acceptable at school, nobody worried about it — except the duck.

The rabbit started at the top of the class in running, but his performance deteriorated when he enrolled in psychotherapy sessions to deal with his low self-esteem, caused, so the psychotherapist said, by his poor swimming grades.

At first, the squirrel was an outstanding climber. But he soon became frustrated when his instructor made him start from the bottom of each tree instead of leaping across the tops. He developed charley-horses from overexertion and received a C in climbing and a D in running.

The eagle spent much of his time in the principal's office, defending his unorthodox techniques. Although he was invariably the first to arrive at the top of the tree, he used unconventional methods that the regents had not approved in the curriculum.

At the end of the program, a snapping turtle, who was a brilliant swimmer and an adequate runner and flyer, graduated with the highest marks. He was able to pass flying by making his dives off rocks look like flight. The snapping turtle was elected valedictorian.

The prairie dogs boycotted the school, campaigning against the school trustees for not including burrowing and digging in the curriculum. They lost every appeal and eventually apprenticed with the badger, later joining the groundhogs and foxes to start the Sanctuary School.

The same principles apply in the real world. Hal Sperlich led the development of the original Mustang under Lee Iacocca at Ford Motor and later invented the minivan while at Chrysler. Reminiscing over these innovations, he observed, "You're walking a very lonely road. Life in a large corporation is easier if you go with the flow and don't support major change. People who propose things that are different make more conservative people nervous, and the corporate environment just doesn't reward people for challenging the status quo." Sperlich didn't just invent the minivan, he saved Chrysler, because the minivan became the company's profit-gusher for

> **Could Hamlet have been written by a committee, or the Mona Lisa painted by a club? Could the New Testament have been composed as a conference report? Creative ideas do not spring from groups. They spring from individuals. The divine spark leaps from the finger of God to the finger of Adam.**
>
> ALFRED WHITNEY GRISWOLD
> QUINN

many of the following years. A minivan prototype had been developed four years earlier in another creative sinkhole — General Motors — and, according to Vincent Barabba, a top GM marketing executive, "We had the minivan market nailed but nobody wanted to do it."[1]

Sperlich developed the idea for the minivan while he was working for Ford. His idea was to create a vehicle for the homemaker that was more serviceable than a station wagon, but had the height, width, and handling to make grocery shopping and car-pooling easier. His design breakthrough was the use of front-wheel drive, but no one at Ford would buy the concept. Being condemned to bear the torch of creativity through an endless rainstorm dampens the soul. Sperlich threw in the towel after twenty years with Ford, to join Chrysler. Once there, he unsuccessfully tried to sell the minivan for another two years.

With Lee Iacocca's* move from Ford to become the Chairman of Chrysler, Sperlich gained a soulmate and the rains no longer doused the flame of his creativity. Sperlich says his failure to introduce the minivan earlier was due to Detroit's rigid product-design thinking. "They lacked confidence that a market existed, because the product didn't exist... in ten years of developing the minivan, we never once got a letter from a housewife asking us to invent one. To the skeptics, that proved there wasn't a market out there."[2]

The minivan is a classic example of the frustration suffered by the creative soul until noticed, and nourished, by the leader. Leaders who create an environment in which the soul can be foolish, whimsical, outrageous and wacky will foster blithe spirits who generate money-making innovations. In 1922, Minnesota Mining and Manufacturing inventor, Francis G. Okie, invented a sandpaper designed to replace razor blades. He reasoned that men would rather sand than shave. The idea was politely received but not widely accepted, although Okie wasn't transferred to Outer Mongolia either. Instead, he was encouraged to continue doing what he did best — generating wacky, out-of-the-box thinking. One day, he came up with a waterproof sandpaper that became a hit with the auto industry: it produced a better exterior finish and created less dust than existing sandpaper products. The

> **The very essence of the creative is its novelty, and hence we have no standard by which to judge it.**
>
> CARL ROGERS

---

*It has always seemed somewhat surreal to me that Lee Iacocca's last name is an acronym for I Am Chairman Of Chrysler Corporation of America.

company became 3M Co. and waterproof sandpaper became the first in a line of legendary blockbuster innovations.

Following convention often inhibits the free-flow of creativity.

Practice in free-form thinking is both good for the soul and valuable when dealing with extreme situations. On her way to Hong Kong airport in the spring of 1995, Paula Dixon was involved in a motorcycle accident. Boarding the British Airways jet to London, she noticed minor pain in her left arm. Twenty minutes after take-off, she started to complain of chest pains. Two of the passengers, Angus Wallace and Tom Wong, were medical doctors. They examined Dixon and determined that she had fractured her ribs, which had punctured her lung. They feared that if the plane landed to get her to a hospital, the change in cabin pressure could kill her. The doctors created a makeshift operating room shielded from the rest of the passengers by blankets. Using a small scalpel to make an incision in her chest, they started to work. Over the skies of India, using an airline knife and fork to hold the incision open, they pushed a catheter into Dixon's chest with a coat hanger sterilized in brandy. A pen top linking the tube to a bottle of Evian mineral water was used to drain an air pocket that had built up around one of the lungs. "Those two big heroes literally saved my life," said Dixon. Added British Airways' Derek Ross, "She actually got some breakfast before she got off the flight!"[3] And Wallace polished off the remains of the five-star brandy. If all our workplaces were regenerated and invited such free-spirited creativity, they would inspire us as never before.

The Editor Within

The willful use of power and fear by traditional managers in mechanical organizations to inhibit creativity is bad enough, but our creative juices are just as likely to be dammed from within as from without. Natalie Goldberg, author of *Writing Down the Bones: Freeing the Writer Within* and *Wild Mind: Living the Writer's Life*, teaches creative writing courses. She describes the little voice in our heads, which makes us cross out, spell-check, and maintain control, as the "editor." This voice benchmarks everything we do against an external standard, and judges what we have written, or what we wish to write as too juvenile, pretentious, illiterate, or awkward. The soul blurts the truth which the edi-

> He writes so well he makes me feel like putting the quill back in the goose.
>
> FRED ALLEN

tor censors by imposing the currently accepted standard. Our editor places speed bumps along our creative highway and is never far from our elbow as we travel through life and work. The soul is no editor, because it is not inclined to judge, but the personality more than makes up for the soul's detachment. Only when the personality silences the editor can the soul be free to create.

The editor focuses on weaknesses, but we need to use a Values Shift from *weaknesses to strengths*. Charles Kettering, inventor of the cash register and founder of Delco, once bet a friend that if he gave him a birdcage, and he hung it up in his house, sooner or later, he would have to put a bird in it. His friend accepted the bet. "So I got him a very attractive birdcage made in Switzerland and he hung it near his dining-room table. Of course, you know what happened. People would come in and say, 'Joe, when did your bird die?' 'I never had a bird,' Joe would say. 'Well, what have you got a birdcage for?' He said it was simpler to buy a bird than to explain why he had an empty birdcage." If you hang a birdcage in your mind, eventually, you will find something beautiful to put into it.

When a young composer came to Mozart to ask for his advice on how to develop creatively, Mozart told him, "Begin writing simple things first, songs for example." "But you composed symphonies when you were only a child," the man exclaimed. "Ah," Mozart answered, "but I didn't go to anyone to find out how to become a composer."

Loosening Our Ties

Our approach to clothing may indicate our approach to creativity. Our clothes are soulful accoutrements. Traditional managers, who would dress us all in the Western equivalent of Mao's Red Army tunic, strip away the precious uniqueness of our soul. Our business uniforms force us into mediocrity and sameness — the opposite of creativity. How can the soul be creative when it is subjugated this way?

Before giving a speech, I have found it prudent to determine the dress code. I prefer not to embarrass my hosts, or myself, by showing up in jeans and cowboy boots when everyone else is wearing an evening dress, or by wearing my business suit when everyone else is dressed in the conference theme and I haven't been told. I always think how silly

Dress is a very foolish thing, and yet it is a very foolish thing for a man not to be well dressed.

PHILIP CHESTERFIELD

this is but I never have the courage to break the habit of conformity. When I was temporarily confined to a wheelchair, following my skiing accident, the rules changed. Fate handed me a license to wear whatever I chose. Who is going to criticize a speaker in a wheelchair for wearing jeans? So running shoes became permanent attire, and I threw the rest together as I was leaving to catch the plane. No one ever gave it a second thought — except me. At last, my personality felt comfortable and my soul liberated. This new-found freedom gave me the courage to top each previous eccentricity and the threshold of my goofiness expanded with each outing.

Yet why is there so much interest in the material I use to cover my exterior, compared to the material I am going to deliver from my interior? Presumably, I am being paid for what I say, not for what I wear. If the environment in which we work — our soulspace — can help to romance the best from our souls — our soulwork — can we not say the same for our attire? Should we not focus on doing everything possible to create soulspaces and dress codes that animate the soul, just as much as the personality? We are, after all, trying to inspire the soul. It would seem that we should encourage people to adorn themselves with whatever liberates their soul and the creative muse within — and not just on "dress-down day."

Dreams and Intuition

To the traditional manager, who combines the five senses with the analytical techniques of the Newtonian thinker, dreams and intuition are at best unscientific and at worst dangerous. Where the personality doesn't take intuition seriously, the soul treats it as the most useful of its senses, the other five being relegated to supporting roles. The soul works primarily on hunches, emotions, premonitions, and funny feelings. It is almost impossible to measure the value of dreams and intuition in progress, but the results can be prodigious. If we can learn to become comfortable with the notion that not everything must be quantified and value the unknowable as a legitimate source of information, then emancipation of the soul is possible, from which will follow a release in creative thinking.

> **If all the dreams which men had dreamed during a particular period were written down, they would give an accurate notion of the spirit which prevailed at the time.**
>
> GEORG HEGEL

Kaizen — Doing It Better

As I mentioned in Chapter 2, there are two ways to grow: by doing things differently, or by doing the same things better. This is a very subtle, but potent, idea. The muse in the soul resorts to creativity.

The Japanese call this *kaizen*: Continuous improvement in personal life, home life, social life, and work life, involving everyone. It is an attitude that honors the act of micro-excellence.

Procter & Gamble (P&G) has been on a four-year drive to reinvent work processes across different divisions, by reducing the variety of its offerings and standardizing ordering and billing. Previously as many as 25 percent of all orders — some 27,000 every month — required manual corrections. Today, if a customer wants both Pampers and Tide, they appear on the same invoice and are delivered on one truck — and the invoice is usually right. During the same period, the company has also reduced the costs of raw materials, packaging, production warehousing, and freight and delivery by 7 percent and has passed these savings on to consumers.[4] These improvements are not glamorous, nor do they win awards, but customers and employees win. By doing the same things better, the costs between manufacturer and retailer have been dramatically reduced and P&G's reputation as a cutting-edge supplier has enhanced their business relationship with customers. Suppliers have upgraded their skills and processes to meet the demands of their customers and the continuing strength of the company gives greater security to employees. *Kaizen* at P&G rewards the planet by being more eco-friendly and shareholders benefit too: in 1994, P&G's return on equity was the highest in their forty-four-year history.

Freedom for the Soul

Traditional managers often fear that if their colleagues generate wildly successful creative thinking, by comparison, they will look like unimaginative dolts. The insecurity that causes this fear produces a lose/lose condition: not only are traditional managers stifling creativity within their teams, but they cannot even be original themselves. As a result, the entire team loses and becomes despondent. TEAM is an acronym for *Together Everyone Achieves More* — our role is to encourage creativity and when this is achieved, we deserve credit for setting up the environment in which creativity can flourish. Who invented the minivan—Hal Sperlich or Lee Iacocca? Who cares? Iacocca has retired a wealthy man; Sperlich is doing his own thing as an independent consultant. Chrysler also won, as did all the souls within. The creative energy that produced the minivan also kickstarted a burst of creativity within Chrysler that had not been equaled in the previous fifty years: breathing new life into the Jeep and generating the cab-forward LHS cars, the Stealth, the Neon and many more.

Preparing an environment that will nourish creativity is, in itself, a creative activity. Spontaneity, dynamism, fun, humor, freedom from fear of failure, incentives, sympathetic values and culture, a soulspace, and celebration are just a few of the essential ingredients of a creative culture. Leaders who seek to liberate the soul through creativity must establish a Sanctuary in which failure is not punished but valued as a learning experience.

Genuine creativity is nurtured by many of the criteria described elsewhere in this book. It requires a culture driven by strong values, where truthtelling and promise-keeping are important. Team members need to feel that they have permission to offer creative thinking that, at first, may not easily fit within the existing mainstream thought of the organization. They need to know that unconventional ideas or positive criticism of current practices will be honored, not punished. The team must sustain a permanent state of grace in which fun, civility, integrity, respect, and good nature are daily practices. Rewards should be personal, soulful, and intentional, and the physical environment designed to inspire soulful work. A successful, creative culture views the notion of competition as irrelevant, provides all necessary information, encourages participative decision-making, imposes few rules, and provides a learning environment. The choice of teammates is determined by the team and profit is placed in its proper perspective. This defines a Sanctuary: the crucible of creativity and a place of regeneration.

Champions of creativity remove the speed bumps for creative thinkers and give permission for the soul to be free, to think freely, *to be.* They ask the right questions: What can I do to help you be more creative? What are the needs of your soul? What will inspire you?

Those who practise creative thinking need to ask themselves two vital questions:

1. How can I do it better? (*kaizen*)
2. How can I do it differently? (creativity)

Love and Creativity

More than anything, creativity depends on love. An old story demonstrates the difference between personality and soul. A good man who died was sent temporarily to the fourth dimension. While there, he was punished by having to eat with spoons longer than his arms. He kept dropping the food and was soon suffering from excruciating hunger. Eventually, he was transferred to the fifth dimension, where he was surprised to find that the spoons were the same length, but no one starved because everyone fed each other.

Creativity flourishes in a loving environment, because love enables the personality's ego to renounce autonomy. In this way, the personality is freed to give itself to the muse and from this transformation springs creativity. The muse resides within the soul.

The three Primary Values of the Values Cycle serve as a useful guide for the kind of love that I'm talking about here:

Mastery Undertaking whatever you do to the highest standards of which you are capable.	**Do I love what I am doing?**
Chemistry Relating so well with others that they actively seek to associate themselves with you.	**Do I love the people that I am doing it with?**
Delivery Identifying the needs of others and meeting them.	**Do I love the reason I am doing it?** (To meet the needs of others)*

The freedom to express our creativity is a birthright of the soul. Reclaiming this right is one step towards reclaiming higher ground. This is the work of the soulful missionary, for if traditional managers are obstructing this right, it is the calling of the soul to remove every obstacle that is in the way.

14

Fuel for the Soul

There has been no recession. We are not going through one nor are we recovering from one. In fact, there probably never was one, and there may never be one. A recession is an attitude. I have had the good fortune to consult with some of the finest leaders and their teams across North America, and during this time, I have learned an important lesson: "recession" is an excuse invented by the irrelevant.

There are two types of recession-blamers. The first is the corporate version, who blames "the recession" for poor corporate performance, weak and declining sales, diminished profits, evaporating markets, and brutal competition. The corporate recession-blamer tells everyone that things will get better when the recession is over. The second version is the employee recession-blamer, who is afraid of possible job loss, being "downsized," furloughed, demoted, or fired and then being unable to find equivalent income and work conditions.

Recession-blamers think this way because they have become irrelevant. The survival and evolution of individuals and therefore their organizations today is achieved when they remain relevant to the marketplace. Companies who are irrelevant to their markets and employees whose skills are no longer relevant start to think like recession-blamers.

The Irrelevant Organization

Let's look at organizations first. Industries are said to be afflicted by cycles in the economic environment. The technology industry is a good example, with the exception of Microsoft. The government is demoralized and obsolete — except the U.S. Army Corps of Engineers. And there are exceptions in steel, hospitality, financial services, and advertising — in any public- or private-sector organization. In fact, some of the loudest recession-blamers can be found in government. Some traditional managers cannot admit that they (and therefore their organizations) have become irrelevant. Their organizations no longer inspire employees and suppliers and excite and delight their customers. They make products or provide services that are *no longer relevant to their customers' needs*. When their customers defect, the leaders of irrelevant organizations blame the recession — never pausing to question why more relevant organizations flourish. In defending their personal reputations, these leaders refuse to see the obvious: that other organizations are searching for bright new talent because, despite "the recession," they are booming and attracting new customers. Instead of overhauling the way they do business — inspiring, motivating, and helping their employees to develop and find and keep customers for life — these irrelevant leaders conduct micro-analyses of the recession. A commitment to learning leads to relevance to customers and therefore rewards for the soul.

The Irrelevant Employee

What about employees? Many of them have become the victims of the unsound decisions of irrelevant traditional managers. But others have allowed their own skills to become irrelevant. In an age of adrenaline-pumping, pulse-racing change, where obsolescence is measured in weeks or months rather than years, none of us can expect to market irrelevant skills. In this climate, assembly-line workers who have been doing the same job for forty years should not be surprised that their skills have become unmarketable. If they had maintained their life and work skills with the same diligence as the equipment they used over those years, things would be different for them today. Unemployment is the pay-off for an irrelevant skill-set. There are few unemployed computer systems analysts and programmers, biochemists, child care workers, guards and home-security salespersons or homeopathic doctors. Learning is the fuel of the soul.

Education is the best provision for old age.

ARISTOTLE

Motorola's CEO, Gary Tooker, says, "With new processes and new technologies, you want to replace yourself instead of letting someone else do it. Success comes from constant focus on renewal."[1] While others blame the recession, leaders who listen to the needs of their customers and suppliers and meet these needs, and employees who constantly refresh their skills will survive and grow. As Darwin could have told them, the future belongs to them both.

In a survey of senior executives, training directors, and human resource professionals, Lakewood Research, publishers of *Training Magazine*, found that only 15 percent of the $100 billion spent annually by U.S. companies on training was deemed to be sustainable beyond the first year. In the knowledge era, it is constant learning (not training, which is as we've said earlier, is for dogs) that is a season ticket to the game of life, and experience is one of the greatest teachers.

The 10 percent Lifelong-Learning Maintenance Contract

Experience has a hidden danger: it teaches us how to be better at the same thing. This alone does not serve our learning need and we must be prepared to step outside of our existing paradigm by learning something entirely new. Change is not something that only affects other people — it will eventually wipe out all of our own existing jobs too. This is especially true of careers where new technologies are replacing people or redefining tasks. Our lifelong learning journey, therefore, should lead us to continuous personal development that ensures that we are always *relevant* to the changing marketplace in particular and to the planet in general. Learning is the fuel of the personality, too.

Recently a client asked me how we could avoid the breach of trust with employees that inevitably results from downsizing. I suggested that both leaders and employees in organizations shared the responsibility for upgrading life and work skills and that this should be treated as an ongoing, never-ending practice. In this way, everyone in the organization can remain relevant and therefore insulated from the risk of downsizing.

He asked me how much time would be required to achieve this condition, and I estimated it to be about 10 percent of every employee's year. He said that this was an unrealistic goal because it would mean that every employee would be away from their jobs for five weeks every year. I then asked him if he believed that a $1,500 yearly service contract was unreasonable for a $15,000 photocopying machine. He didn't think so. "So why are you prepared to invest 10 percent annually in the maintenance of the physical plant and equipment but are not willing to do the same for the most valuable and important assets in your business — the people who make it work?" Why would we even blink at the thought

A man who carries a cat by the tail learns something he can learn in no other way.

MARK TWAIN

of spending the same percentage to maintain intellectual capital as we would for physical assets?

Not long ago, it was customary to encourage our children to study medicine, dentistry, or law. We believed that they would then be set for life. Not any more. Today it is not uncommon to hear about unemployed doctors, dentists, and lawyers. We used to think that once we had been trained for our jobs, our heavy-duty learning days were over and our future secured. *But we are not our jobs.* Thinking like a plumber, auto-mechanic, or sales person is dangerously limiting. Besides, those jobs may also go the way of the railroad fireman, the elevator operator, and the punch-card operator of yesterday and the airline reservation clerk, bank teller, and travel agent of tomorrow. Yet in all of these fields there are pioneers reinventing themselves while others flounder — Southwest Airlines, BancOne, and Rosenbluth Travel are some examples that come to mind.

> **Experience is not what happens to you. It is what you do with what happens to you.**
>
> ALDOUS HUXLEY

The most important "fringe benefit" is not health care or a pension. It is the right to learn. It is an inoculation against irrelevance. Our challenge is not just to learn in order that our skills remain relevant to our careers, but that we learn fast enough to keep pace with the changes in life. Those who commit to a practice of lifelong learning — intellectual maintenance — can rest easy, knowing that they will stay relevant — and young. What's more, it's good for the soul: learning leads to regeneration.

Learning and Self-Esteem

A recent article in the *Wall Street Journal* suggested that "Service providers treat customers similar to the way they as employees are treated by management. In many such organizations, management treats employees as unvalued and unintelligent. The employees in turn convey the identical message to the customer." Outstanding customer service is the direct result of high employee self-esteem. Poor service is the direct result of low employee self-esteem.

Self-esteem is a gift from the personality to the soul. It is achieved through learning. Self-esteem functions as the soul's immune system; the greater our self-esteem, the more robust our soul. Self-esteem is one of the most critical elements in determining the outcome of one's life because self-esteem dictates how we relate to ourselves and therefore how others relate to us. Self-esteem is a prerequisite for truth-telling, because if we do not feel self-assured, that is, at ease about expressing our views, we will distort the truth about ourselves and our organizations.

When we love what we do, we do it well, because it is joyful and fun. High levels of *Mastery* create a "rush" that is hard to match in other ways. Indulging in activities that inspire us is a very human way to reward ourselves. We can reach rare moments of bliss through exquisite levels of *Mastery*, which can only come from a dedication to learning.

Mihaly Csikszentmihalyi has described a state of consciousness that he calls *flow* — a state of concentration so focused that it amounts to absolute absorption in activity.[2] Everyone experiences flow from time to time and will recognize its characteristics: people typically feel strong, alert, in effortless control, un-self-conscious, and at the peak of their abilities. Both the sense of time and emotional problems seem to disappear, and there is an exhilarating feeling of transcendence.

Figure 18: Mihaly Csikszentmihalyi, *Flow: The Psychology of Optimal Experience*

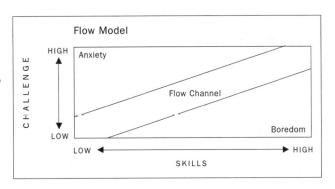

The two most important dimensions of the flow experience are *challenge* and *skill*. These are represented on the two axes in Figure 18. A challenge that demands greater skills than those currently possessed leads to anxiety; an excess of skills compared to the challenge being currently presented leads to boredom. Flow occurs in the channel where challenge and skills are balanced and growing — what I have referred to as *Mastery*.

Flow is a state of consciousness that is very closely related to self-esteem. If, however, our work produces flow, we are on purpose and our work may develop so that it becomes as great as our soul. If, however, our work is smaller than our soul, we must ask ourselves what lesson we are learning through this occupation, how long it will take to complete the lesson, and how we may graduate and move on to a greater lesson.

We all have a powerful and constant need to feel good about ourselves. Treating employees like parts or production units undermines their self-esteem, which results in the deterioration and eventual destruction of the quality of service we give to customers and to each other. This undermines the quality of life within the organization and thus imperils our souls.

How do we achieve greater self-esteem? Much has been written on this subject (Nathaniel Branden is among the best authorities) and there has even been a state commission (the Task Force to Promote Self-Esteem, chaired by California State Assemblyman and Chair of the Ways and Means Committee, John Vasconcellos), but we have learned one key lesson: self-esteem does not come from repeating daily affirmations or blowing kisses into the mirror every morning.

The only way to get positive feelings about yourself is to take positive actions. Man does not live as he thinks, he thinks as he lives.

THE REVEREND VAUGHAN QUINN

If we want to feel better about ourselves, we have to do something or accomplish something *real* that we can feel better about. This means achieving a greater level of *Mastery* in something — anything — as long as it is a real accomplishment. So the key to self-esteem is *Mastery*, which is achieved through learning. This relationship is illustrated in Figure 19: The Learning Model.

Figure 19:
The Learning Model

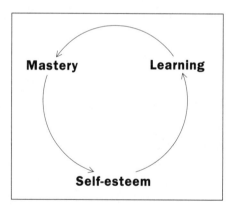

Mastery   Learning

Self-esteem

The Learning Self-Check

Try this technique when you are next in your office. Open your diary and turn the pages back to the beginning of the year. Scan each day that has passed to determine how much time you have dedicated to learning so far this year. Calculate the percentage of time you *actually* spent on learning and reflect on what you would like it to be. Map out a path of learning for the year ahead that will lead to significant development in personal *Mastery*, self-esteem, and relevance. Aim as closely as you are realistically able to the 10 percent standard. A middle-aged woman considered learning Russian but changed her mind when she heard that it would take ten years to become proficient. She told her friend, "I am fifty now — that would make me sixty by the time I become competent." Her friend reflected for a moment and said, "But my dear, you will be sixty anyway!" The skinny branches of learning bring temporary feelings of insecurity, because we suddenly realize how much we have to learn, but learning has a big pay-off: *Mastery*, which, in turn, leads to self-esteem. Few prizes are more fulfilling for the soul.

The Responsibility for Learning

Who is responsible for learning — the company or the individual? Here is how this subject was discussed in a recent *Fortune* article:

> Does this sound familiar? You're expendable. We don't want to fire you but we will if we have to. Sorry, that's just the way it is. And one more thing — you're invaluable. Your devotion to our customers is the salvation of this company. We're depending on you to be innovative, risk-taking, and committed to our goals. Okay?

The article went on to describe how the old social contract, based on loyalty in exchange for security, has given way to a new ethic:

> There will never be job security. You will be employed by us as long as you add value to the organization, and *you* are continuously responsible for finding ways to add value. In return, you have the right to demand interesting and important work, the freedom and resources to perform it well, pay that reflects your contribution, and the experience and training needed to be employable here or elsewhere.[3]

Intel's vice president of human resources, Kirby Dyess, puts it this way: "You own your own employability. You are responsible."

I believe that this explanation covers only half of the picture because it is not sensitive enough to the needs of the soul. Personal development and evolution — learning — are shared responsibilities; a partnership between employees and their organizations. The soul is adaptive; it is continuously learning. It responds to its environment, becoming enchanted or dejected as a result of what it learns from the people and events it encounters. The soul also seeks to be safe and fears becoming irrelevant through loss of *Mastery* and therefore self-esteem.

Anyone who stops learning is old, whether at twenty or eighty. Anyone who keeps learning stays young. The greatest thing in life is to keep your mind young.

HENRY FORD

But the personality thwarts the ambitions of the soul by inventing excuses to postpone learning: "I can't afford it at the moment"; "I have other priorities now"; "I will do it next year." The personality is forever debating with the soul about the need and the relevance of learning, and, more often than not, the personality wins the argument. This leads to irrelevance.

It is not coincidental that so many successful authors publish their first books in their fifties, for at this stage of their lives their soul tells their personality, "You have been making excuses all our life; if we don't get this done soon, the book is going to die within us." It works the same way with learning: the baby-boomer student market is exploding. The soul knows that the personality is mortal and it waits patiently; its wisdom eventually prevails.

Of all the beautiful truths pertaining to the soul which have been restored and brought to light in this age, none is more gladdening or fruitful of divine promise and confidence than this – that you are the master of your thought, the molder of your character, and the maker and shaper of condition, environment and destiny.

JAMES ALLEN

As the learning model above illustrates, learning leads to *Mastery*, which, in turn, leads to self-esteem, all of which result in personal evolution — the opposite of personal irrelevance. Therefore, learning is an essential fuel for the soul, propelling it to a state of expansion, inspiration, and grace. Creating opportunities for learning individuals leads to the development of the learning organization, and this, in turn, leads to a critically important learning goal — the learning society.

PART THREE

AND
THE
BOTTOM
LINE

15

Soul Proprietor

A Sanctuary is a whole system. Its components are not independent New-tonian parts but an interdependent blending of human and financial cap-ital, working together in perfect harmony as a unified system. The sum of all the energy, creativity, evolution, love, and intellect generated by the souls within an organization is its lifesource. Although an organization may have adequate financing, plants, equipment, and facilities, it remains a dead organization without its *lifesource* — it does not come alive until it is animated with the talent, goodwill, and spirit of people. Without this lifesource, organizations are no more than a set of legal documents. Orga-nizations generate capital growth and profit but only the lifesource of the organization can make this happen. Any attempt to unlink the lifesource from the output of the organization is regressive, illogical, and Newton-ian. Consider a tree: its lifesource — the nutrients from the earth, the sun, and the sap — is not separate from the new growth it generates, any more than the efforts of owners are separate from the capital and profits they produce.

Traditional managers have removed, and largely ignored, this vital relationship between ownership and the lifesource of the organization. As a result, employees often have no stake in the future of their enterprise beyond its survival. Their main hope is limited to the short-term results of their organization and its continuing capacity to pay their salaries. Since these salaries are often largely disconnected from performance, there is lit-tle incentive to add value, be more effective or efficient, innovate, find new business, encourage bright people to join the team, invent new processes, or create new wealth. In fact, because there is no connection between per-formance and the soul, there is little incentive to do anything that might strengthen the heart, mind, or bottom line, and yet these are the goals of the organization with spirit.

When Bernard Marcus, chairman of the Home Depot, is invited to sit on another company's board, he always purchases at least 2,000 of the company's shares. When Home Depot invites a new director to sit on their board, Marcus says, "We insist that they make a personal and serious financial investment in the Home Depot—either by purchasing stock or by investing in an options program that we make available to them. It is important that the amount is significant enough that each person feels that he or she is at risk."[1] There is no better way to cultivate the ground than with the owner's footprints.

Hollywood and the Soul

The entertainment industry is the classic example of evolving thinking about equity and ownership. Few industries stimulate as much commitment, passion, and rapture. When Jeffrey Katzenberg, the former chairman of Walt Disney Co.'s studios, resigned in 1994, he immediately attracted two soulmates in David Geffen and Steven Spielberg. Together, they formed DreamWorks SKG, the hottest studio in Hollywood. They didn't do it for the money—all three are wildly rich. What fired their spirits was the passion that permeates their work—the fun, exhilaration, the *Chemistry*, the opportunity for the three to forge their *Mastery* into an organization that will lift the hearts of millions around the world. This blitheness of spirit is driven by the connection all three have developed between their talent and passion and their material performance.

Part of the reason for the success of this unique industry is its structure. The giant, soulless dinosaurs of the past are gone. In their place has grown a network of many small teams—flexible, collaborative, and highly entrepreneurial. They form alliances around projects, such as a film, and when the project is completed, they disperse to other projects. In these interdependent clusterings, they have chosen to live and work with *Mastery*, *Chemistry*, and *Delivery*. Everyone's money and reputation are on the line and there is a visceral connection for everyone involved, between lifesource and results.

This energy has developed into America's second-largest exporter, with annual foreign sales of entertainment services approaching $4 billion. In a delicious irony that puts a new spin on the old dictum, "Make love, not war," the slack caused by devastating job and spending cuts in defense in Los Angeles County has been taken up by art, fantasy, and fun. This area is now home to 92 percent of the 370,000 people who earn their living from the Californian entertainment business. In one of the most demanding industries in the world, *Mastery* is the key to survival and success. In Hollywood, this *Mastery* has been achieved through specialization, flexibility, *kaizen*, learning, and intense collaboration among these networked teams.

The success of the entertainment industry rests equally on the very direct connection its members have made between their lifesource and their material performance. If it's a box-office hit, you will be enriched in many ways, but if it's another box-office bust like *Heaven's Gate* or *Ishtar*, you will have time to reflect on the lessons learned, while eating porridge until, hopefully, the next project comes along. This is a world in which one's soul is engaged by being connected directly with the results. Many Hollywood entrepreneurs see themselves more as artisans than as business people. Their remuneration is variable, and is derived partly from their prior reputation for *Delivery* and their *Mastery* of craft skills, and partly from the positive impact their contribution can have on box-office receipts. This becomes the equivalent of equity for Hollywood entrepreneurs, who therefore identify with the whole result, not just their piece of it.

Hollywood's combination of networked structure and linkage between lifesource and results encourages commitment to the success of the entire project — what one might call a big-picture perspective. A clear sense of ownership, responsibility for the end result, taking the whole view, and being connected to the results — these are ways to inspire the soul. Although the personality gets paid well, the soul earns the big psychic payoff. This will be the model for all evolved organizations in the future.

Equity Ownership

It is confusing to the soul to be in the organization but not of it. I often wonder why the lights are left on all night in major downtown skyscrapers. Is it an ego statement or an advertisement, or just careless or forgetful behavior? Would these buildings be darkened if the people who work in them shared the electricity costs? Would ownership help them to relate to the waste of this habit, and many others, and their effect on the bottom line and the precious resources of the planet? If every employee were asked to share in the hundreds of thousands of dollars spent in lighting the building through the night, which is what being an owner would require them to do, would their attitude to nocturnal lighting change? Applied to every aspect of an organization, this shift in attitude would drive operating costs downward, improve maintenance standards, conserve the Earth's resources, engage the hearts and minds of all employees, and inspire the soul.

The soul seeks to be connected to the whole, including the results of the organization. Linking the organization's lifesource with its equity is not a material goal but an emotional one. The purpose of equity ownership for employees is not to create a get-rich-quick scheme, but an attempt to shift attitudes and establish connections between the performance of the organization and each of our souls. The goal of ownership is not just to enhance personal wealth through stock option plans and the like (a direct appeal to the personality) but also to enhance personal evolution—a direct appeal to the soul. Except in a few cases such as United Airlines, UPS, and Avis, this practice is largely absent from larger organizations.

> **The instinct of ownership is fundamental in man's nature.**
>
> WILLIAM JAMES

Providing equity ownership turns people into soul proprietors, enabling them to heal organizations and make them whole again. It removes the class barriers and artificial labels that separate shareholders and employees. They become one and the same because they *are* the same—they share the same objectives and are invigorated by the same aspirations that vitalize all owners.

Ownership connects people with performance as measured by the profit-and-loss account, thus making them accountable. But ownership also confers responsibility. A soul proprietor owns the results flowing from the actions and decisions that he or she makes. As a result, ownership carries the responsibility for performance. This is a radical departure from conventional practice in most commercial and nearly all not-for-profit organizations. This shift in culture amounts to a revolution, a declaration of democracy, in which real authority and accountability, as well as participation in the financial and spiritual success or failure of the organization, is shared among all, not just a few, senior executives. This is easier to achieve when the hierarchies are flattened and the traditional structures, dismantled.

Real financial equity, such as stock ownership, is the desirable route to true organizational democracy. It is a necessary condition for creating a sense of soul proprietorship. The exact mechanism by which we effect the change in ownership is not the important issue. What is critical is that we all *behave* as though we own a piece of the organization. Nor is this evolution of ownership intended to threaten existing ownership structures. The market will determine how ownership can be transferred fairly, and there are no limits on the creativity or the design of the ownership structure. Nor is this ambition to transfer equity driven by a political or intellectual agenda — it is the result of an evolution in human consciousness, a process that flows from a desire to inspire the soul, intending to heal not harm.

To see the future, one need look no further than the phenomenon of franchising, which vividly demonstrates the potency of ownership. About one-third of all retailing is now undertaken through a franchised outlet. It is the fastest-growing sector of the economy. A very large proportion of these new entrepreneurs are refugees from organizations where they experienced no sense of ownership. Many of them have opted for a far more arduous and less lucrative lifestyle than their former corporate lives, in exchange for the personal renewal experienced through ownership — an exchange of personality for soul.

Franchising is simply one of the indicators of the revolution to come. Our society will be transformed over the next twenty years as ownership concepts and practices are overhauled. The current model does not work anymore and has resulted in concentrations of power and competing agendas that have led to alienation, fear, and helplessness in the workplace. Our goal is to steer this remarkable transformation safely so that organizational ownership and thinking are repositioned, converting old concentrations of power and equity to new ones. While most of us are indirect owners, through pension and mutual funds, this does little to encourage feelings of control or involvement. Direct ownership is the most ambitious and definitive step in this transformation. I do not mean pseudo-ownership, but real ownership.

> **Happy the man who far from schemes of business, like the early generations of mankind, works his ancestral acres with oxen of his own breeding, from all usury free.**
>
> MARK TWAIN

For enlightened and evolved leaders, developing plans for the transference of ownership will be a priority, because they will understand the quantum difference ownership can make to the soul, and therefore to organizational performance. Traditional managers will continue to struggle with the implementation of concepts based on personality — restructuring, delayering, TQM and the like — but real breakthroughs cannot be made this way. The real breakthroughs will come in Sanctuaries that take bold steps to forge permanent connections between the life-

> **What the world needs is some "do-give-a-damn" pills.**
>
> WILLIAM MENNINGER

source of the organization and its customers, employees, and partners. As ownership is transferred, a new culture of accountability and responsibility will emerge, based on involvement and aliveness, rather than detachment and disinterest.

In the end, our goal is to engage the soul, to inspire it and to put a spring in the step of the eight out of every ten people who currently despise working. Since the days of our youth when we operated our five-cent lemonade stands, we have each sought the one missing piece that excites our souls — ownership. Reflect for a moment on that childhood lemonade stand, and the good feelings it aroused. Though the money was appreciated by the personality, there were greater gifts to the soul: self-esteem, pride, diligence, concern, service, stewardship, friendliness, housekeeping, economics, thrift — and happy exhaustion.

Ownership rekindles these same feelings, polishes our character, and inspires our souls. We all yearn to experience this happiness again and to harness the energy of our souls to the transformation of organizations. Becoming a soul proprietor will transform work and raise us all to a higher consciousness.

16

When Team Members
Come and Go

Let's pretend for a moment that you are a member of an Olympic rowing eight. A new member is about to be added. Who should make this decision? The coach? The captain? The president of the Olympic Rowing Committee? Since you will depend on this new team member — very literally — to pull his or her weight, doesn't it make sense that you should be consulted beforehand and participate in the eventual decision?

Since most of us are similarly affected, shouldn't we apply this principle across the board? What criteria will be used to select the new team member? Will the criteria appraise the condition of the personality as well as the state of the soul? In short, when additions and replacements are planned, will the opinion of every team member be considered? Is there any difference between a corporate team and a rowing eight? The process of adding and removing members of corporate teams is perhaps the most entrenched and contentious example of personality-based decision making in organizations today.

For traditional managers, the need to control the decisions affecting selection and replacement of employees is very deep-rooted, often bordering on paranoia, as they bitterly resist attempts to shake loose their control over employment. The advancing wisdom however, is not on their side, because the logic of transferring control of hiring to those most directly affected by the performance of a new team member is irrefutable. Evolution in organizations will eventually usher in a more democratic approach, unless revolution brings it about first.

The Dark Night of Re-engineering

One of the reasons people are so fearful at work is that they have every reason to be. Over the last decade, they have been terrorized with growing intensity by a succession of management fads. Most of these have been euphemisms for "slash-and-burn" tactics that remove people from the corporate overhead. Employees live in fearful anticipation, expecting any day that an anonymous grim reaper will tear through their organizations and leave no employees in their wake. Before Jack Welch, CEO of General Electric, became more humane, he was known as "Neutron" Jack, after the bomb that destroys all the people but leaves the buildings intact. At Xerox Canada Inc., former CEO Richard Barton fired an entire level of management in one day. According to one ex-Xerox employee, "It was around New Year's Day [1993]. There were ambulances parked in front of the building because there was a real fear that people would suffer a heart attack from the news."[1] When the Chemical Bank and the Chase Manhattan Bank announced their merger, the executives cheerfully trumpeted the projected savings from job cuts when the two operations joined.

To make matters worse, all this cost-cutting (that is, slashing payrolls) has not worked. All the lay-offs, plant closures, delayering, and brave speeches about becoming lean and mean haven't delivered the promised goods. Non-farm productivity in the United States rose an average of 1.2 percent annually throughout the 1980s — virtually no improvement over the 1970s. Half of the restructured companies surveyed by the Society for Human Resource Management reported that productivity worsened or remained unchanged after the lay-offs.

A recent study by Deborah Dougherty of McGill University and Edward Bowman of Pennsylvania's Wharton School found that companies were less innovative following their downsizing experience than their unshrinking peers. Another study by Massachusetts consultants Mitchell & Company found that although shares of downsized firms outperform the stock market for the first six months they lag after three years.

In a study by Right Associates of Philadelphia, 74 percent of surveyed managers in recently downsized firms reported that their employees suffered from low morale, feared future cutbacks, and distrusted management. Teams who have been advised that they are empowered are especially embittered — they are frightened and confused when being "empowered" by traditional managers who continue to retain total control. It feels a little like painting stripes on a horse and yelling "Zebra!" In a few years, we will look back on the dark night of re-engineering and view it as one of most sterile and brutal eras of modern management.

It Doesn't Have to Be This Way

In the mechanical organization, the personality has been encouraged to follow "slash-and-burn" strategies to maintain the balance between costs and prices. But this is the coward's way. There is more to life than re-engineering and downsizing ("'ING management,"according to a friend of mine) and we owe it to ourselves to be more imaginative than to simply copy everyone else in using these tactics that are so barbarous to the soul.

Wisconsin Public Service Corporation (WPSC) is an investor-owned electric and gas utility, with 2,500 employees who provide service to 400,000 customers in a 10,000-square-mile area of Northeastern Wisconsin and an adjacent part of upper Michigan. This is a passionate company, with a passionate leader who is building a Sanctuary. The company mission is "to provide customers with the best value in energy and related services," and their vision is to be a team of "people creating the world's premier energy company."

When faced with the challenge of aligning costs with market forces, they chose a more difficult, but more soulful path — a path that respected the sacredness of people, a path leading to higher ground. WPSC was already an industry leader, but they wanted to be even better. They had worked hard to develop positive labor relations and Daniel A. Bollom, President and CEO, took advantage of these to avert a looming crisis. He and his management team knew that the overhead structure of his company would eventually cripple its future prospects. Annual labor negotiations were approaching and he saw the opportunity to move further away from the adversarial negotiating style that has historically characterized union/company relationships. Dan and his team knew that without fundamental changes in human attitudes, WPSC stood little chance of surviving in an industry with a locomotive called deregulation coming down the track. The company had earlier adopted a negotiating practice called win/win bargaining and Dan's team used this in their contract sessions.

> **If men have the talent to invent new machines that put men out of work, they have the talent to put those men back to work.**
>
> JOHN F. KENNEDY

In the 1990 three-year labor contract, the groundwork was laid for strengthening the communications and building cooperation. As the 1994 contract negotiations began, the two sides laid out their issues and concerns: the union wanted to avoid lay-offs; the company wanted flexibility in job structuring. Traditionally, the two parties would have gone head-to-head from these opposing positions. But this time was different. They asked each other, in the spirit of trying to fashion a win/win deal, whether everyone was prepared to strive in good faith for *both* goals. Dan made his proposition: "We guarantee that there will be no lay-offs, if you guarantee to be flexible." History was made that day at WPSC — both sides agreed to face the future as partners instead of warriors.

A new set of beliefs had been developed for the entire company, which were used to guide them on their new journey:

- Our customers are the primary focus of our efforts;
- Our actions must always be rooted in honesty and integrity; and we should always foster trust, faith in others, fairness and respect;
- Our learning through study, review, dialogue and experimentation benefits our customers, ourselves and our company;
- We must continuously work together to create and improve processes, and eliminate those that are no longer valuable;
- We cannot tolerate actions that crush people's self-esteem, aspirations, individuality, or dignity;
- We must recognize that every employee adds value to the company; therefore we must not allow job titles to stand in the way of an employee's ability or willingness to contribute;
- We must acknowledge and use the experiences and insights brought to the company through people's diverse backgrounds, choices, life-situations and perspectives; and ensure the freedom to express our diversity;
- We must be flexible as individuals and as a company;
- We must share ideas, information and knowledge freely, quickly, candidly and unencumbered by organizational structures or individuals;
- We must responsibly act as faithful stewards of the resources entrusted to us by others;
- Work should enrich and bring joy to every employee.

These beliefs have guided the partners in their dialogue and in the development and implementation of the strategies that have followed. In the years that have passed, virtually every other utility has produced the carnage that flows from downsizing and re-engineering, but WPSC has remained a low-cost energy producer in the region. There are 109 nuclear power plants operating in the United States and WPSC's Kewaunee Plant is one of four that have won the industry's Award of Excellence five times. WPSC's bond rating remains among the top two or three in the industry and the company's compassionate and innovative style has caught the attention of some financial analysts.

All this has been achieved by creating a Sanctuary in which WPSC has been able, among many things, to honor its no-lay-off pledge, rather than resorting to re-engineering or downsizing. As Dan Bollom put it, "We are not willing to sacrifice our future to gain an advantage today. We will not arbitrarily cut staff or budgets nor stunt our growth." As the champion of the WPSC Sanctuary, Dan Bollom has shown that honoring the soul can be both efficient and lucrative.

Dan Bollom and his team asked all employees to reinvent themselves and their services. In order to protect their security, employees have been going back to school, learning new skills and shedding old ones, augmenting leadership and communications abilities, and asking customers how the company could change and what new services they would like WPSC to provide. In one case, the company advertised internally for twenty volunteers to transfer to a new gas marketing group. Each was offered the equivalent of one year of technical-school training before being transferred to a new position, which was created to meet newly defined customer needs. The customers are loving it, the employees are revitalized, and the organization is excited. One executive confided to me, "I love this place!"

Today, survival is no longer the greatest threat to WPSC. Of greater concern is that their extraordinary success and soulful culture might attract a larger utility that would acquire them. This raises an issue of whether the new company would respect the Sanctuary that Dan Bollom's team has created, or whether WPSC would be overrun with traditional managers from a mechanical organization who would snuff out a shining example of the kind of leadership that reclaims higher ground and inspires the soul.

Empowering the Team and Inspiring the Soul

Earlier, we contrasted the wide use of the word *empowerment* with its scarcity in practice. On the rare occasions where a team is fully and properly empowered, it owns the responsibility for achieving team goals. This concept is still so new and untried that it is uncommon. Assuming that readers of this book accepted the principles of empowerment long ago, there remain several vital steps that must be taken before full empowerment can be said to exist within teams. One of these is entrusting the team with the unfettered right and responsibility for adding new members and deciding when existing colleagues no longer meet the agreed standards of the group—and what should be done about it.

The world of sports offers many examples of player selection decisions being made over the heads of team members. The detrimental effects on team morale and performance are all too obvious. Owners of sports teams, increasingly desperate to short-circuit the process of winning, are negotiating contracts and compensation with superstar players that virtually guarantee that they will never win a championship. In 1994, Glenn Robinson, the top draft choice for the NBA for the year, signed a ten-year contract with the Milwaukee Bucks for $68 million. He had yet to play a professional game and had just dropped out of Purdue after his junior year. One wonders what team members are murmuring behind the scenes. There is a natural law in team sports: *a team of champions cannot become a championship team.* Of course, teams need input from coaches, specialists, and outside advisors—not to mention the bankers—but in the end, it is the team that must perform, and therefore it is the team that must assume responsibility for player selection.

Flavor-of-the-month-style managers have hijacked and hopelessly corrupted the word *team.* Everyone is doing "the team thing." We indiscriminately use the *team*-word, linking it with anything: service team, team-building, team-work, teammates, team-spirit and team effort, without consideration for the significant, sacred underpinnings needed for a true team to exist. A team is defined in the dictionary as a group of people working together in a coordinated effort. Teams are united by a common purpose. They share harmony, trust, truth-telling, respect, support, courage, *Chemistry,* shared vision, goals, and values. A high-performing championship team epitomizes the concept of the Sanctuary.

Selecting Team Members

Decisions that affect people are just as important as decisions that affect profits. Indeed, *every* decision first affects people, who then affect profits. Therefore, no decision affecting people should be made in isolation of their colleagues. This is more than a matter of economic wisdom; it is a matter of integrity, trust, and ensuring that each team becomes a Sanctuary within a Sanctuary.

Ricardo Semler, CEO of Brazil's Semco, has created a Sanctuary where freedom has invigorated the soul. Semco's employees virtually run the company—in fact Semler shares the CEO title with six senior executives, each of whom carries the title for half the year. One-third of the employees set their own salaries, and are required to reapply for their jobs every six months. Managers retain their positions at the pleasure of those they lead, based on feedback surveys of manager's performance. Semler, whose company is privately owned, shares 23 percent of the company's profits with employees; on 1994 revenues of $30 million, Semco shared $278,000. Fifty satellite companies operate on the Semco premises, some of which are managed by former Semco employees who work part time for Semco and part time for themselves. Says Semler, "When I describe Semco to other business people, they laugh. 'What do you do?' they ask, 'Make beads?' And I say, 'No, among other things, we make rocket-fuel-propellant-mixers for satellites.'"

Semler says that trust is the important thread running through his philosophy, adding, "This system sounds chaotic, can be frustrating, and is in some ways uncontrollable.... It requires daily leaps of faith. It has destroyed any semblance of corporate security." Semler took over the business fourteen years ago, when he was twenty-one years old. Since then, sales per employee have risen from $10,800 to $135,000—more than four times the average of other companies in Semco's business.[2]

Cynics will say that this is all too difficult in a modern organization faced with the pressures of contemporary markets. If we don't change the paradigm and we continue to use the old concepts of the mechanical organizations, the cynics will be right. But if we change the paradigm, we can change the possibilities. When we add new members to the team, we are adding a new soul as well as a new personality. We therefore need to search for the appropriate characteristics of both. To strengthen and shape the character and direction of the team, we need to clearly define the level of soulfulness achieved by its members. We also want to know if these members are growing and evolving as spiritual beings, not just ego-driven overachievers.

Every team needs to screen new members to determine the characteristics of their personality as well as their soul. Hundreds of psychometric profiling tests are available in the market to measure aspects of the personality; in fact, hardly any other types can be found. We have become experts at assessing personality, but we are novices at trying to understand the soul. The *Soul Screen* on the following page helps teams to determine some of the criteria that are not easily identified through an analysis of the personality. When we add a new member to a team, we are interested in knowing, "To what extent does this person possess soulful qualities?" "How evolved is this person?" The first five questions are based on the front wheel Values Shifts of the Values Cycle discussed in Chapter 2. Of course, I do not intend to suggest that these are the defining characteristics of a soulful person—only that they are some of the important questions, that they may point to additional areas of inquiry, and that they may be more important than those questions that deal only with personality. As a minimum, they should indicate whether this new team member will add to the qualities you are seeking as you build your Sanctuary.

The Soul Screen—New Member

To what extent does the prospective team member display these characteristics? Please answer each question on a scale of **0-10**

1 From ME to YOU: A profound appreciation of the value of YOU (the other person), and a recognition that other people and their needs are as worthy as ours. A vigorous commitment to the soulful needs of others.

2 From THINGS to PEOPLE: A higher concern for PEOPLE and their intrinsic value and sacredness than for the acquisition, accumulation, and stewardship of material things.

3 From BREAKTHROUGH to KAIZEN: A deep dedication to KAIZEN (continuous improvement, doing the same things better) that more than equals the personal commitment to achieving breakthroughs (doing things differently).

4 From WEAKNESSES to STRENGTHS: Celebrating and building on STRENGTHS, rather than dwelling on weaknesses, and recognizing the spiritual value of doing so.

5 From COMPETITION and FEAR to LOVE: Practising LOVING-KINDNESS in every aspect of life, based on compassion and generosity instead of competition, fear, and aggression; using the language of LOVE, rather than the language of war.

6 Being in the MOMENT: Bringing a deep sense of joy and contentment to life that is derived from the pleasure of being in the MOMENT rather than from a constant craving for something more or different that is based on insecurity.

7 TRUTH-TELLING and PROMISE-KEEPING: Honoring the TRUTH in every aspect of life and supporting the right of others to do the same. Honoring the spirit as well as the letter of all PROMISES, verbal or written, once they have been made.

8 INTEGRITY: Seeking the inherent honesty in all things and ensuring that all acts are noble and virtuous.

9 FAITH: Enjoying a sense of inner peace, based on a connection with a superior being or higher consciousness that transcends the universe.

10 PERSONALITY to SOUL: Continuing to travel a spiritual path that nourishes personal development and evolution, balances yin with yang, and assists in the transition from ego and personality to SOUL.

A team is an interdependent system. It is therefore vital that every team member endorses the addition of new members. Equally important, teams must agree on the criteria for inclusion, and especially the kind of Sanctuary that they wish to create and the spiritual standards they seek to encourage. Further, great teams consciously plan their spiritual development, catering to the current evolutionary stage of each individual as well as the needs of the entire team as a system. The goal is to coach the team to higher ground.

Parting with Existing Team Members

Insensitive handling of employee terminations in organizations has reached epidemic proportions across North America. In many ways this is not surprising, if we consider that most of these decisions have been based on personality. Hard-pressed traditional managers, faced with a choice between accepting new and demanding performance goals or finding a new job, start slashing and burning. Many faithful employees have been victims of this tyranny and psychotherapists have never been busier. What has made these events so painful to the survivors as well as those who have been "downsized" has been the betrayal and lack of truth-telling.

Although only one person becomes a casualty, everyone knows — even if it is never admitted — that when relationships break down, more than one person is responsible. By being part of a team, members accept the obligation of team performance and they also own the covenant that goes with it — selecting and changing team members. This includes a significant obligation for the success and development of individual team members. In a Sanctuary, this is not the right of an outsider; it is a collective trust of the team. If the team reaches an agreement that overall performance will be enhanced by replacing one of its members, this trips another responsibility — to handle the matter in a sacred way. We are not just saying goodbye to John Doe whose name we will have forgotten in a few weeks. This is another soul, and in a Sanctuary, each soul assumes exacting commitments to the other. *He ain't heavy, he's my brother.*

We raise the standards of the entire team by becoming aware of our responsibilities to the soul, and as we do so, we build our Sanctuaries. How we treat each other is therefore one of the most important responsibilities within teams. If we treat labor as trash — something to be thrown away as soon as it is no longer of value — we will be stripped of our spirit. If we treat labor as a commodity, to be exchanged or traded as a *thing*, we will be treated the same way. If we treat labor as a spirit seeking a human experience, we will begin to operate at an entirely different level. This is the higher ground, where trust, respect, dignity, and compassion nourish the soul and build worldwide reputations for great teams. These are the Sanctuaries where the soul is sacred and where people are no longer afraid. It is to such a sacred place that the soul yearns to come home again.

The Soul Screen—Departing Member

To what extent has the team fulfilled its obligations to the departing member? Please answer each question on a scale of **0-10**

1 From ME to YOU: Have we appreciated the real value of the other person, and have we always been as keen to meet their needs as we have been to meet our own? Are we meeting the needs of the soul? Have we created the opportunities necessary for their development and learning?

2 From THINGS to PEOPLE: Have we shown greater concern for the innate value and sacredness of PEOPLE than for the acquisition and stewardship of material things? Are we putting the souls of people before their cost? Are we doing so now?

3 From BREAKTHROUGH to KAIZEN: Have we practised KAIZEN (helping others to continuously improve and do the same things better) as diligently as we have striven for breakthroughs (doing things differently)? Are we doing so now?

4 From WEAKNESSES to STRENGTHS: Have we consistently applied the spiritual practice of celebrating and building on STRENGTHS, rather than dwelling on weaknesses? Are we doing so now?

5 From COMPETITION and FEAR to LOVE: Have we practised LOVING-KIND-NESS in every aspect of our relationship, showing compassion and generosity instead of competition, fear, and conflict? Have we embraced the language of LOVE, rather than the language of war?

6 Being in the MOMENT: Have we been bringing a deep sense of joy and contentment to life, derived from the pleasure of being in the MOMENT rather than from a constant craving for something more or different that is based on insecurity?

7 TRUTH-TELLING and PROMISE-KEEPING: Have we always honored the TRUTH in every aspect of life, and supported each other's right to do the same? Are we being truthful now? Are we adhering to the spirit and the letter of our PROMISES?

8 INTEGRITY: Has there been an inherent honesty present in all things? Have all our acts been noble and virtuous?

9 FAITH: Have we in the past maintained, and are we now adhering to the standards inherent in our FAITH?

10 PERSONALITY to SOUL: Have we offered the spiritual support necessary to nourish personal development and evolution, balance yin with yang, and assist in the transition from ego and personality to SOUL?

17

Community

Throughout these pages, we have been discussing the concept of the Sanctuary — a safe place for the soul, where fear has been banished and inspiration is a constant companion. A Sanctuary is a closed community of like souls, but it exists within a larger, open community. The concept of the Sanctuary can save the organization and all the souls within it. The concept of community has a larger ambition, for it can save the world.

If It's Going to Be, It's up to Me

Redesigning the world so that it inspires the soul can only be achieved through *our own* efforts — if it's going to be, it's up to me. We can continue to complain, say we can't fight city hall, and throw up our hands in despair, or we can draw a line in the sand and resolve that, from this day on, we will each become part of the solution. This is the means by which we can retrieve the collective soul that has been lost in our communities.

There can be no change in our larger community until we decide to make it so. Therefore, our opportunity is to release the enormous latent talent residing in organizations today and set it working in a positive way in our political system. This is a thrilling prospect and there is much to be done.

In Chapter 3, Truth-Telling and Promise-Keeping, we showed how half-truths, what I have called *truth decay*, slowly steal from the soul, progressively wounding and weakening it. We can

There is no God higher than Truth.

MOHANDAS K. GANDHI

reclaim the higher ground by refusing to compromise with the truth, recognizing that there is only one standard — the truth. In Chapter 9, Competitive Spirit, we have argued that violence works the same way. There is only one standard — non-violence — and even minor acts of violence, like rudeness, bad manners, or hurtful behavior, are on the same continuum as the ultimate violence — war.

Similarly, changes in community are made in very small steps by one person at a time. Healing the soul is an incremental affair, and it always begins with the individual—me. It is just as dangerous to consider our indifference to the community as trivial as it is to

Snowflakes are one of nature's most fragile things, but just look what they can do when they stick together.

VESTA M. KELLY

downplay the dangers of truthlessness and violence. We cannot be half-pregnant. Each of our actions is important—every one of us is mighty. When all of the members of a Sanctuary resolve to become involved, the community will start to heal too. It is the incremental magic of numbers. Thinking about ourselves as insignificant parts is

Newtonian thinking—thinking as evolved and enlightened souls enables us to see the whole and thus changes the perception of our potential.

Change happens one person at a time and it happens when people decide to take less and give more. With his father gone, his mother lost to cancer when he was twelve and his adored elder brother killed in a domestic dispute, seventeen-year-old Steven Hines of Pine Bluff, Arkansas, appeared to be off to an inauspicious start in life. Local police viewed him as a school drop-out and troublemaker, since he had served two terms in delinquency schools for fighting and theft.

As he cycled through the poor part of his neighborhood one evening in 1994 to buy a soft drink and some potato chips, he noticed flames leaping from the roof of a trailer home. He dropped

I believe that every right implies a responsibility; every opportunity, an obligation; every possession, a duty.

JOHN D. ROCKEFELLER, JR.

his bike and sprang to action. "I knocked and shouted, but no one answered," he recalled later. "I could see kids sleeping on the couch and floor." Without a further thought, he was through the door and bringing out children singly and in bunches

through the inferno. "When I got all the way inside, I could see these flames go across the ceiling. They were moving real fast. The heat was intense. I said to myself, 'If I don't get them out of here, the ceiling's going to cave in.'" Before he reached the bedroom of the elderly couple with whom the children were staying, Hines rescued twelve children between the ages of four and thirteen. "The woman was in her wheelchair, and I was guiding that with my hands," said Hines. "Her husband was having to hold on to the back of my shirt to follow us out 'cause it was harder to see."

When the fire fighters arrived, they learned that a slender youngster had quietly left the scene, without a word to anyone, having just saved fourteen people from a certain fiery death. Hines later explained, "You do what you have to do and if I'd been killed, it would have been for some good." The well-wishers, among them President Clinton, have renewed Hines' spirit, strengthened his bank account, and helped him to return to school and eventually to college. "I see I have a heart, and I see you can do more in life by doing good," says Hines. "I want to help other people because people are helping me now. I don't want to let them down; I don't want to let myself down."

This is a wonderful story of one person who chose a path of generosity and compassion instead of selfishness and greed — a Values Shift *from me to you.* Examples such as these inspire others and, paradoxically, attract recognition to the converts, boost their self-esteem, and teach them and the rest of us about the importance of contributing more than we take. The example is not confined to individuals but also extends to our organizations.

The price of greatness is responsibility.

SIR WINSTON S.
CHURCHILL

Many corporate leaders seem to think that becoming involved in the political community is limited to industry lobbying, supporting political action committees, attending swanky $500-a-plate political fundraisers, and schmoozing at political/business associations. This shallow and often cynical relationship between organizations and politics has contributed to negative public perceptions of both. Our challenge is to recognize the value that can come from rekindling a sense of community that offers people at work a deeper experience for the soul.

This can be achieved when people can place their hands on the levers of authority and influence outcomes that positively affect their own lives and those of others who share the same earthspace. To know that what we do at work *and* in our communities has real meaning, is a fundamental need of the soul. In a Harvard study of volunteers who altruistically gave up their time to help others with no prospect of material reward, it was found that 98.3 percent of them experienced a phenomenon known as "helper's high." Psychologists found that this rush came from the joy of giving — the natural path of the soul. When climbing into bed at night, few things are as gratifying to the personality, as well as the soul, as knowing that the day's efforts contributed positively to customers, employees, suppliers — and the larger community. These are the different communities with whom we spend most of our waking hours.

I want to stress that I am not promoting advocacy here; it is our long history of self-interest that has produced the karma we are experiencing today — the triumph of personality over soul. The need of the personality to take has eclipsed the desire of the soul to give. This is too often the general pattern of business/community relationships. Instead, we need to become ambassadors from the closed community of the Sanctuaries that we are creating to the open communities where we live.

This means more than a commitment of money. We need to contribute something much more valuable: our commitment of time, energy, will, intellect, love, collaboration, and spirit. This commitment must rest on partnership, not competition; on a philosophy of abundance, not scarcity. It must be built on the principle of circulation, allowing the spiritual, intellectual, material, and financial resources to circulate freely between the Sanctuary and the community. The Chinese conception of illness, which is an imbalance of energy, applies here. We are suffering from too much energy within our organizations and too little within our communities.

Implementing Commitment to Community

Some leaders believe that unless employees give 110 percent of their lives to the company, by working eighty-hour weeks and sacrificing their personal lives for the good of "the team," they are showing disloyalty. When a team of software developers were designing a video server for Oracle Corp. in 1993, they worked round the clock for weeks to create the product. At a quarter to midnight one Saturday night, the programmers called Lawrence J. Ellison, founder and chairman of Oracle, who was at home with his date. Ellison arrived within the hour, accompanied by his date. "I wanted to see it," said Ellison, "I couldn't just leave her there."

Later, when William Bailey, a member of the development team was asked how Oracle pulled off in two months what Microsoft took one year to do, he said, "Microsoft programmers need more sleep than we do."[1]
Of course, if we stand back from this workaholism and distance ourselves from personality for a moment, we realize that the company is not our whole life, but *part* of our life. It is a very important part, but still, it is just a part. We are not just employees, we are also members of a larger family — "team Earth."

So how should the missionary and spiritual leader relate to the community? Earlier, we discussed the need to commit 10 percent of our time to learning. The argument was made that this is not a luxury but an investment imperative if we wish to avoid personal and corporate irrelevance.

Similarly, having created a Sanctuary, we must secure its setting, for a Sanctuary cannot survive without the community in which it exists — the relationship is symbiotic. It is not someone else's job, it is *our* job and it is time for us to roll up our sleeves and do it. Though the need to serve our communities is great and urgent, timing is very important; we must reclaim higher ground within our own organizations, practising and perfecting the characteristics of the Sanctuary before attempting to integrate these notions into the wider community.

Mooses's Law of Solution:
Complaining makes
you part of the problem.
Defining successful
solutions makes you part
of the solution.

THE WAY OF THE TIGER: GENTLE WISDOM FOR TURBULENT TIMES

Leaders are often reluctant to become involved with partisan politics, claiming that it is a matter for the conscience. They hold an often unwarranted fear of alienating customers and employees by becoming involved in a particular party or cause. So who is going to do it? Them? Who is "them"? If we do not get involved and contribute our *Mastery*, *Chemistry* and *Delivery*, how will we be able to change things for the better?

Mid-term Political Report Card

Many people believe that a politician with values is an oxymoron. While this may be true in a few instances, it is too cynical for a general view. We need to use all our enormous resources in a positive manner to become the instruments of change. The principles of the Values Cycle can be helpful in this regard. Outlined below is a survey that my company designed for a state association of municipal elected officials. Its purpose was to produce a mid-term report card that enabled elected officials to adjust to the needs of their customers — the constituents. Although it was designed as an anonymous mailing to a representative sample of constituents, the Values Cycle could just as easily be used to guide a discussion between a constituent and a politician, a meeting with selection committees, a review with staff assistants, and so on. The survey was precoded (though this information is not shown on the recipient's copy) so that the data can be tabulated and the *vector*, calculated (see Chapter 2, Culture and Values). This produces a measure of the personal effectiveness of the politician and can be used to build a personal development program that will help the politician to learn, develop, and serve constituents more effectively.

Mid-term Survey of Constituents

This survey is designed to measure your current feelings about your local elected representative. Please complete every question, even if you do not know your representative well.

If you are not sure of your response, please offer your best opinion — it is your *impression that is important*. This survey is anonymous but we would like to know four things about you:

1. In which Municipality do you reside?

_____

2. Have you ever met your representative...
○ NO   ○ YES, once   ○ YES, more than once

3. Have you attended local political meetings?
○ NO   ○ YES, once   ○ YES, more than once

4. Do you see your representative as
○ a delegate (voting as you would) or
○ a representative (voting as he/she thinks is best at the time)?

Please complete the survey as soon as possible and return it in the reply paid envelope provided. Thank you for your cooperation.

#	How is Your Representative Doing? (please rate on a scale of 1–10)						
	The Back Wheel						
1.	My representative is open-minded						
2.	My representative understands the issues of our community						
3.	My representative easily identifies with the feelings and ideas of others						
4.	My representative is a good listener						
5.	My representative sticks with a task until it is finished						
6.	My representative is always there for others when he or she is needed						
7.	My representative forms strong emotional bonds with people						
8.	My representative always responds promptly to inquiries						
9.	My representative always tells the truth						
10.	My representative genuinely cares about the problems of others						
11.	My representative understands the goals of our community						
12.	My representative makes good decisions						
13.	My representative strongly represents the interests of others						
14.	My representative understands people						
15.	My representative is a true professional						
16.	My representative tries to do the right thing rather than always doing things right						
17.	My representative spends a lot of time learning about issues relevant to his or her responsibilities						
18.	My representative goes beyond the call of duty to satisfy the needs of others, inside and outside his or her constituency						
19.	My representative is trusted by his or her colleagues						
20.	My representative is at the top of his or her game						
21.	My representative keeps his or her promises						
22.	My representative sees "the big picture," not just his or her own personal or "turf" interests						
23.	My representative is willing to be inconvenienced if it will help others						
24.	My representative values consultants, external experts, and nontraditional options						
25.	My representative works effectively as a member of the team to which he or she belongs						

26. My representative readily accepts criticism						
27. My representative seeks win/win combinations with people						
28. My representative possesses exceptional standards of job-related skills						
29. During dialogue, my representative focuses exclusively on our conversation, never permitting interruptions						
30. My representative is a caring and compassionate person						
The Front Wheel						
31. My representative puts the interests of others before his/her own						
32. My representative puts people before results and meeting targets						
33. My representative believes that doing the same thing better (kaizen) is as important as doing things differently (breakthrough)						
34. My representative builds on strengths rather than focusing on weaknesses						
35. My representative achieves results through compassion and partnership rather than fear and power						

Guidelines to Representatives for Completion and Interpretation of The Values Cycle Vector

1. Total the answers for the questions as follows, placing the sum of your score in the appropriate box:

   MASTERY: Total questions 5, 12, 15, 20, and 28 divided by 5—place your score in the Mastery box below

   Learning: Total questions 2, 17, 22, 24, and 26 divided by 5—place your score in the Learning box below

   CHEMISTRY: Total questions 7, 9, 14, 19, and 27 divided by 5—place your score in the Chemistry box below

   Empathizing: Total questions 3, 6, 10, 25, and 30 divided by 5—place your score in the Empathizing box below

   DELIVERY: Total questions 8, 16, 18, 21, and 23 divided by 5—place your score in the Delivery box below

   Listening: Total questions 1, 4, 11, 13, and 29 divided by 5—place your score in the Listening box below

The Primary Values	Score 1–10	The Accelerators	Score 1–10	Vector
MASTERY *I undertake whatever I do to the highest standards of which I am capable.*		**LEARNING** *I seek and practice knowledge and wisdom.*		
CHEMISTRY *I relate so well with others that they actively seek to associate themselves with me.*		**EMPATHIZING** *I consider the thoughts, feelings, and perspectives of others.*		
DELIVERY *I identify with the needs of others and meet them.*		**LISTENING** *I hear and understand the communications of others.*		

2. Subtract each *Primary Value* score from the corresponding *Accelerator* score and enter the result in the Vector box.

3. Check the absolute scores and the rank order of each of your *Primary Values*. Note that the higher the score (out of a possible 10) the higher you value and practice the *Primary Value*. This list, therefore, indicates the order in which you tend to rank the three *Primary Values* in yourself and in others. It suggests that if you had to choose between the three you would choose the descending order of preference shown.

4. Check the absolute scores and the rank order of each of your *Accelerators*.

5. Knowing in which order you rank and practice the *Primary Values* and the *Accelerators* is only half the story. You will also want to know whether you are growing or declining in each of these *Primary Values*. Personal growth is indicated when the level of energy ascribed to the *Accelerator* is greater than the equivalent number for the *Primary Value*. Positive numbers indicate that you are experiencing growth in a *Primary Value* while negative numbers indicate the reverse. Thus, for example, if you are experiencing growth in *Mastery*, the number for *Learning* will be greater than that for *Mastery*. This relationship is called the *Vector*.

6. Note the rating that you have scored for your *Shifts*.

7. The final step is to validate this information. Does it correspond with what you currently understand about yourself? What direction does it suggest for you? What lessons are there for you in this information and how will you ensure that you are growing in each of your *Primary Values*? How will you learn from the *Shifts*?

Turning Communities into Sanctuaries

The soul seeks encouragement. We all know that things are not as we would like them to be and we yearn to change them, but we lack the encouragement necessary to become actively involved in creating that change. Our souls see the need but not the support. Our role, therefore, is to supply that encouragement — moral and financial, and even more important, spiritual. Employees who are willing and capable should be encouraged to run for political office and receive the appropriate time off, as well as the funding, coaching, technology, and supplies necessary to become elected and work effectively for their constituents and the community.

Faith Popcorn has written about cocooning — the tendency to become so disenchanted and afraid of our communities that we turn inward, making our homes into fortified entertainment centers. This is a philosophy of despair and hopelessness. If we concede this ground, we are finished as a human race. Dr. Dean Ornish, a California specialist in coronary heart disease and a medical advisor to President Clinton, writes in *Dr. Dean Ornish's Program for Reversing Heart Disease*, "...anything that promotes a sense of isolation leads to chronic stress, and often, to illnesses like heart disease. Conversely, anything that leads to real intimacy and feelings of connection can be healing in the real senses of the word: to bring together, to make whole. The ability to be intimate has long been seen as a key to emotional health; I believe it is essential to the health of our hearts as well."

> **No snowflake in an avalanche ever feels responsible.**
>
> STANISLAW JERZY LEE

It is as unrealistic to give up hope as it is to expect a miraculous transformation overnight. The sensible position is to assume our roles as the new missionaries, to have faith and to serve. Faith and service will arrest the slide into despair and harness the energy of the soul to heal our communities. But we need every soul to accept this challenge, not just a few. We are all needed in the work of rebuilding our communities; after all, reclaiming higher ground is a task for all souls.

Recently, I was working with a public utility of 2,600 employees in the town of Green Bay, Wisconsin. I asked the chairman to consider asking every one of those 2,600 people to contribute 10 percent of their year to the community of Green Bay, by becoming actively involved in its politics and infrastructure. At first, this might seem an unrealistic request, especially

> **Everybody talks about the weather but nobody seems to do much about it.**
>
> MARK TWAIN

when it is added to the 10 percent of each year already committed to learning. But consider the spiritual and material benefits that could accrue from such a visionary policy. The impact would be incredible. With a population of 100,000, Green Bay would gain about 13,000 hours or 250 person-years of knowledge, service, love, intellect, wisdom, and spirit each year. Green Bay is a wonderful town today, but through the practical energy of these volunteers serving their community, it would become enriched even more.

Now consider how Green Bay could be transformed if every organization in the area did the same thing. The fresh release of some of the finest talent available in the community dedicated to a shared vision, accepting leadership, solving issues, building a greater sense of community and quality of life, would be breathtaking. Taxes would decline and services would rise as a result of this new influx of wisdom and talent. Organizations would find their relationship with the community changed from one of coexistence to one based on synergy. Others would hear about the renewed spirit of Green Bay and seek to become a part of it. This would draw new investment and attract new talent, because the soul loves kinship and yearns to belong to a community with spirit. These new arrivals would fuse with the existing citizens into a reinvigorated partnership of friendship and goodwill — a community of souls eager to participate and live in a win/win atmosphere, a community regenerated.

Now pause for a moment and reflect on the impact that a similar commitment would have on your own community. This surge of energy and renewal would transform the area where you work and live as well as the relationships among people, organizations, and government. It would be a gigantic gift to the soul.

In the Arthurian legend, the Fisher King is a sorry figure because his domain has been rendered into the Wasteland. He is both a symbol of the devastation and the cause of it. Like Perceval, we have the opportunity to ask the question that will break this spell: "Whom does it serve?" But do we have the resolve and the spiritual responsibility to do so? Asking the right questions will break the spell — restoring the Wasteland of our communities to their original bounty.

18

A Profit with Honor

Profit, like wealth, is a rightful desire of the soul. It can nourish both the personality and the soul. However, this cannot be done unless our profits are acquired with grace.

In my work with corporate executives, I frequently encounter mission statements that include the ritual declaration that the primary purpose of the company is to make a profit. Econ-

> **Profit is like oxygen, essential for our survival, but not the point of our existence.**
>
> *THE WAY OF THE TIGER: GENTLE WISDOM FOR TURBULENT TIMES*

omist Milton Friedman engraved this in our minds and shareholders never fail to reinforce the message. But the primary purpose of an organization is *not* to make a profit. It is to help human beings grow, express their creativity, contribute their lifesource, and make the world a better place. Above all, the role of an organization is to be an efficient means of distributing knowledge, and improving human conditions and happiness.

While profit is necessary for human fulfilment and liberation of the soul, it is by no means sufficient in itself. Indeed, most entrepreneurs did not start their businesses to make a profit. They started them to fulfil their dream about doing something better than it had been done before, and they believed that if they succeeded in realizing their dream, they would become very profitable. Profit, to a certain degree, is the material yardstick for measuring how well we meet the needs of others.

Profit: Dollars or Value?

When we refer to profit, do we mean making money or creating value? There are different classes of profit. For example, when we measure profits in the traditional way — by deducting expenses from income — we must add all of the profits generated from the sales of all organizations, regardless of the *quality* of those profits. Using this criteria, we must include repairs to people, infrastructure, and automobiles resulting from road crashes; absenteeism caused by stress-related illness; health costs caused by tobacco and the abuse of other substances; retribution and foreign aid to countries where the use of military weapons has resulted in death and destruction; crime, espionage, prostitution, and smuggling. Indeed, we must include any activity that exploits the frailties and vulnerabilities of humanity. But isn't there another side to the balance sheet? Should we not calculate more than just the profit from cutting old-growth hardwoods in the Amazon jungle, and include the hidden costs to the planet that some estimate at twenty times the retail price of the wood from the rain forests? If we did our calculations this way, insisting that all our profits flowed from grace, we might rethink our actions. By continuing to calculate profits in the conventional way, we delude ourselves into believing that we can conduct business as usual forever.

The thinking within the Sanctuary requires a different approach, which urges us to set aside an additional portion of our profits to pay for the hidden costs to people and the planet, of our indiscriminate quest for more profit. These more accurate calculations, determined by the leaders of Sanctuaries, would look very different from those we are used to.

In addition to the $20 trillion of derivatives that are on the books of international banks and corporations, international currency speculators shuffle about $1 trillion of yen, pounds, marks, and francs between themselves every single day. In the same period, the total of all manufactured goods throughout the world only amounts to $30 billion. Every day, $1.3 trillion passes through the cyber-stockmarket of Wall Street in New York—the world's largest financial center. This is the equivalent of the entire output of the world passing through New York every three weeks. Both the "real" and the speculative transactions make a profit, but is there a qualitative and measurable difference between the two? Does the soul distinguish between them? I believe that Anita Roddick, Thomas Chappell (founder of Tom's of Maine), and Ben Cohen (co-founder of Ben and Jerry's Homemade Ice Cream) sleep better at night than Gordon Gekko, Ivan Boesky, or The Donald. In the long run, this shows up quite clearly on the bottom line.

Contrary to popular opinion, socially responsible business is not an oxymoron—but maximizing shareholder value in a socially responsible way is. The view of many corporate leaders can be summed up in the recent comment of Robert Goizueta, Chairman of Coca-Cola: "I get paid to make the owners of Coca-Cola increasingly wealthy. Everything else is just fluff." Is inspiring people just fluff? Are integrity, truth-telling, authenticity, respect, collaboration, and fun just fluff? Is it just fluff to honor and inspire the soul? Does the modern leader "win" by being "lean and mean," or is there also room for benevolence, loving-kindness, and stewardship?

Profit is vital for our survival, but we all have to make a choice: will it be our master or our servant? The corporate objectives of The Service-Master Company place profit and values in their proper context. This global organization, founded in 1947 by Marion Wade, embraces among other things, cleaning, maintenance, lawncare, food services, and pest control services to consumers and industry. The reader of the firm's annual report gets the message quickly — *on the first page* are the words "*Each of us should use whatever gift he has received to serve others, faithfully administering God's grace in it's various forms.* 1 Peter 4:10." The company's values are just as clearly stated on the same page. Chairman Bill Pollard and his management team want to make sure that everyone knows the commitment to these values is permanent, so they have chiseled them, in letters nearly a foot high, into a curving marble wall that stretches 90 feet and stands 18 feet tall which greets visitors as they step into the lobby of the firm's headquarters in Downer's Grove, Illinois:

1. To honor God in all we do
2. To help people develop
3. To pursue excellence
4. To grow profitably

It doesn't get much clearer than this. The first two are *ends goals* and the last two are *means goals*. Says Pollard, "Profit is a means in God's world to be used and invested, not an end to be worshipped." For employees, customers, partners, suppliers, and franchisees, this dedication to serving God and humanity is palpable and practiced daily. The notion of *Delivery* — service to others — is translated into their marketing: *1-800-WE-SERVE*. Of course the paradox is that a commitment to being of service to others makes money — over the last 25 years, ServiceMaster has generated annual compound growth in net income of 23 percent on systemwide sales of $4.5 billion provided in 30 countries by 200,000 people to 6 million customers. *That's the value of values.* Says Pollard, "For us, the common link between God and profit is people."

The Power of the Heart and Mind on the Bottom Line

We have come to know profit as the bottom line, but there is a *top line* too. Peter Barnes, President of the San Francisco–based telecommunications company, Working Assets Long Distance, describes the top line as promoting change, regardless of whether we make a profit, and he points to the success of his own company as an example. Founded in 1985, by 1993 revenues had reached $35.8 million, with profits of $2.7 million. Barnes builds the costs of social responsibility into his business, whether his company makes a profit or not.

If you don't do it excellently, don't do it at all. Because if it's not excellent, it won't be profitable or fun, and if you're not in the business for fun or profit, what the hell are you doing there?

ROBERT TOWNSEND

Another example is Dayton Hudson Corp., the $21-billion retailer that invests substantial time and 5 percent of federally taxable income directly into the communities where they operate. They do this through social action and arts programs and Dayton's Chairman and CEO believes that these communities are stronger as a result, and that these initiatives have created an advantage for his company in the marketplace — in sales, purchasing, and recruiting. It has even helped, he believes, in strengthening the company's defense in a recent unsuccessful takeover attempt.

Special Olympics, named "the most credible charity in North America" by the *Journal of Philanthropy*, is the largest international program dedicated to children and adults with mental retardation. Conceived by Eunice Kennedy Shriver and Sargent Shriver twenty-five years ago and supported by the Joseph Kennedy Foundation, there are today over 1 million mentally handicapped athletes training and participating in twenty-three Olympic-type sports in 140 countries. The mission of the Special Olympics is to provide year-round sports training and athletic events to these Special Olympians, and they are called "special" for a good reason. The looks on the faces of the athletes tell it all.

When they receive their medals, when they assist a fallen contestant, when they celebrate the triumph of their will over their mental challenges and when they hug their families, coaches, and friends, the tides of joy flooding their hearts, though evident, can only be imagined by others. The hearts of volunteers and sponsors burst no less with pride and love for them too. For Special Olympians, there are no contract lawyers, no multi-million dollar endorsement deals, no tantrums, and no egos — just big hearts and beautiful souls.

As the Chairman of the Advisory Board of the 1997 World Winter Games, I felt privileged to attend the 1995 World Summer Games in New Haven, Connecticut, the largest multisport event on the planet that year. During ceremonies in which John Scott and I accepted the Special Olympic flag on behalf of Canada from former Governor of Connecticut, Lowell P. Weicker Jr., I learned a lesson about the generous heart and reciprocal altruism from Jean-Pierre van Rooy, the president of Otis Elevator. A division of United Technologies, the company is the world's largest elevator manufacturer, employing 66,000 people in 1,700 international offices. United Technologies had participated for seventeen years in the Connecticut Special Olympic Summer games and when J.P. van Rooy was transferred from Europe to become the president of Otis, he was asked to attend the Sunday track and field events sponsored by the company. He described it as one of the best days in his life and he made a personal commitment that in future he would participate every year.

In 1994, United Technologies made a cash commitment to Special Olympics of $1 million of which Otis pledged $250,000. J.P. was not looking for an opportunity to support a charity—he was looking for a partner that would involve all of Otis' international employees as volunteers in a worthy and noble venture. One year later, this ambitious initiative resulted in "Team Otis" embracing 4,000 Otis employees from operations in thirty-eight countries who were deeply committed to supporting the games—coaching, fund-raising, assisting athletes, finding sponsors, and managing events. In addition to the corporate pledge, another $350,000 was raised through employee contributions and many national operations of Otis defrayed the travel costs of their country's athletes, enabling Malaysia, for example, to participate in the games for the first time. Over 100 Otis employees from twenty-seven countries, many of them traveling with their nation's Special Olympic team, joined with 600 United States–based volunteers at New Haven, where they worked round the clock, creating unparalleled camaraderie among themselves, and celebrating the gifts of mentally handicapped athletes. As J.P. said to me later, Otis has participated in many teambuilding and leadership programs, but none has come close to matching the results of the partnership between Otis and Special Olympics. It cut across all boundaries of race, country, creed, function, and division; hierarchies disappeared and previously undiscovered leaders emerged.

How does one measure the impact of such a venture on the bottom line? Perhaps one should not try. The lessons learned through cooperation, sharing a vision, helping others to realize their dreams, forming new friendships and striving without competition, have all been immense for

If you would hit the mark, you
must aim a little above it;
Every arrow that flies feels
the attraction of earth.

HENRY WADSWORTH
LONGFELLOW

Otis. The strengthening of internal morale and the lessons of leadership and activity management are yielding growing and lasting benefits for everyone — on and off the job. Team Otis is so exhilarated by their experience, that they have made a long-term commitment to their partnership with Special Olympics that will create a legacy

affecting millions of people well into the next century. From this, they are profiting today and will continue to do so in their financial statements and their souls. That is the bottom line.

Anita Roddick, founder of The Body Shop, says, "All we make is skin and hair products, and we can't take a moisture cream seriously. What we take seriously, though, is how we use the ingredients, where we find the ingredients, how we manufacture, and what we do with the profits. We know instinctively that the human race knows that its spirits will soar if its basic material needs are being provided for in an honorable way."[1] Viewed this way, how should we measure profit? As Anita Roddick puts it: "If I put a campaign in my window for elder flower eye gel, I will sell billions of bucks worth of the stuff. I do not sell billions of bucks worth of my shampoo when I am campaigning on human rights, but my soul feels better, my staff are happier, and that's all that's necessary."[2]

The Body Shop's experience supports my view that something much more subtle is going on. If people identify with Anita Roddick's latest cause, this may attract them — some for the first time — to The Body Shop. They may reason that although there is no appreciable difference between the skin care products they are buying from another company and those of the Body Shop, the difference in values that the company stands for justifies a change. If people perceive a difference in how companies relate to the soul, and if they feel that the only major difference between the products of one company and those of another is, for example, Anita Roddick's current cause, this may invite them to switch their allegiance. If consumers can make a social statement by shopping at The Body Shop, without any loss to their personality, this represents an unusual opportunity for the soul to win too. In this way, values, integrity, grit, honesty, and passion are doing double service — as instruments to heal the planet and as a powerful marketing strategy. The resulting sales translate into profits.

There is an overwhelming case to be made that profits achieved through greed and dishonesty gratify the personalities, not the souls, of everyone involved—customers, employees, and suppliers. When combined, the twin diseases of the soul—greed and dishonesty—have lethal force on the bottom line. On the other hand, profits created with integrity inspire the souls of everyone involved, and lay the foundation for future profit growth.

Business is more than a vehicle to provide jobs and profits. It is one of the most elegant forms ever designed for all of us to make a sacred contribution to each other and the planet. It is measured two ways: by calculating the financial returns derived from our efforts, and by measuring how much we have inspired the soul. Profit is not just a measure of what we take out. It is a measure of what we put back in. It is a spiritual ratio as well as an economic ratio that must satisfy the personality as well as the soul.

The Hidden Costs in Profits

International Gizmos Inc. has just had its best year ever. Profits have soared and shareholders are ecstatic. The CEO is a hero and is awarded a huge bonus. The company declares a record dividend and announces ambitious plans for expansion. An acquisition is rumored and foreign expansion is in the cards. The press celebrates the company's prowess and consulting gurus add to the company's fame by featuring them in quality and customer-service video training programs.

Behind the scenes, however, some of the suppliers are muttering that the company's success has been achieved on their backs. They claim they have been mercilessly jaw-boned in efforts to trim costs and lower prices, and while they have been grateful to do business with such a successful company as International Gizmos, their margins have never been slimmer and continuing declines are forecast. As a result, they are feeling neither prosperous nor fulfilled and their business successes feel strangely hollow.

Employees of International Gizmos are also feeling left out of the party. Their budgets have been cut, headcounts have been slashed, and they have been asked to produce even more next year with fewer resources. Getting budgets approved is becoming more difficult and internal competition for resources is growing. A new quality program is about to be introduced and the company's two least productive factories are scheduled for closure early next year. There is a growing fear that this will bring more lay-offs. The employees are tired, burned out, and resentful.

Suppliers are beginning to ship late and quality is declining. Absenteeism and substance abuse is on the rise within the company. These and other hidden costs are rising, but they are currently masked by International Gizmos' recent record profits. Paradoxically, the profit-and-loss account does not tell the whole story, since it is a historical picture rather than a barometer of the future. What are the chances that their outstanding financial performance this year can be repeated next year? What kind of drag on performance is represented by the hidden costs of resentment, demoralization, and stress? Most insidious of all, how can the company, being so steeped in personality, learn about and then reverse the defections of the souls it has caused? How can it regenerate itself? Where are the missionaries? How can it recover from the leaching of its lifesource, without which, any aspirations about future profitability are pure pipe dreams?

A business that makes nothing but money is a poor kind of business.

HENRY FORD

Although the names are made up, the example is real.

Profits are not measured by money alone. There are elements of yin and yang to profit. The yang is defined by financial criteria; the yin is defined by the soul. The yang of organizational performance is measured by the financial statement, the yin by its soul. Though the soul is often subordinated to the personality, it cannot last that way for long. Eventually, the disenchantment of the soul infects the personality.

A friend of mine runs one of the largest service organizations in North America. A retail client that accounted for 30 percent of his revenues rewarded the personalities of his teams with handsome profits but punished their souls with toxic and unpleasant behavior. The retailer relentlessly demanded more services and results but was unwilling to pay for them. The relationship was abusive, profane, insulting, and dishonest. The retailer sneered at integrity and accused my friend's staff of incompetence. Many organizations suffer similar demeaning affronts to the soul in the misguided belief that it is the price we must pay for rewarding the personality.

My friend sensed that the pain this customer caused his employees was too great, and, following the code of the Sanctuary, he called a meeting with them to discuss the customer and to develop a future strategy. Why were relationships so difficult? What were the problems? Were they legitimate? What would it take to resolve the issues? A plan was developed to improve communications and a high-level visit was made to the retailer to discuss their relationship openly. Together, a strategy was laid out, and commitments were made to improve the relationship; it seemed that a new leaf had been turned.

But the relationship didn't heal and the harassment and abuse continued. My friend's employees felt their client had little respect for their own customers or employees and, in the longer term, their virulence would lead to a breakdown in relationships and eventually a complete corporate failure. This risk, together with relentless daily punishment to the soul, was deemed to be unfair to the team. My friend called another meeting and made a radical suggestion — resignation of the account. They openly discussed the impact of this decision on each of them. Resigning the account could result in the loss of one-third of their business, and in personal risks and lay-offs. On the other hand, the customer would receive nearly a year's notice and during that time, the company would make every effort to offer opportunities elsewhere in the organization to those at risk. At first the team members were afraid and apprehensive, but one by one, they chose the higher ground. During this emotional meeting, one employee reflected for a moment and then asked my friend, "What took you so long?"

Having secured this profitable account only five years earlier, it was with a heavy heart that my friend wrote a letter to the client informing him that the two companies' corporate culture and values were in such extreme conflict that they could no longer do business together.

At first the customer was furious. He offered better financial terms and incentives. In these situations, it is tempting to listen to the demands of the personality, and overlook the needs of the soul. The personality is afraid — it thinks of the ego and the potential damage to security, the financial statement, and image. But my friend remained resolute. The business was handled normally as the client's contract period ran out, and during this time the retailer's attitude improved, the insulting and abusive behavior declined, and the toxicity abated. At my friend's firm, people felt good about the decision, no jobs were lost, the resigned business was slowly replaced, and the souls for whom he cared within his Sanctuary were no longer forced to compromise or make excuses. The yin and the yang were harmonized.

The soul can enjoy profits as much as the personality and it is very straightforward to create profits that please the soul, by establishing the kind of practice that one finds in a Sanctuary. This is a place where profit is valued and the process of profit generation is graceful and sacred. As profit growth is attained, everyone and everything are treated with grace. The soul is promoted to equal partnership with the personality, so that both participate in the benefits that profits produce.

At the end of this chapter, there are some questions that the reader may find useful in testing the soulful qualities of the organization's profits. These questions are not intended to be definitive, but rather to suggest the questions we should ask about profits in order to produce a satisfactory profit statement for the soul — and to break the spell that, like Percival, so many of us are under. The reader may find this Profit Scorecard useful as a basis for adding further questions.

Profitability erected on the firm underpinnings of grace and sacred actions will attract new customers, suppliers, employees, and investors, because they too live with grace and regard life as sacred. The arrival of these new souls is welcomed by our own and we thrill to the prospect of their contribution. The profits we achieve through grace are therefore our ultimate advertisement, because they gain the attention of other talented souls who seek to join our Sanctuary and help it to expand. By welcoming them to our team, our Sanctuary can evolve and develop our soulwork. In time, our team is able to establish a reputation for creating a Sanctuary — a higher ground where souls are inspired. In this way, our Sanctuary will attract more souls, who seek to help and support our soulwork even more. And so a miracle takes place among non-believers. First, we change ourselves, then our organization, then our community — and then the world.

The Sacred Profit Scorecard 0-10

1 From ME to YOU: Have our profits been generated without exploiting people or their souls? Have all of the people who contributed to our profits been enriched in material and non-material ways as a result? Have we met the soulful needs of those contributing to and benefiting from our profits?

2 From THINGS to PEOPLE: Have we shown greater concern for the innate value and sacredness of PEOPLE than for the acquisition and accumulation of profits? Are we continuing to do so?

3 From BREAKTHROUGH to KAIZEN: Have our profits resulted from KAIZEN (helping others to continuously improve and do the same things better) as well as from breakthroughs (helping others to do things differently)?

4 From WEAKNESSES to STRENGTHS: Has our pursuit of profit helped us to celebrate and build on our STRENGTHS? Have we avoided the use of negative incentives that penalize weaknesses in our efforts to produce greater profits?

5 From COMPETITION and FEAR to LOVE: Have our profits resulted from LOVING-KINDNESS, compassion, and generosity? Have we rejected the use of competition, fear, conflict and aggression as methods of stimulating greater profits? Does the creation of our profit depend on the language of LOVE, rather than the language of war?

6 Being in the MOMENT: Does our profitability bring a deep sense of joy and contentment to the lives of our partners, customers, employees and shareholders, derived from the pleasure of being in the MOMENT rather than from a craving based on insecurity, which constantly drives us to earn more?

7 TRUTH-TELLING and PROMISE-KEEPING: Have we ensured that the TRUTH has never been compromised in our pursuit of profits? Have we adhered to the spirit and the letter of the PROMISES we make to employees, customers and partners, regardless of the pressure to generate increased profits?

8 INTEGRITY: Have our profits been generated with honesty? Have they been achieved through noble and virtuous acts?

9 FAITH: Have our profits been produced in a manner that is consistent with the standards inherent in our FAITH?

10 PERSONALITY to SOUL: Have we ensured that our profits were not achieved at the expense of the spiritual support necessary to nourish personal growth, balance yin with yang, and assist in the transition from ego and personality to SOUL?

Epilogue

Some Thoughts about
Building a Sanctuary and
Questions for
Soulful Missionaries

Whenever I run public seminars or workshops about transforming organizations into Sanctuaries that nourish the soul, participants from different organizations tell me how they too yearn for the regeneration that will transform their workplaces into soulful places. Some talk about how they have achieved remarkable successes in creating a Sanctuary, and their stories are thrilling to hear. Others talk about how they long for change, about how dysfunctionality, pain, and anger run rampant in their organizations, and how they hate their work and the damage being done to their own souls. They usually say, "I wish our senior management had come to hear this." Then they tell me why their organization is not ready to become more soulful.

Not long ago, I was speaking at a conference where another keynote speaker had also presented. A famous futurist, he spoke of the amazing developments in technology that lie ahead in the early part of the next century. At the end of my speech, a member of the audience told me how much she had enjoyed the futurist, but that during his presentations she had kept writing on her notepad, the words: "Where is the *soul*? Where is the *soul*? Where is the *soul*?" I told her that we need to take care of both the personality and the soul, and that synchronicity had caused her to sign up for his speech — as well as mine.

People become anxious when they consider the prospect of introducing major changes in values within their own organizations. The tasks of regeneration and organizational and personal renewal often look too daunting. In some cases, this may be true and the answer may be that only a move to another, more soulful place of work will offer hope. For the majority, however, the chances of success are not as bleak as they may first appear; in fact, they are very good. We simply need to sharpen the ax before we chop the wood.

Here are some ideas about how to implement spiritual renewal and change. I hope that in your new role of missionary for the soul, a modern Perceval, you will find them heartening.

Congruence

Trust and integrity are good examples of words that are more widely used than practised. This causes a sense of incongruity in people's hearts. Some traditional managers talk about how much they respect people and then show the shallowness of their beliefs by shutting operations and terminating employees without notice. If we ask people to tell the truth, we need to be sure that we are doing the same.

> **It's no use walking anywhere to preach, unless the walking is the preaching.**
> SAINT FRANCIS OF ASSISI

The best teaching is not achieved through talking, but by modeling.

Behavior that reveals an absence of commitment and congruity makes people nervous. In soulwork, it is vital that we always walk our talk. For example, it is critical to be scrupulous about keeping promises, while introducing the concept of promise-keeping. I have seen so many programs driven into the ditch because the words and music have not been aligned.

Emotional Maturity

There are many words and emotions that some people find awkward. These include love, fear, loneliness, please, thank you, failure, spirituality, death, and termination. It takes a long time to achieve a measure of emotional maturity and we need to make it safe for each other to do our inner work. As we grow, we become more evolved. As missionaries, it is our responsibility to each other to make it safe to experiment, make mistakes, look silly, and take criticism from those outside our Sanctuary, as we pursue, however clumsily, our personal growth. We might call this growing by groping along.

Handling Power, Control, and Fear with Grace

Soulfulness is threatening to the unevolved person. When power has been the drug of choice for so long, it is difficult to kick the power habit without experiencing severe symptoms of withdrawal. The most useful antidotes in the soulful revolutionary's tool kit are grace and courage. The style of a person who thrives on power is to intimidate and threaten, but grace will melt their aggression. Try not to match their anger with any of your own — aggression depends on the laws of mechanics: it is unrewarding when it has nothing to push against, as every bully knows. But those who use power to achieve their ends are devious and courage will be required to ensure that your plans for soulfulness are successful. Just when everything looks hopeless, no one appears to be listening, and there are no champions for your cause — this is when the passionate missionary will need to dig down deep and pull out every last atom of courage that can be mustered.

Introducing soulfulness into organizations is a test of stamina and faith — those with the deepest reservoirs of courage will emerge refreshed and renewed with a strength they never knew was in them. At those most testing moments, remember that everyone wants more love — not fear — in their lives and they yearn to let their souls fly — they just don't know how to do so safely. Your mission is to teach them how. They also know that they want to move their lives onto a more spiritual path but, very often, they are not sure how to articulate their desires. They have the same sense of alarm and need for hope that the rest of us do, but they are not sure how to put it all into words. This, too, is your mission.

Listening

Effecting regeneration — organizational transformation and spiritual renewal — is sometimes seen by traditional managers as irrelevant to the personality needs of people and corporations. There is an answer to this: listen to the goals of traditional managers and then fit your objectives around them. If, for example, there are demands for greater productivity, link your soulful aims with these targets, showing how your work will not threaten these goals and may even help to meet them. Form a partnership with and elicit help from the traditional manager, and give credit for his or her contribution. The goal is to listen and use the information to achieve a soulful purpose. Giving away the credit is a small price to pay for success. Argument is nearly always counterproductive because the traditional manager controls rational argument in the mechanical organization and will use it to promote short-term thinking. Short-term thinking is the nemesis of soulful change because it is easy to interrupt the process at any moment and then declare it to be a failure. More than anything else, keep listening and encourage everyone to wait until the end of the movie before passing judgment on the success of soulwork. Building a Sanctuary is a journey, not a destination.

Benchmarking

It is difficult to measure progress in building a Sanctuary. There are few models. Practice is the only meaningful yardstick because people need to experience the energy and emotion of soulfulness in order to appreciate the benefits. Tools such as financial statements, balance sheets, attitude surveys, and turnover ratios offer only limited insights into the calibration of the soul. Try to resist attempts to rationalize and measure everything with standard tools rooted in personality. Some things just are and do not easily submit to the rigors of quantification.

Patience

A Sanctuary is a timeless thing. It does not become standard operating practice in ninety days, and it may not have a positive impact on next quarter's financial statement. It takes time to implement programs of renewal and change, and failure is invariably caused by unrealistic timetables and impatient demands. Guard against being superseded by the latest management fad that suddenly appears and threatens to sweep aside important soulwork, because it promises results in a shorter time frame. Fad-flitters always try to distract the attention of Sanctuary-builders. Set reasonable deadlines for your soulwork, and then triple the estimated time for completion. Building a Sanctuary requires patience, and spiritual work has its own rhythms, like the seasons and the harvest.

Consider how the bamboo grows. After the seed falls to the ground, it is watered by the rains and nourished by the nutrients of the soil. During the first year, nothing happens. The rains and the earth continue to do their good work for the second year, but again nothing happens. This pattern is repeated during the third and fourth years; still nothing happens. Suddenly, in the fifth year, during a span of not more than six weeks, the bamboo grows ninety feet. Did the bamboo grow to be ninety feet in six weeks or five years? If nature had become impatient, abandoning her nurturing duties at any time during those five years, the bamboo would have died. We should try to resist the temptation to abandon our journey before we reach the destination. If we dig up the bamboo to see if it is growing, it will die. The bamboo grows ninety feet over five years, but during the first four years, it appears to the untrained eye that nothing is happening. Nature teaches us wonderful lessons about patience.

Rivers know this: There is no hurry. we shall get there some day.

WINNIE-THE-POOH (A. A. MILNE)

Courage

In a few years, implementing the ideas described in this book will look easy. Today, especially in places where the soul has never been allowed to enter, it may look impossible. I want to ask you to have courage. Let me share my experiences with you. As the former CEO of a company that grew from zero to $100 million, I often look back wistfully, trying to understand what we did that worked so well. I have concluded that we discovered the advantages of building a Sanctuary long ago, but we didn't use these words, probably because we didn't truly understand the magic upon which we had stumbled. If we had, bankers, lawyers, customers, suppliers, and employees would probably have thought we were crazy. So we just did it without talking about it.

We know too much and feel too little. At least, we feel too little of those creative emotions from which a good life springs.

BERTRAND RUSSELL

Strangely enough, it is a lot easier to practise grace, loving-kindness, and truth-telling, than it is to teach it to others. If you get cold feet, think about my dilemma. I am known for my work in corporate culture, personal and organizational renewal, strategy, values, and leadership. Often when I begin to talk about love, integrity, promise-keeping, grace, and joy, people start to look at me as if I don't have any fingerprints. So I just tell the truth.

I can tell you that I never address large audiences about creating Sanctuaries without first digging deep for courage. I know that we are describing the next frontier of leadership thinking, but I am mindful of the audience and where they are coming from, and often, what they have been living with and how they have been struggling to survive. As a client once told me, "We want to get to Sunday too, but today is Monday and we have to get to Tuesday first."

There is nothing more difficult to take in hand, more perilous to conduct, or more uncertain in its success, than to take the lead in the introduction of a new order of things.
NICCOLO MACHIAVELLI, *THE PRINCE*

As fellow missionaries, you and I run a lot of risks as we design spiritual renewal programs based on moving away from rewarding personality towards the development of an ethic that romances the soul. But we should both keep reminding ourselves that transforming people and their organizations is not unimportant work. You and I must understand, perhaps in ways that no one else is able to, that we are pioneers — evolving humans — on a mission to make the world a better place. Your workplace is your laboratory, and your mission here is to help cast off the feelings of emptiness that haunt the souls of your colleagues. *Play to win.*

You are dedicated to building a Sanctuary. The people in your soul-space are about to be transformed. Your goal is to use all of your *Mastery, Chemistry,* and *Delivery* to create a new culture within your Sanctuary, so that your team will bounce out of their beds in the morning, throw open their windows, and shout to the sun, "I want to go to work; I love what I do; I love the people I work with; my work is a special part of my life; I am having fun!"

You will be criticized: cynics will sneer and joke about your dream. When they do, just remind them about the ineffectiveness of doing what we have done before — MOTS, and remind them that, *"The mediocre person is one who has stopped climbing."* We are destined to climb to the higher ground, for it is there that we shall inspire the soul.

"Come to the edge," he said.
They said, "We are afraid."
"Come to the edge," he said. They came. He pushed them . . . and they flew.
(Guillaume Apollinaire)

RECLAIMING HIGHER GROUND
Creating Organizations that Inspire the Soul

Please answer each question YES or NO

1. I am brave enough to ask the right questions at work. _____
2. I consistently honor my deepest values at work. _____
3. I tell the whole truth, in everything that I do at work. _____
4. I keep my promises, even the smallest ones, at work. _____
5. At the day's end, when I leave my work, I have made peace with everyone. _____
6. Fear and competition have been banished from my work and personal life. _____
7. I love the people with whom I work. _____
8. I have fun at work. _____
9. My work fills my life with joy. _____
10. My work *richly* rewards my soul. _____
11. My soul is inspired by my physical working environment. _____
12. I help my competitors to prosper. _____
13. When I win, no one else loses. _____
14. I have all the information and authority I need at work. _____
15. Trust is widespread in my organization. _____
16. I am free of bureaucracy and hierarchy at my work. _____
17. I am able to use all my creative potential at work. _____
18. My organization invests 10 percent of payroll in personal development and learning for all employees. _____
19. Our employees spend 10 percent of their time in community involvement and service. _____
20. Every dollar earned by my organization makes my soul proud. _____

How to Score the Soulscreen

Total up all the number of Yes's in the right-hand column, and check your score against the numbers below, and read the interpretation that is appropriate for you.

0–4: The Soul of your organization is endangered; 5–8: The Soul of your organization is beginning to stir—encourage it. 9–12: Your organization is doing valuable Soulwork. There is much to do but you are on your way; 13–16: Congratulations! Your workplace is becoming a Sanctuary—a community of kindred Souls; 17–20: In your organization, work is a spiritual practice. Cherish it!

The Primary Values	
Mastery	Do I undertake every task as well as I possibly can? Am I utilizing my talent fully? Am I drawing the full potential from my soul as well as my personality?
Chemistry	Is what I do good for people? Is it truthful? Does it respect the soul? Is it courageous? Does it have Grace? Does it honor male and female energies?
Delivery	Do I meet the needs of the personalities and souls of others? Is my energy positive? Do I respect the sacredness of other people and things?
The Accelerators	
Learning	What must we learn to achieve greater Mastery? What can my soul teach me? How can I grow? Who is my mentor? Is the learning process leading to self-esteem? What are the lessons my life is teaching me?
Empathizing	Am I practicing empathy? Is my work sufficiently empathetic? With whom must I develop greater empathy to build superior chemistry?
Listening	How can I listen better? To whom must I listen? Am I listening to the souls as well as to the personalities of others? Have I listened to my own soul?

The Shifts	
From Me to You	Are the soulful needs of others being placed before the needs of my personality?
From Things to People	Do I place a greater value on people and their souls than on their things and on money? Is this the practice for all my work colleagues?
From Breakthrough to Kaizen	Do I strive to achieve a better result as well as a different result? Does my life and each activity improve every day? Do I invite my soul to guide the improvement?
From Weaknesses to Strengths	Do I build on strengths rather than correcting weaknesses? Do I reinforce rather than criticize? Do I encourage the soul?
From Fear to Love	Do I encourage love instead of creating fear? Do my actions inspire joy and healing instead of hostility and competition? Do I win without creating losers?

A Note on Terminology

A number of words are given special meaning throughout *Reclaiming Higher Ground*. For the ease of the reader, some of these are defined below. First, I have described the dictionary, or formal, definition and then I have added some notes of personal interpretation:

Chemistry: *Relating so well with others that they actively seek to associate themselves with you.*

Chemistry is one of the Primary Values of the Values Cycle. People with *Chemistry* possess characteristics and attitudes that favor building strong relationships; place a high value on harmonious association with others; take the initiative to repair, maintain, and build relationships; and seek connections that go beyond the superficial. They establish deep friendships, bond with others at an emotional level, and build win/win partnerships. They trust others and enjoy their company, preferring collaboration to operating as a loner. They are gregarious and easy to get along with. In the commercial world, those with *Chemistry* develop deep relationships that often result in long-lasting and profoundly rewarding business and personal friendships. They develop material and non-material connections with employees (and their partners), suppliers, customers, industry associates, and strategic alliance partners. *Chemistry* addresses issues of communication by creating relationships built on trust that flows from truthfulness, accountability, energy, honesty, respect, compassion, integrity, and love.

Customer: *A customer is anyone who comes to us with a need. Therefore everyone is a customer, but there are three main kinds:*

Employee: An individual who provides services to the company on a full- or part-time basis and who undertakes to meet certain work-related responsibilities in exchange for an agreed package of material and spiritual rewards.

Customer: An external customer who is an individual or organization seeking to meet their perceived needs through the use of the products or services we provide.

Partner: A person or organization supplying services or products. Through their successful utilization and the human relationship they develop with customers, partners help their customers' organizations to meet perceived needs.

In our professional lives, *customers* exist in many other roles: unions, regulators, bank managers, accounting firms, bosses, colleagues, head office, other companies in our industry, trade associations, and many more. In our personal lives, we also have many *customers*, such as a spouse or partner, parent, child, relative, friend, neighbor, and all of those with whom we have developed a relationship based on interdependence.

Delivery: Identifying the needs of others and meeting them.

Delivery is one of the Primary Values of the Values Cycle. People with *Delivery* respect the needs of others and are passionate about meeting them. Their focus on other's needs is motivated by enlightened self-interest and altruism. They place the meeting of customer needs above short-term profit, taking the long view that profits flow from this philosophy. They develop and implement "win/win" deals and relationships, treat customers as partners not adversaries, are concerned with doing the right thing, more than doing things right, and measure their personal standards of performance through the results they achieve with employees, partners, and customers.

Empathizing: Considering the thoughts, feelings, and perspectives of others.

Empathizing is the Accelerator for *Chemistry* in the Values Cycle. Empathizers put themselves in the shoes of others, walking in their moccasins, and realize that this is the first essential in building relationships. They take the trouble to see things from the other person's point of view, being keenly interested in the other's challenges and aspirations. Their worldview is altruistic, compassionate, kind, and caring. They are more concerned with cooperation, collaboration, and partnering than competition, conflict, and power. An individual who is skilled in Empathizing is call an *empath*.

Empowerment: Trusting people.

Trusting people, and giving them all the information, training, encouragement, and authority they need to make the right decision for the customer.

Evolved (person or organization): An unfolding, opening out, or working out; process of development, as from a simple to a complex form, or of gradual, progressive change, as in a social or economic structure.

Evolved people are those who have discovered through their learnings, that the questions of life are seldom found in superficial or material answers alone. They know too that the right questions are more important than answers. The evolved person challenges traditional logic, attempts to align beliefs and practices with his or her code of integrity, searches for the connection between spirituality and work, and seeks deeper meaning in life. Evolved people respect differing views, understanding that life's meaning is to be found everywhere. They are open, always learning and growing, they avoid premature judgment or criticism, and they are ever-ready to hear ideas that might lead to an improved condition for humans and our planet. An evolved person knows that there is only one truth, but that there are many different ways of seeing it.

Grace: Beauty or charm of form, composition, movement or expression; an attractive quality, feature, manner, etc.; a sense of what is right and proper, decency; thoughtfulness towards others; good will.

Those with grace appreciate the natural elegance of human relationships. They turn every communication and relationship into beautiful music. Those with grace use charm and integrity to maintain symmetry in all of their relationships. Those with grace seek to integrate themselves with people with whom they interact. They guide relationships with a sure hand that seeks to make every soul whole — first with itself, but also with the universe. Grace in a graceless world requires immense personal courage. Our personal mission is to be in a state of grace, with everyone with whom we have been in contact, when our soul leaves this planet.

Kaizen: Continuous improvement in personal life, home life, social life, and work life, involving everyone.

Kaizen is one of the Values Shifts from the front wheel of the Values Cycle. The literal Japanese translation of *kaizen* is "better way." It is the art of doing the same thing better rather than doing things differently (breakthrough); *kaizen* is the practice of making small improvements in the status quo through continuous, ongoing efforts. It is a solution-based, rather than problem-based, philosophy. *Kaizen* incorporates *warusa-kagen* (which means "things that are not yet a problem, but are somehow not quite right"). *Warusa-kagen*, if left unattended, may eventually lead to significant problems. Those who practise *kaizen* seek constant improvement in their work, social, personal, and spiritual lives and are therefore always growing.

Learning: Seeking and practicing knowledge and wisdom.

Learning is the Accelerator for *Mastery* in the Values Cycle. Those committed to learning place a high value on experts, teachers, and a mentoring relationship. They maintain lasting relationships with their teachers and experts. They devote above-average amounts of time to reading, studying, practising, and perfecting, being constantly open to new ideas and alert to opportunities for improvement. Learners ensure that those around them have the right tools for learning and for their work, improvising where finances or circumstances require. They are restless in their quest for knowing and, always being unsatisfied with current levels of wisdom, they are always seeking. They establish choices, timetables, and budgets that meet their learning objectives so they can gain greater understanding and therefore *Mastery*.

Listening: Hearing and understanding the communications of others.

Listening is the Accelerator for *Delivery* in the Values Cycle. Listeners have the capacity to shut down "mental chatter," and are skilled at giving their undivided attention to others. They know the value when listening of looking for a variety of signals besides the words, such as body language, intonation, and expression. They have the capacity to "hear the words as well as the music," tending to listen openly, and in the most effective ways possible, in order to understand, without being defensive or manipulative. Listening is not easy and understanding its full implications is made simpler by knowing that the words LISTEN and SILENT have the same letters.

Mastery: *Undertaking whatever you do to the highest standards of which you are capable.*

Mastery is one of the Primary Values of the Values Cycle. People with *Mastery* possess a commitment to doing whatever it takes to reach the very highest standards. They seek ambitious ends, being devoted to continuous improvement in their personal and professional lives (see *kaizen*), and constantly questing for excellence. In general, they possess highly developed skills, competencies, and practices and are expertly knowledgeable in their areas of specialty, usually being among the best in their field. They maintain a lifetime respect for knowledge and are often blessed with a mentor. *Mastery* is based on core competencies, tasks, knowledge, learning, teaching and professional development, skills, expertise, information systems and technology, science, efficiency, accomplishment, technique, artistry, and sophistication.

Sacred: *To sanctify; consecrated, or belonging to God; regarded with the same respect and reverence accorded to holy things; venerated; hallowed; secured as by a sense of justice against any defamation, violation, or intrusion; inviolate.*

Here is the question: If it is sacred, would we harm it? Anything that is sacred, we deem to be holy and protected. We are all sacred; so is the planet and all of Earth's creatures. Our personal space is sacred, as are all of our Sanctuaries. We may choose to designate anything or anyone as sacred. Our journey is sacred, the truth is sacred, and our positive purpose in life is sacred. All living things and everything that enhances the human condition, the generations before and that follow and our biosphere is sacred. Violations of sacred things are violations of the soul.

Sanctuary: *From the Latin:* sanctus, *sacred, holy place, as a building set aside for the worship of a god or gods; a place of refuge or protection, a shelter.*

A Sanctuary is not so much a place, but a safe environment, a state of mind. We may not be able to change the world around us, but we can change ourselves. In this way, though the world around us may be crazy or dangerous, in the Sanctuary of our own space, we are secure. A Sanctuary is like a shield, repelling the toxicity around us. But a Sanctuary is even more than a physical location—it is an attitude. Sanctuaries are often formed by groups of like-minded individuals who seldom meet, but who share values, and love, trust, and respect each other, enjoying a common code. A Sanctuary is a holy place, a place where we give reverence to all of the people and things within it. It is a place where we practise a sacred code, living with grace and all of the other soulful ways described in *Reclaiming Higher Ground*.

Soul: An entity that is regarded as being the immortal or spiritual part of the person; the life force; the vital essence of a human; innermost being or nature, nobleness of spirit or its desired expression.

For me, the soul is the immortal or spiritual part of us. It is our essence, our moral and emotional fiber, our warmth and our force. It is the vital part of us that transcends our temporary existence. It is our psyche, which is the Greek word for soul. We are souls with bodies, not bodies with souls. Our minds are limited to dealing in possibilities, but our souls are capable of reaching beyond the traditional, to the magical and the richly elaborated dream. What the limited mind considers a miracle, the soul considers possible. The soul is the essential "more" that exists in our work, our play, our friends, our families, our environment, our material objects, and all of life's activities. This "more," this magic that inspires the soul, is what I contend is missing from our work and therefore our lives.

Endnotes

Introduction
1. Hammer, M., and J. Champy, *Reengineering the Corporation*, Harper Collins, New York, p. 32.

2. "The Straining of Quality," *The Economist*, 14 January 1995, 55.

3. Stratford Sherman, "Big Blue Shows Signs of Life," *Fortune*, 6 February 1995, 16.

4. Christopher A. Bartlett and Sumantra Ghoshal, "Changing the Role of Top Management: Beyond Systems to People," *Harvard Business Review*, May–June 1995, 132–42.

5. Peter Russell, "Who's Kidding Whom? Is Western Civilization Compatible with Sustainable Development?" *World Business Academy Perspectives* 8, no. 1 (1994): 7–8.

6. B. Joseph Pine II, Don Peppers and Martha Rogers, "Do You Want to Keep Your Customers Forever?" *Harvard Business Review*, March–April 1995, 103–14.

Chapter 1
1. "Improving Executive Thinking," *For CEOs Only*, 12, no. 2: 2.

2. Thomas Moore, *Care of the Soul*, HarperCollins, 1992, xi.

3. John D Hull, "The State of the Union," *Time*, 6 February 1995, 42–53.

4. Ibid.

5. "CEO Interview," *Fortune*, 6 February 1995, 24.

6. Diane Brady, "The Roots of Chaos," *Maclean's*, 19 November 1990, 46–48.

7. "From Catastrophe to Crisis," *The Economist*, 12 May 1990, 85–86.
8. Dan Lavin, "Millionaires@Work," *Fortune*, 3 April 1995, 20–21.

9. "The Business of Business?" *Utne Reader*, September–October 1993, 72.

10. Patricia Galagan, "Bringing Spirit Back to the Workplace," *Training and Development Journal*, September 1988: 37.

Chapter 2
1. Donald Krause, *The Art of War for Executives*, Perigree.

2. Russel Mitchell and Michael O'Neal, "Managing by Values," *Business Week*, 12 September 1994. 38–43.

3. Readers wishing to explore the concept of the Values Cycle in greater depth will find a thorough treatment in *The Way of the Tiger: Gentle Wisdom for Turbulent Times,* (Toronto: The Thaler Corporation, 1989).

Chapter 3
1. Weston Kosova, *Washington City Paper,* 16 August 1991.

2. Lance H. K. Secretan, *Managerial Moxie,* (Prima Publishing, 1993).

Chapter 4
1. Marjorie Kelly, "Michael Novak: The Theology of Business," in *The New Paradigm of Business,* ed. Michael Ray and Alan Rinzler, (Jeremy P. Tarcher/Perigree Books, 1993), 197–98.

2. Hal F. Rosenbluth, *The Customer Comes Second and Other Secrets of Exceptional Service,* William Morrow, 1992).

3. Ronald Henkoff, "Finding, Training and Keeping the Best Service Workers," *Fortune*, 3 October 1994, 110–22.

4. Hal F. Rosenbluth, *The Customer Comes Second and Other Secrets of Exceptional Service,* (William Morrow, 1992).

5. Andrew Kupfer, "Success Secrets of Tomorrow's Stars," Fortune, 23 April 1990, 77–84.

Chapter 5
1. Al Reis and Jack Trout, *Marketing Warfare.*

2. Jon Franklin, *Molecules of the Mind,* (New York: Dell, 1987), 25.

3. Norman Cousins, *Head First,* (New York: E. P. Dutton, 1989).

4. Ibid., 4.

Chapter 6
1. *Utne Reader*, January-February 1994, 64.

2. Stephan Rechtschaffen, *Psychology Today,* November–December 1993.

3. Kathryn Leger, "Peladeau's Poker: All Guts and Gall," *The Financial Post,* 27 May 1995, 16–17.

4. Mark Sutcliffe, "Racket Scientist," *Canadian Business*, June 1995, 52–58.

5. Tamsen Tillson, "The Last Patriot," *Canadian Business,* July 1995, 26–30.

6. Elizabeth G. Conlin, "A House Divided," *Inc.*, February 1995, 72.

7. Lance H. K. Secretan, *Living the Moment,* (Toronto: The Thaler Corporation Inc., 1993), 56.

8. Thomas Moore, *Care of the Soul,* (New York: HarperCollins 1992), xvi.

9. Brian Dumaine, "Why Do We Work?" *Fortune,* 196–204.

Chapter 7
1. Brian O'Reilly, "The New Deal: What Companies and Employees Owe One Another," *Fortune*, 13 June 1994, 44–52.

2. Mary Kay, *Mary Kay Director's Guide,* (published by Mary Kay Cosmetics), 1993, 3–4.

Chapter 8
1. Address to the 31st Congress of the International Chamber of Commerce, (Mexico: 1993).

Chapter 9
1. Jaclyn Fierman, "When Genteel Rivals Become Mortal Enemies," *Fortune,* 15 May 1995, 90–100.

2. Brian Dumaine, "Why Do We Work?" *Fortune*, 26 November 1994, 196–204.

3. Cynthia Joba, Herman Bryant Maynard Jr., and Michael Ray, "Competition, Cooperation and Co-creation: Insights from the World Business Academy," in *The New Paradigm in Business*, (New York: Jeremy P. Tarcher, 1993), 53.

Chapter 10
1. Jay Finnegan, "Everything According to Plan," *Inc.*, March 1995, 78–85.

2. George Gendron, "The Roots of Evolution," *Inc.,* June 1995, 11.

3. Russell Mitchell, "Managing by Values," *Business Week*, 12 September 1994, 43.

4. D. Dreher, quoted in *The Tao of Inner Peace*, Harper Perennial, 1991), 186–87.

Chapter 11
1. Rita Koselka and Randall Lane, "What Matsushita Left on the Table," *Forbes,* 3 July 1996, 46–48.

2. "Corporate Reputations," *Fortune,* 6 March 1995, 56.

3. Ibid., 57–58.

4. Rolf Osterberg, *Corporate Renaissance: Business as an Adventure in Human Development,* (Mill Valley, CA: Nataraj Publishing, 1993) 139.

Chapter 12
1. Christopher A. Bartlett and Sumantra Ghoshal, "Changing the Role of Top Management: Beyond Systems to People," *Harvard Business Review,* May–June 1995, 132–42.

2. "The Horizontal Corporation," *Business Week,* 20 December 1993, 44–49.

3. Christopher A. Bartlett and Sumantra Ghoshal, "Changing the Role of Top Management: Beyond Systems to People," *Harvard Business Review,* May–June 1995, 132–42.

Chapter 13
1. Alex Taylor III, "Iacocca's Minivan," *Fortune,* 30 May 1994, 56–66.

2. John Huey, "Nothing is Impossible," *Fortune,* 23 September 1991.

3. Jay Tokasz, "Winging It—Scalpel, Knife, Fork," *USA Today,* 24 May 1995, 5A.

4. "Corporate Reputations," *Fortune,* 6 March 1995, 57.

Chapter 14
1. "Corporate Reputations," *Fortune,* 6 March 1995, 56.

2. Mihaly Csikszentmihalyi, *Flow: The Psychology of Optimal Experience,* (New York: Harper and Row, 1990).

3. Brian O'Reilly, "The New Deal: What Companies and Employees Owe One Another," *Fortune,* 13 June 1994, 44–52.

Chapter 15
1. "Redraw the Line Between the Board and the CEO," *Harvard Business Review,* March–April 1995, 153–65.

Chapter 16
1. Mary Teresa Bitti, "McGarry Queen of the Xeroids," *The Financial Post Magazine,* June 1995, 18.

2. Jaclyn Fierman, "Winning Ideas From Maverick Managers," *Fortune,* 6 February 1995, 66–80.

Chapter 17
1. Richard Brandt, "Can Larry Beat Bill?" *Business Week,* 15 May 1995, 38–46.

Chapter 18
1. "Anita Roddick: Eco-business," *Utne Reader,* September–October 1990, 47.

2. Ibid.

Index